G000146347

1 09

3

TEN ADVENTUROUS WALKS IN WEST KENT

Raymond Hugh

Illustrations by
Jackie Hei and Philip Allsop

ISBN 1 874476 17 9

Published by Morning Mist Publishing 1996
This edition 1996 ©
P.O. Box 108, Reigate, Surrey RH2 9YP
©Raymond Hugh and Jackie Hei 1996

Designed by
Morning Mist Publications

INDEX

INTRODUCTION

THE ADVENTURE

The adventure must be yours, it is the thrill of exploration, the pleasure of experiencing something new and the surprise of the unexpected. You could do the same walk several times and each time it will be different. In Spring, apple blossom compete with woodland bluebells for the most colourful display whilst autumn brings a myriad of reds. You may spot a kingfisher, common along the many rivers which snake across the county or a kestral hovering in the sky in search of food. In Summer hops hang golden in the air whilst orchards grow heavy with fruit. In Winter the trees bare, the countryside can appear dark and forbidding and the next day dazzling white under a crisp frost beneath welcoming blue skys. The weather cannot only change the appearance of a walk, it can also change the feel. The adventure is discovering the secrets of the route on the day.

THE REWARD

The reward is the sense of achievement and the knowledge that not only have you completed a respectable distance, you have learned and experienced something of West Kent which before was a mystery. There is no greater satisfaction than to discover the county as our ancestors did - on foot.

WHEN TO GO

Many walkers make the mistake of only walking in fine weather, leaving the hills at the slightest sign of rain. In wet and windy weather the countryside is untamed and with the majority of the population safe in their houses, one can really get a feeling of remoteness and a better idea of what Kent was like several hundred years ago. My suggestion is that you try and do the walks in all seasons and all weathers. At the end if you don't hate me, you will really begin to feel an affinity with the Kent countryside and the satisfaction of knowing Kent well. As for the time of day, I recommend that you try and time your walk to include either dawn or dusk. Theses to me are the best parts of the day, unfortunately often missed by the majority.

PREPARATION

Planning the walk is as important and as enjoyable as doing the walk itself. firstly consider whether you want to make a weekend of it. If you do, then I suggest that you book local accommodation. This not only cuts down on travelling on the day, but creates a seemingly longer weekend and allows you to remain familiar with the area at night. There is nothing better in my mind than to finish a long walk and retire to local accommodation for a hot bath before a well earned visit to the local village pub, without having to worry about driving home. A selection of recommended accommodation is listed at the end of each walk.

Once you have decided on your walk, familiarise yourself with it. Read the walk through, following it on the map, to ensure you understand where it is you are going. The route descriptions contain points of interest and you may want to take time to stop and visit these. If you do, it might be worth borrowing a book from the library to read up before your visit. When you have made up your mind on the points of interest to visit, try and estimate the length of your walk. The timings given on each walk are meant as a rough guide only and are based on a person being reasonably fit. If you are unsure, then I suggest you allow for approximately two miles per hour. Timing is important as you could find yourself stumbling back to the start in the dark.

Finally, make sure you are fit, the walks in this book are longer than the average walking book and can be hard work if you are unprepared, To help identify the gradients, a cross section is included at the start of each walk.

WHAT TO TAKE

A good map is essential. I recommend you use the Ordnance Survey Landranger maps and the start of the walk details the map(s) required. You can use the Ordnance Survey Pathfinder maps which have far more detail such as field boundaries, but they can be harder to find and can ultimately be more expensive.

Once armed with your map, make sure you have sensible clothing, this means clothes which are loose and comfortable. Tight jeans and high heels are not recommended! No matter how good the weather is at the start of the day, always pack some waterproofs. Being caught out in the rain without the necessary protection is not an experience I would recommend. In summer if you are walking in shorts, waterproof trousers are also particularly useful as a temporary protection against nettles. There is a wide range of waterproof clothing now available, the two recommendations I would make are:-

(1) Make sure you are completely covered, that is by trousers and a jacket.

(2) Buy clothing made from one of the breathable materials - your local stockist will advise you on these.

If the weather is cold, then gloves and a hat are always advisable. No matter what time of year, I always pack a jumper and have never regretted it. Keeping warm helps avoid tiredness. Most importantly, make sure you have a good pair of shoes. If you can afford it, then buy a pair of walking boots. If not, then make sure your shoes are strong, comfortable and have soles with a good grip. Equally important are good socks. If you have boots then two pairs are advisable. Do not think that the socks you wear to the office will do!

Sensibly clothed, you can now think about any other equipment you may need. A camera and a pair of binoculars are always useful and can enhance your day out. I always carry a pocket book on birds, you could do the same or add to this with a book on local flora or history. You will find the walk all the more enjoyable for a little bit of knowledge. Do not though get over enthusiastic and take a library or you may find yourself requiring a book on first aid!

A basic first aid kit though is always advisable. The Kent countryside may appear tame and so it is compared to the Himalayas but it must still be treated with respect. The book and the map should be enough to find the route without difficulty, however a compass is always useful for finding your way when paths are undefined.

Refreshments are always an important consideration. There are places where you can get a bite to eat on every walk but even if you wish to use their facilities it is important to carry some basic snacks, especially in cold weather. You should always carry water and a thermos flask with hot soup or drink can also be very welcome. To carry all this one should have a comfortable day sack or small rucksack These are now available from a wide assortment of shops, but before you purchase one, make sure it's strong and more importantly ensure it's comfortable.

Finally, take your five senses with you - these are essential if you are to fully appreciate the walk, but most importantly, **ENSURE YOU TAKE THIS BOOK.**

GETTING THERE

Most people will be mobile, i.e. a car or bicycle. Where practical I have listed railway stations, however buses are far more difficult as their routes and timetables tend to change with the wind. For those people relying on a bus to reach the start, I have listed the main bus companies serving the area below:-

Inland Travel Tel: 01580 879339
Kentish Bus Tel: 01474 321300
London and County Tel: 01737 242411
Maidstone Motor Services Ltd Tel: 01634 832666
National Express Tel: 0990 808080
Stagecoach Tel: 01233 620342
Wealden Beeline Tel: 01892 833830
Kent County Council also operate a public transport information line which is free Tel: Freefone 0800 696996

ROUTE FINDING

The route descriptions are instructional rather than poetic and should be followed without difficulty. To assist you a series of symbols in the left hand margin enable you to identify specific points on the walk at a glance. A good map is essential and should be used in conjunction with the route description . Please remember that like everything else, the countryside changes with time, a fenced path can become unfenced and vice versa.

Before setting out, make sure you have identified the route on the map. To pinpoint a starting point or place of interest I have used grid references. These are six figured numbers which identify a particular point on the map. Every Ordnance Survey map is covered by a national grid. The grid's lines are identified by numbers printed on the map's surround. To find a grid reference, take the first three numbers which refer to the vertical lines on your map and locate them on the top or bottom (north or south) of the map. The third number is an imaginary line in the square following the first two numbers. To find this line, divide the square into ten equal parts. Then take the last three numbers, which refer to the horizontal lines and locate them on the left or right (east or west) of your map and follow the line of this reference until it meets the line of the first reference. Their meeting point is the grid reference point itself. Do not rely on the maps in this book, these are not to scale and are meant as a rough guide only.

It is important that you recognise the various types of footpath signs. Most are fairly obvious, i.e. wooden post with a sign marked "footpath" or "public bridleway", pointing in the direction of the right of way. Some will have the name of a specific route, for example, "The North Downs Way."

Over recent years many County Councils have standardised their signs to follow national guidelines. Footpaths are now shown with a yellow arrow and bridleways with a blue one. Like the old wooden signs the arrows will point in the direction of the right of way. Some arrows will have the initials of a recognised walk imprinted, the most common one you will see is "WW", which is the Wealway or the Greensand Way which is marked by the name encircling an Oast House. In the wooded areas of Kent you will often find yellow or blue circles painted on the trees indicating a footpath or bridleway. On top of all this, you will often find custom built signs. These can mark an official route but more often than not, are the work of local farmers guiding the walker across their land. An example of the former, is "The North Downs Way", which is highlighted by a white acorn on a black background.

An important rule on route finding is to take your time, follow the map and read the route description thoroughly. If you do this, then you will return to base without mishap.

LONG DISTANCE WALKS

Many of the routes meet long distance linear walks which run through Kent. In case you want to try any, I have listed their names with distances below, along with the publisher that produces a description of the walk.

Darent Valley Path (leaflet) - 12 miles (Sevenoaks Council)
Eden Valley Walk - 15 miles (Kent County Council)
Greensand Way (Kent) - 52 miles (Kent County Council)
High Weald Walk - 27.5 miles (Kent County Council)
London Country Way - 205 miles (Constable)
Medway River Path - 27 miles (Medway River Project)
North Downs Way - 141 miles (Aurum Press)
Saxon Shore Way - 140 miles (Ramblers Association)
Sussex Border Path - 150 miles (Ben Perkins)
Vanguard Way - 63 miles (Cicerone Press)
Weald Way - 90 miles (Cicerone Press)

TOURIST INFORMATION CENTRES

If you require any further information on transport, tourist facilities or accommodation, I have listed the local Tourist Information Centres below:-

Maidstone	Tel: 01622 602169
Sevenoaks	Tel: 01732 450305
Tonbridge	Tel: 01732 770929
Royal Tunbridge Wells	Tel: 01892 515675
Westerham	Tel: 01959 565063

PROTECTING THE COUNTRYSIDE OF WEST KENT

The special beauty of West Kent is protected by a number of organisations. Apart from protecting and managing the environment, they also organise a variety of activities and events throughout the year.

Supporting these organisations will ensure their survival and the continued protection of a landsape threatened by urbanisation. I have listed below the organisations which deserve special praise along with a telephone number or address from where you can obtain membership details.

Kent Trust for Nature Conservation
Tyland Barn
P O Box 23
Maidstone
Kent

The National Trust
Scotney Castle
Lamberhurst
Kent

AUTHORS NOTE

Every effort has been made to ensure that the route descriptions are accurate. Time changes things however and can alter the description of the route. If you have any difficulty in finding any part of a route, please write with details giving a grid reference to enable me to re-examine the route. A free copy of the next publication will be forwarded for any suggestions used in the next edition. Enjoy your walks.

THE CHIDING CHALLENGE

Distance: 9½ miles (15.25km)

Time: Allow approximately 4½ hours

Map: Ordnance Survey Landranger Map 188

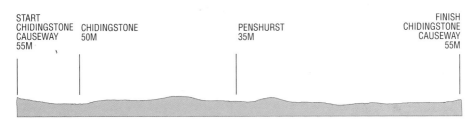

START			FINISH
CHIDINGSTONE	CHIDINGSTONE	PENSHURST	CHIDINGSTONE
CAUSEWAY	50M	35M	CAUSEWAY
55M			55M

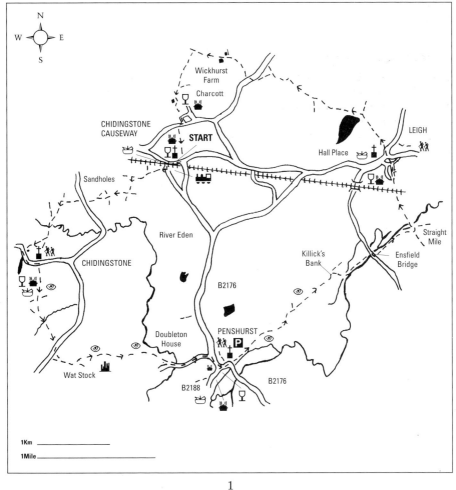

Walk Summary

This is a classic Kent walk through classic Kent countryside, visiting two of Kent's most famous villages. Never a dull moment, this walk is perhaps the perfect introduction to Kent. Following a mixture of well trodden and scarcely known paths, the Chiding Challenge makes for a day out that you will cherish for time to come. As a bonus, there are no fewer than six pubs en route, though be warned as in several places the route follows the course of rivers and if you do not wish to end up in another "drink", go easy on the pub testing! Seriously though, parts of the route are liable to flooding and therefore, unless you fancy a swim, do not attempt this walk during prolonged wet weather.

Start - GR. 521465 Map 188

The walk starts from the layby opposite St. Luke's church at Chiddingstone Causeway. Close by is the popular "Little Brown Jug" pub and (confusingly), Penshurst railway station. Chiddingstone Causeway is on the B2027 between Edenbridge, Crockham Hill and Tonbridge. Tourist signs for Hever Castle, Penshurst and Chiddingstone all guide you close to Chiddingstone Causeway. One request, please do not park in the "Little Brown Jug" pub carpark. Please either park in the layby opposite the church or in the station carpark. Trains to Chiddingstone Causeway run approximately every hour.

Alternative starts can be made from all three villages visited en route, namely Chiddingstone, Penshurst or Leigh.

One last tip, at weekends if you intend starting at Chiddingstone or Penshurst, then start early as car parking can become difficult.

THE CHIDING CHALLENGE

To start the walk, from the layby opposite the church and facing the church, turn right along the road towards "The Little Brown Jug" pub. The pub is famous for its food as well as its beer, but if you are tempted for "one before ye go", remember that there are five more pubs en route. On reaching the pub, cross the road to arrive at Penshurst railway station. *The railway line which connects Redhill with Tonbridge was opened in May 1842. The following year it opened to Folkstone and then Dover and for several years after was the only rail link from London to the Channel ports.* Go over the railway bridge to the platform the other side and exit the station into the station carpark. Continue ahead passing to the left of a yard supplying fencing and look out for a signposted footpath ahead. Take this, going over a stile beside a gate, to thereafter, follow a track along the right hand side of a field. To your left now, are fine views of the rolling countryside of Kent and its distinctive oasthouses.

At the far side of the field, pass through a gate into another field and continue straight across this field to, at the far side, turn left and follow the field perimeter, a line of trees and a small stream. After approximately one hundred metres, look out for a gap in the line of trees on your right and go through this into another field, thereby crossing over the small stream. Take care not to miss this. Continue straight ahead along the left hand perimeter of the field and at the far side, go through a metal gate ahead. This is sometimes closed and may necessitate your climbing over it.

Alternatively, if you are not a keen climber, turn left just before the gate into a hop field adjacent and then turn immediately right along the field perimeter. After a short distance, ignore a stile on your right (this is where the official route rejoins) and continue at the corner to follow the field perimeter round.

To follow the official route, after climbing or passing through the gate ahead, continue in the same direction along the left hand perimeter of the next field and after approximately fifty metres, look out for a stile on your left which you should cross into a hop field. (This is where you join the alternative route). Turn right along the field perimeter and at the corner, continue to follow the perimeter round and at the far side, at the next corner, pass through a gap in the hedge ahead into the next field. After a few paces, turn right over a stile into yet another field and carry straight on along the left hand perimeter, enjoying good views to your right of "Beckett's Farm", with its two oasthouses. When the perimeter of the field bends left, you should ignore this to continue straight on, heading for a red tiled house, "Sandholes", visible in the distance ahead.

At the far side of the field, go over a footbridge to cross a meandering stream and continue ahead, bearing very gently left, to meet and follow a hedge on your left. Further up, pass through a gap in the hedge on your left to cut across the corner of a field, heading for a point just left of the house, "Sandholes". Pass between the house on your right (a fine old Wealden farmhouse) and a pond on your left and follow the perimeter fencing to the property round to your right, to reach a stile which you should cross, beside a gate. After the stile, follow a driveway ahead, past a converted barn, to meet a lane **(GR. 508459)**. Cross the lane and join a signposted footpath the other side by going over a stile into a field, where you should continue ahead along the left hand perimeter. To your left here is a fine view to "Larkins Farm".

"Larkins Farm" is in fact a brewery, one of only three remaining in Kent, a   **i**
tragedy when you consider that less than a hundred years ago there were over fifty breweries in the county, a county supposedly famous for its beer making! The brewery is a successful family run concern, started in 1986, the brewing process being housed in a 1930's barn which was once part of the Astor estate. The farm on which the brewery is sited has existed since 1200 and the name "Larkins" is derived from the name of the original farmer, Theobald Lavikins. The farmhouse is excellently sited for brewing, close to a good source of local fresh water renowned for its sweetness and built on a rock which acts as a natural cool cellar - it's a wonder brewing didn't start earlier! The brewery gives a tour on Saturday mornings for around £5.00 per person and at the end, there is a free tasting where the owners claim that they give much of the entry fee back by way of free drink!

At the far side of the field, go over a stile and continue ahead along the left hand perimeter of the next field. After approximately twenty to thirty paces, turn left to cross a stile beside a gate (the stile is slightly hidden behind a tree), into another field. Carry straight on, keeping to the left hand field perimeter with a house on your right. Ahead of you now should be the tower of Chiddingstone church and far more visible, Chiddingstone Castle. As you near the far side of the field, or at a point where you meet a gateway on your left, bear diagonally right to head for a wooden plank footbridge, ignoring as you continue a stile on your right. The footbridge takes you into another field where you should continue ahead along the right hand perimeter until you reach a stile on your right. Go over the stile and turn left onto a well walked public footpath to soon cross the pretty river Eden.

i *The River Eden flows for just fifteen miles from its spring in Surrey to the river Medway. Today Kent County Council promote the river as a tourist attraction and have even designed a walk, the "Eden Valley Walk", based on its course. This is a far cry from earlier days when the river was considered more of an inconvenience. So much so, that there is some dispute as to the original name of the river, a name being of little consequence to an inconvenience! The river therefore, has the dubious and rare distinction of being named after a bridge and not the reverse which is more usual. The bridge in question is of course, Edenbridge, just a few miles to the west. After the Romans, a bridge (now gone) was built by a Saxon Chieftain, Eadhelm. Over the centuries this was corrupted to Eden and gradually became the name of the river also. A red brick pill box beside the river indicates that it has served at least one purpose in its lifetime, that of defence.*

After the bridge, carry straight on following a prominent path across a field and at the far side, where the path meets the corner of a wood, turn right to cross a stile into another field. Take care not to miss it. Go straight across the field bearing gently left as you continue and at the far side cross over a stream, pass through a gap in a hedge and continue ahead along the left hand perimeter of the next field. On a clear day there are fine views here to the Greensand Ridge, including Ide Hill and Toys Hill featured in "The Churchill Challenge". At the field corner, the route leads into what is best described as a natural funnel, passing a small pond on your right, to come out at a lane after a small metal kissing gate. Ahead of you now are more good views to Chiddingstone Castle. Turn left along the lane passing over a bridge which also acts as a dam to one of the lakes to the castle (a good point to stop for a breather). Thereafter, continue to follow the lane into the village of Chiddingstone itself and arrive at what is possibly its main attraction, "The Castle Inn", owned by the National Trust.

i *Chiddingstone (GR. 501452 Map 188) is one of the great unspoilt villages of England. It is virtually a perfectly preserved Tudor village with all the essential ingredients, a church, a shop (reputedly the oldest in England), fine half timbered houses, a castle and of course, a pub. As a result of its perfect preservation, the village has been much painted and photographed over the years and every good coffee table book on our green and pleasant land will include its picture. As a consequence, people drive here in their droves at weekends, somewhat spoiling the Tudor atmosphere. Therefore, if you want to really appreciate the undoubted beauty of Chiddingstone try and come on a weekday or alternatively, start early. My first encounter with Chiddingstone was on a fine early spring morning with the sun spreading dappled golden waves on the ancient "Castle Inn". There was not a car in sight and I almost half expected a couple in Tudor clothing to come strolling down the street.*

The village, of course, goes back long before the Tudors and in all probability was originally Saxon. The origin of its name is one of constant argument. The "stone" is obvious, for a path (passed later) beside the village school leads to a large boulder of Ardingly Sandstone. Many legends surround the boulder or stone, including one that suggests townsfolk were taken there as a form of punishment

4

and were made to stand on the stone and be given a chiding (telling off) by the other villagers. This tale conveniently explains the village's name and though colourful is sadly for the romantics only and is probably nothing more than a legend. Far more likely, is that the stone was named after a Saxon, possibly Cidd or Cidda, both common Saxon names. Another legend suggests that the stone was used as a Druids' altar or place of worship before the arrival of the church. Both are quite probable, indeed the latter was a common practice when there were no local churches to attend. People would gather instead at a prominent local landmark such as a large stone or tree. This is why you often see named trees, for example "Red Oak", marked on ordnance survey maps.

The earliest building in the village is the church which still has a few traces of its 13th century origins. Built of local stone, it was virtually destroyed in 1624 when lightening struck its tower and started a fire. If you look closely at the tower, you can still see some of the fire-blackened stones. Facing the church is the village's famous line of fine Tudor house with overhanging upper storeys and intricate leaded windows. All have a history of their own, but the two most famous are the village shop and Post Office and the pub. The shop is thought to have been built in the 15th century and at one point belonged to the father of Anne Boleyn. The shop started trading around 1620 making it probably the oldest in England. The postbox was originally at St. Pancras goods station. The village pub also dates back to the 15th century but only became an inn during the early part of the 18th century. It was known then as "The Three Bells" but changed its name to "The Castle Inn" when, in 1737, it was sold to Henry Streatfield of Chiddingstone Castle.

The High Street used to continue straight on past the pub where a set of iron gates now stand and a row of houses used to continue past the pub to Chiddingstone Castle itself. Then, Chiddingstone Castle was known as "High Street House". "High Street House" like the rest of the village was originally Tudor, but was rebuilt in the 17th century and in the late 18th century heavily Gothicised to become a castle. The castle is open to visitors and is well worth a visit, if only to see the exotic display of Eastern art. The most famous residents of Chiddingstone Castle were the powerful Streatfield family who were squires for over four hundred and fifty years, from the reign of James 1 until 1936. The Streatfields played their last major role in the village by selling the village, at a reduced price, to the National Trust. The family still live in and around the village today and also offer the best B&B in the area at nearby "Hoath House".

Approaching Chiddingstone

5

As mentioned at the beginning, the village is steeped in local legend and is reputed to have a number of ghosts. One, a cavalier, who is said to have climbed the church tower actually turned out to be the verger winding the clock! Less well explained however, is the little girl who haunts the flat above the shop. Strange noises and doors opening and closing are said to be a regular feature.

Depending on what time you arrive at the village, the pub is well worth a visit. It stocks the local Larkins beer and also sells the beer of another local brewery, Shepherd Neame. The interior is very nice but in summer the garden is an absolute delight. The ancient village shop stocks a good range of provisions.

As you leave the village with historic dates and tales of ghosts whirling around your head, don't be too alarmed if you see a coach and horses coming towards you. The village has acted as a set for several films, including Elizabeth 1, starring Glenda Jackson, and you could just be witness to the making of another.

To continue our walk, in front of "The Castle Inn", follow the lane as it bends left and continue, following the lane, for approximately ten metres beyond the footpath for the Chiding Stone, to join another footpath on your right, marked by a low stone Kent Footpath sign. Pass through a metal kissing gate to join the footpath and follow it, between fences, running parallel to the drive of a house on your right. Thereafter, the footpath continues between fields where, in winter in particular, there are good views to your right back to Chiddingstone Castle. On meeting a pair of stiles, cross the stile on the right (the left leading to a playing field) and carry straight on to, after a short distance, go over another stile ahead and continue across the centre of a field, walking gently downhill and heading for a small copse slightly to your right. On a clear day, visible in the distance ahead to your left, is a large rectangular pink and rather grand building. This is "Wat Stock Farm" and is passed later on our walk, when you will discover that the building is not all that it seems! The path soon meets the copse which hides a hollow and continues along the edge of the copse to, after a few paces, arrive at a stile. Ignore a path on your left to go over the stile and carry straight on, ignoring another path on your right, keeping a fence, as a guide, on your left.

The path continues gently downhill to arrive at a track just after passing beside a disused kissing gate. You are now following the old coach road between Penshurst, Chiddingstone and Hever. This stretch is said to be haunted by a headless coachman driving a coach and horses. If a coach and horses passes you here, it probably has nothing to do with modern day film making! Turn left along the track and shortly after, pass through a wooden kissing gate adjacent to another gate, the track now being marked as the Eden Valley Walk. At this point you will also cross over a stream. After the stream, follow a wide track ahead and later, when this forks, take the left hand fork in the direction of the yellow arrow and the Eden Valley Walk sign, to soon after arrive at a road. Turn right along the road and after approximately ten metres, join a signposted public bridleway on your left **(GR. 504440)**.

The bridleway immediately leads into a field which you should cross, bearing diagonally left, heading for a gate and stile at the far side. As you cross, on a clear day, you will gain some superb views to your left. At the far side, go over the stile and turn left along a wide track, passing a large pond on your left. As you continue, look out for a collection of barns ahead to your left with a pink and white frontage. These are part of "Wat Stock Farm" and make up the "grand *i* building" seen earlier on our walk. Follow the track past a house and another pond before entering the farmyard of "Wat Stock Farm". Ignore a turning off to your right as you enter the farmyard and continue ahead, passing between the farmhouse on your right and three barns on your left. Notice the barns are joined by two walls of breeze blocks to give the appearance the other side that the barns are one rather grand building - a very clever modern-day folly and illusion. Did it fool you?

After the farmyard, keep to the track which runs between fields and enjoy the views, where gaps in the hedge on your left allow, over the rolling Kent countryside. Stay on the track, ignoring all turnings off, for approximately one mile, to eventually meet a narrow tarmacced lane. As a point of note, on one part of the track before meeting the lane, there is a magnificent view to your left over ◉ the river Eden across the valley to "Doubleton Farm" and oasthouse. The oasthouse is one of the oldest in Kent and the farm originally dates back to the 13th century. The name "Doubleton" is derived from the farm's original owners the "Dubbells".

On meeting the lane turn left to follow it and shortly after, cross the river Eden for the last time today. After this, continue along the lane to eventually arrive at a road, the B2176, in front of "Penshurst Place", which in winter is clearly visible ahead but in summer, hidden behind a leafy hedge. Turn left along the road for approximately fifty metres and go over a stile on your right to enter the grounds of "Penshurst Place". Thereafter, continue in the direction of the public footpath sign, pointing diagonally right (the Eden Valley Walk) and not the one pointing left. You will now find yourself walking through open parkland with the magnificent "Penshurst Place" on your left and heading for the tower of the village church. If you can take your eyes off "Penshurst Place", behind to your left is Penshurst cricket pitch. It is arguable the second oldest in England and certainly must have one of the most prestigious locations. To continue, go over a "V" stile *i* just before the church tower and follow a tarmacced footpath past the bottom of the tower to arrive at the church porch. The church is well worth a visit.

Penshurst Church, dedicated to St. John the Baptist, is over eight hundred *i* *years old. Built of mellow sandstone, the church retains an air of olde worlde* † *charm. This is in spite of "improvements" by the Victorian architect, Sir Gilbert* ▪ *Scott, more famous for the Albert Memorial and St. Pancras Station in London.* *Inside, is a memorial window to Thomas a Becket. Becket appointed the first* *recorded priest at Penshurst the day before his murder at Canterbury Cathedral.*

To continue, from the porch, follow a brick path through the churchyard and pass beneath the upper storey of a cottage (much used in period dramas) to arrive at a delightful tiny square, the original Leicester Square. Note the old white post box in the wall of the building on your right and to the right of this, a charming half-timbered cottage which looks as though it is on the verge of collapse. This was once an inn and what a shame it is not open to make the arrival at Penshurst even more perfect. Our way from the square, is left along the road and through the gateway to "Penshurst Place". First though, I recommend you turn right to explore the village and enjoy a half way rest at the village's hostelry, "The

Leicester Arms", a Wayside inn offering character accommodation. If alcohol is not your cup of tea, then the village also has a number of tea rooms. Whatever your decision, it is a good point at which to tell you more about the village and "Penshurst Place".

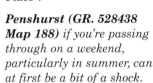 

i **Penshurst (GR. 528438 Map 188)** *if you're passing through on a weekend, particularly in summer, can at first be a bit of a shock.*

The original Leicester Square

Suddenly, after following miles of quiet paths you emerge to face the 20th century. Daytrippers crowd the streets in their cars looking for the best parking space and camera clutching and colourfully dressed tourists express their delight in a multitude of languages. Try and see beyond all this and you will appreciate the reason why so many people travel to Penshurst, for quite rightly it is the jewel in Kent's crown. A friend once said to me, "all routes lead to Penshurst" and he was right as set in a bowl and surrounded by hills with white-topped oasthouses, Penshurst lies at the junction of the rivers Eden and Medway, as well as two major roads, the B2176 and the B2188. Footpaths too, some hundreds of years old, all appear to converge on Penshurst, a sign of the village's importance.

The main reason for the village being so important is "Penshurst Place", originally one of the most powerful manors in England and certainly one of the best preserved. I will cover the house a little later but what I will say now, is that over the centuries its powerful inhabitants brought international politics to the heart of this little village and with it, wealth and national recognition,one reason for the large number of quality and well preserved houses in the area.

With "Penshurst Place", it is easy to overlook the village which is a shame, for even with the exclusion of "Penshurst Place", the village is equal to the best in the area. The main street is made up of many different styles of buildings, all with a wealth (wealth being the operative word!) of character. At the south eastern edge of the village, on the B2188 in the direction of Fordcombe, there is a small garage which now occupies what was once the old forge. The entrance to the garage is through a timber reconstruction of a horseshoe. Today, the garage also doubles as a Post Office and general stores and if you are in need of provisions, is the only place which allows you to stock up. At the main junction in the village stands the relatively modern Village Hall. Built of local stone, it blends in well even if it is a little grand. One of Penshurst's houses has a very unusual claim to fame. In the grounds of "Redleaf House" (private) is what is claimed to be the very first example of crazy paving.

At the eastern end of the village and where we entered, is Penshurst's most famous collection of buildings. Just before the B2176 bends right on its way to Southborough, lies a small and perfectly preserved 16th century square,

8

surrounded by half timbered buildings. Close to the road stands a cherry tree, making the square even more enchanting in spring. Throughout summer you can also admire the swallows whose ancestors have been nesting in these houses virtually since they were built, over six hundred years ago. Facing the square from the road, at the near left hand corner a small office now occupies the old Post Office. The white post box (not in use) is known as a "Ludlow Box" and is one of the earliest in existence. Before this, "The Leicester Arms" acted as the Post Office and kept a stable of horses to run letters to most of the local towns and villages. Beside the old Post Office stands the "Guild House", now a private residence, but which was once the village's other inn. How sad it no longer welcomes the weary traveller. The square is called "Leicester Square" after Robert Sidney, 1st Earl of Leicester. The villagers proudly boast (just get talking in the pub) that this is the original Leicester Square! They are actually correct as the better known Leicester Square in London was built later and it too commemorates the !st Earl of Leicester, who just happened to own the land.

Another good topic of conversation to introduce at the pub, is the age of the village cricket pitch. Most historians believe the pitch to be the third oldest in England, though locals insist on it being the second oldest. The undoubted original is located at a rural spot near Hambledon in Hampshire, the birthplace of cricket, and is featured in "10 Adventurous Walks in Hampshire".

Original squares and second or third oldest cricket pitches, whatever your opinion, you cannot help but be impressed by "Penshurst Place". Its attributes and history are far too great to pen in a walking book and though I will give a brief overview, I recommend you take time to visit and buy a local guide book. The original house dates from the 13th century and its course to today's grandeur started in 1338, when Sir John de Pulteney, Lord Mayor of London no less than four times, and a wealthy merchant, received permission from Edward III to embattle his house. He also added The Great Hall or Barons' Hall as it was once known, still the most impressive room in the house. Incredible, is the huge oak ceiling and such is the hall's preservation, that it is easy to imagine a meeting of Barons sitting at long tables around a central open hearth. A succession of owners were wise enough to keep de Pulteney's original house and instead of condemning it to modernisation, they simply built around it leaving the house of 1338 complete to this day.

The next owner, after de Pulteney, was the Duke of Bedford, brother of Henry V. The Duke was then followed by three generations of the Stafford family, better known as the Dukes of Buckingham and one of the most powerful families of their time. The last of the Stafford heirs was beheaded and as a reward, the Royal family inherited the house! In 1552, King Edward VI awarded the house to Sir William Sidney for his loyalty and service. The same family have owned and lived at the house ever since.

The most turbulent times at the house were undoubtedly during the Tudor period. The Sidney family was close to the Royal family and were active participants in the politics of the day. Queen Elizabeth I was a regular visitor to the house and is known to have enjoyed dancing in The Great Hall. Indeed, it is one of the great mysteries of the day as to whether or not Elizabeth I had a romantic relationship with Robert Dudley, 1st Earl of Leicester.

Perhaps the best known member of the Sidney family was Sir Philip Sidney. Born at "Penshurst Place", he is today well respected for his literary talents, though none of his works were published during his lifetime. Like his younger brother, the 1st Earl of Leicester, Philip was a great favourite of Elizabeth I. She evidently enjoyed his company and on more than one occasion prevented him from attending foreign expeditions "lest", as her famous words ordered, "we shall lose the jewel of our dominions". Ironically, it was Her Majesty's insistence in appointing him to the position of Governor of Flushing in present day Holland, that led to his death. In 1586, at the age of thirtytwo, he died of an infection from a musket shot wound he received at the seige of Zutphen. Poet first and soldier second, he nevertheless never swayed in his loyalty and duty to his Queen and country. Whilst fighting in the low countries he earned the respect of his men and is perhaps most famous for an act of kindness on the battle field. When offered a drink of scarce water he refused and instead gave his ration to a dying soldier with the immortal words, "Thy necessity is yet greater than mine". Even today, these few innocently spoken words are more famous then those he penned. Such is the road to fame! Tragedy and bravery have walked hand in hand with the Sidneys right up to the present day. So much so that a walking book can never do the family history justice. To find out more therefore, as suggested earlier, I do recommend you purchase a local guide book.

"Penshurst Place" is open daily to the public (except Mondays) from 1st April to September. In addition, the house has one of the best preserved Tudor gardens in the country which can also be visited.

After perhaps toasting the Sidneys and enjoying some friendly local banter at "The Leicester Arms", we can return to our walk.

Continue by following the road past the original Leicester Square and as the road bends right, leave it to carry straight on through the magnificent stone and brick gateway to "Penshurst Place", also marked as a public footpath to Killick's Bank and Ensfield. Before you pass through the gateway however,take another opportunity to admire the original Leicester Square on your left. After the gateway, follow the drive which is flanked by a grand old brick wall on your left, topped by a superbly manicured yew hedge. The river Medway is also on your right. As the wall to "Penshurst Place" on your left ends, do not turn left into the carpark but carry straight on to continue along the drive, following the signs for the Eden Valley Walk. The drive soon passes to the right of a pond and as you near the end of this, it is worth taking time to pause and look back at the magnificence of "Penshurst Place".

Keep to the drive to pass a second pond and just as the drive begins to climb uphill, leave it to cross a stile on your left beside a gate, into a field. Turn right to follow the field perimeter and go over another stile ahead into a second field, where you should bear diagonally left to go uphill across the centre of the field, heading for a lone post. As you climb there are more excellent views back to the ⊚ lakes, Penshurst village and "Penshurst Place". After the post, continue in the same direction now heading for a gate at the far side of the field. Go over a stile 🏔 beside the gate and carry straight on along the right hand perimeter of a field. Shortly after, go over another stile beside a metal gate and continue ahead along a concrete drive. Ahead now is a very different view over a part of Kent so far not ⊚ seen on our walk today. In the distance, the North Downs stretch away to the east on their way to Dover and over to your right, on a clear day, the famous Medway town of Tonbridge is just visible with the spire of St. Stephens church rising at its centre.

Follow the drive for some distance to reach a small group of pretty and very typical Kent houses, collectively known as Killick's Bank. The Killicks were farmers here during the early 19th century. Follow the drive past the house and immediately after, turn right onto another drive and go over a stile on your left into a field. Take care not to miss it. Walk diagonally right across the field following a line of posts (which could disappear), to reach and cross a footbridge at the far side going over a narrow strip of water, once the original course of the river Medway. After the footbridge, continue straight on across a narrow field to arrive at the river Medway itself, where you should turn left along the river bank.

Follow the Medway, the river being particularly sleepy at this point, to *i* eventually arrive at a lane which crosses the river via a fine stone bridge known as Ensfield Bridge and named after Ensfield Manor (**GR. 547453**). The current bridge dates from 1940. Go over a stile and turn right over the bridge and follow the lane for approximately ten more metres before crossing the lane, to reach and cross a second stile. This takes you into a field where you should continue ahead following the left hand field perimeter, in the direction of a footpath sign. At the far side of the field, which is a large one, go over a stile into a second field and cut across the left hand corner to, after approximately twenty paces, go over another stile and enter an area of scrub with water either side. Ignore a path off to your right and carry straight on to cross a concrete bridge, thereby leaving the Eden Valley Walk.

The Straight Mile and the River Medway *The concrete bridge spans what* *i* *was to be a canal. During the 1820's, a local entrepreneur, James Christie, set out to build a canal from Tonbridge to Forest Row and then on to join up with the Wey Navigation in West Sussex, which eventually enters the sea at Arundel. The only part of the canal to be constructed was a tiny stretch one mile in length and straight as an arrow, which led to its current name "Straight Mile", though the local water company now use it for drainage and its more formal name has now evolved into the unkind "Straight Mile Drain"! With the coming of the Tonbridge to Edenbridge and Redhill railway, the scheme was out of date before it started and James Christie fled the country leaving many people out of pocket.*

The river Medway at this point is very susceptible to flooding and a little further down river (not on the walk), a number of flood gates and water storage lakes have been constructed as a result of serious flooding in the 1960's, which caused massive damage to Tonbridge. The project is so big that it can boast as being the largest on-river flood storage system in the UK. As an aside, I hope at this point you've heeded the early note at the beginning of the walk about wet weather and are not experiencing the flooding for real!

After the bridge, fork left, ignoring a path right, and head for a metal bridge. Cross the bridge, going over the river Medway for the last time, to enter a field where you should continue straight ahead across the centre. At the far side, cross over a ditch into another field and carry straight on, following the left hand field perimeter and heading for a railway line visible ahead. Before reaching the far side of the field, pass through a kissing gate beside a metal gate and thereafter, follow a fenced track over a mound (a flood barrier) and then under the railway line. After this, follow the track uphill and through another kissing gate ahead to arrive at a road at the village of Leigh. Follow the road ahead which soon leads out to the pretty village green at Leigh beside the cricket club.

i **Leigh (GR. 550465 Map 188)** *is at once a surprise and a delight. Unlike Chiddingstone and Penshurst which can feel cramped, Leigh with its massive green has a feeling of space. Surrounding the green are a jumble of cottages and houses, some weatherboarded, others of local stone and brick. At the northern edge of the green are some attractive Tudor style houses which unlike the genuine article at Chiddingstone, are Victorian imitations. At the far side of the green, on a rise above the village, towers the church of St. Mary, standing as though on constant watch. It is believed the site has been a place of worship for over one thousand years, though the current church is essentially 13th century. Like many of the churches close to London, St. Marys was heavily "restored" by the Victorians. Inside, there are a couple of interesting memorials, one, a brass on the north wall, depicts a lady rising from her tomb. The epitaph reads, "Behold O Lord I com willingly". Another is a memorial to Sir Arthur Page, QC, Chief Justice of Burma.*

From the churchyard there is a lovely view over the village. Also, at the far side of the green, stands the interesting village sign depicting some of the trades of the village and almost opposite, the old blacksmiths, still with its trading sign, though sadly no longer working. Close to this is a small general stores and your last chance to stock up. If you are determined to try another pub (or two!), then facing the blacksmiths and following the road left (not part of our walk), will bring you to "The Bat and Ball", Shepherd Neame. Note the unusual pub sign. A little further on, is the attractive "Fleur de Lys" pub, Greene King. In between the two pubs is the old covered village well, now protecting a village information board.

Incidentally, before you speak to anyone local, the village name is pronounced "Lie". The original spelling was "Lyghe" and is derived from the Saxon word for a clearing in a wood, a hint back to the village's humble origin.

Our route is straight across the green (unless there is a match being played, in which case you will have to walk round), heading for the white memorial the other side. On reaching the far side of the green cross the road, walk past the memorial and cross the B2027 to follow it ahead, in the direction of the sign to Hildenborough and Tonbridge. After approximately thirty metres when the road bends right, leave it to follow a narrow tarmacced path ahead across a small triangular green. On your left now is the entrance to the village church and the mock Tudor gateway to "Hall Place".

i **Hall Place** *a quite magnificent mansion, was built in 1876 for a Nottinghamshire merchant, Samuel Morley, MP. The original house dates from*

12

the Elizabethan period and the current house is constructed in the same style using local brick. Superb grounds surround the house and these are sometimes open to the general public in summer. If this is the case when you pass, don't miss the opportunity to have a look around.

Continue to cross the driveway to "Hall Place" and pass through a small gate the other side onto the drive for "Porcupine House". After a few paces when the driveway bends right to enter "Porcupine House", leave it to follow a narrow footpath ahead and shortly after go through a kissing gate into a field. Once again, continue ahead following the left hand perimeter of the field with the grounds of "Hall Place" on your left. As you continue, particularly in winter when the trees are bare, there are views of the house itself. At the far side of the field, pass through another kissing gate and carry straight on along the left hand perimeter of the next field and at the far side take care not to cross the footbridge ahead, but instead pass through a kissing gate on your left.

After the kissing gate, follow the path which continues to run along the edge of the grounds to "Hall Park" with the old perimeter fencing just about intact. To your right a small stream runs parallel and is shortly crossed by a small and quite ornate disused bridge. (Crossing the bridge is not part of our route). The wooded bank to your left at this point conceals a man-made lake, part of the landscaping to the grounds of "Hall Place". The path continues in a straight line, almost tunnel-like at times and as it begins to gently climb there are marvellous views back to your left over the lake and "Hall Place" itself. The path then leaves the open parkland to continue ahead through stately woodland, dominated by some magnificent rhododendron bushes which are a blaze of colour if you are passing this way in late spring.

The path eventually meets a stile which you should cross into a field. Continue straight on along the right hand perimeter of the field and at the far side, pass through a gate into a second field where, again, you should follow the field perimeter, making for "Leigh Park Farm" directly ahead. As you continue, ignore a stile on your right and at the field corner, pass through a gate ahead to continue along the right hand perimeter of a third field. After approximately forty metres, go over a stile beside another gate ahead into a fourth field and maintain your direction, this time keeping to the field's left hand perimeter. At the far side of the field, technically the footpath is through a gate on your left and then immediately right through another gate to reach a concrete drive in front of a pair of oasthouses. However, these gates are normally locked and it is much easier (as the farmer pointed out to me) to simply go through a gate ahead beside an old disused petrol pump and then turn left along the concrete drive. The drive almost immediately bends right to skirt the pair of derelict oasthouses. From this side, with a pond lapping at their base, it's a scene worthy of a pause.

After the oasthouses, follow the drive for approximately four hundred metres or until you see a stile between two gates on your left. As a guide, in case this arrangement changes, this is just before a line of trees meets the drive on the same side. Go over the stile (or through the gate) and continue ahead along the right hand perimeter of a field with the line of trees on your right. Continue to a point approximately three quarters of the way across the field to then go over a footbridge, crossing Wickhurst Brook, on your right (take care not to miss it) and over a stile to arrive at a lane in front of some cottages **(GR. 531477)**.

Cross the lane and join a track the other side, signposted as a pubic footpath. The track runs gently uphill between hedgerows heading for "Wickhurst Farm" with its twin oasthouses. As you near the farm the track becomes tarmacced and it is well worth pausing a moment to take in the scene behind. As you approach the twin oasthouses ignore a drive leading off to your right and shortly after passing the oasthouses, keep to the track as it forks right (do not make the mistake of wandering into the farm entrance), to pass to the right of the farmhouse. After the farmhouse the track bends right to skirt an outbuilding and as the track then leads left around the outbuilding, you should leave it by passing through the second gate on your right, in the direction of a yellow arrow on a post on your right (take care not to miss it). Do not make the mistake of following the track round the back of the farm.

Pass through the gate and follow a track the other side along the left hand perimeter of a field with fine views right to the Greensand Ridge at Chartwell. At the far side pass through a gate ahead and after a few paces, pass through a second gate to thereafter continue ahead along the left hand perimeter of the next field. At the far side of this field, do not pass through the gate ahead, but turn left instead through a gateway into the adjacent field and then continue along the right hand perimeter of this field, with good views left back to "Wickhurst Farm". Later, when the field perimeter ends, continue straight on across the centre of the field to, at the far side, go over a stile beside a gate and continue straight on across more fields. After a short distance, on meeting a hedge, maintain your direction, keeping the hedge on your right, and at the far side of the field, go over another stile beside a gate ahead and continue straight on across the next field, passing to the left of "Charcott Farm" (recommended accommodation). After passing the farm, make for the far right hand corner of the field and at the field corner, go over a stile and then turn left along a track to soon meet a lane at a bend **(GR. 521471)**.

Our route is straight ahead along the lane. However, if you wish to discover one more excellent hostelry, then turn left for a few metres to arrive at "The Greyhound", a freehouse. Only just over a hundred years in age, the pub feels much older. It is a true local and some of the locals can still remember its busiest period during the last war, when it was a haunt of airmen from the long gone local airfield. Have a couple of drinks here and you may, if you haven't already, regret not having booked in for B&B at "Charcott Farm"! Apart from the well kept beer, the owners serve some good honest food from a well thought out menu.

Returning to our route, continue along the lane and at a "T" junction turn right along another lane and follow this for approximately thirty metres before turning left onto a signposted public footpath. This is fenced and leads between fields heading for St. Luke's church at our homing beacon, Chiddingstone.

i *Chiddingstone Airfield The fields to your left, incredible though it may seem, once housed an airfield. It first saw use during the first World War and between the wars was primarily used for a flying circus. The circus often took people up for stunt rides and the owner and entrepreneur, during one such ride, spotted the potential of a nearby flat area and shortly after, Gatwick Airport was born. During the second World War the airfield was a base for aircraft specialising in dropping spies behind enemy lines. Not long after the war, the airfield closed and*

14

apart from a few low brick buildings and gun emplacements, scarcely nothing remains today which would recall its existence. Perhaps one day someone will erect a memorial to avoid the danger of the airfield being forgotten forever.

At the far side of the field, on meeting a road, turn right to arrive at the layby opposite St. Luke's church and the start of our walk. If you have energy and capacity for some more refreshment then "The Little Brown Jug" is only a few paces away. A comfortable freehouse, this pub serves a wide range of food and also offers B&B, a nice idea as after toasting the many memories of the day, B&B may be the only thing you are fit for!

ACCOMMODATION

The Leicester Arms, Penshurst. Tel: 01892 870551
On the walk, this is an inn simply oozing with history. It is situated at the centre of Penshurst, just across the road from the famous "Penshurst Place". All the rooms are comfortably furnished and all are en suite. A stay here also allows you to experience Penshurst in the evenings, at its quietest - a memorable experience.

Charcott Farm, Charcott. Tel: 01892 870024
On the walk, this is ideal if you want peace and quite in country surroundings. The comfortable accommodation is in a period farmhouse with lots of character. The proprietors are used to walkers and to get you going in the morning, try the "Charles Royal Porridge" with milk straight from the cow.

Youth Hostel, Kemsing YHA, Kemsing. Tel: 01732 761341
Approximately nine miles from the walk, the hostel was once a vicarage in an attractive village at the foot of the North Downs. Quite a large hostel with fiftyeight beds, it can be busy in summer with school parties, so be warned and book ahead.

Camping and Caravanning, Oldbury Hill, Styants Bottom. Tel: 01732 762728
Approximately eight miles from the walk, this is a Camping and Caravanning Club site which is open to non-members. Quite a small site, it is set in a beautiful location surrounded by National Trust woodland.

THE WRATH OF WROTHAM

Distance: 9³/₄ miles (15.65km)

Time: Allow approximately 4¹/₂ hours

Map: Ordnance Survey Landranger Map 188

START
WROTHAM
120M

FINISH
WROTHAM
120M

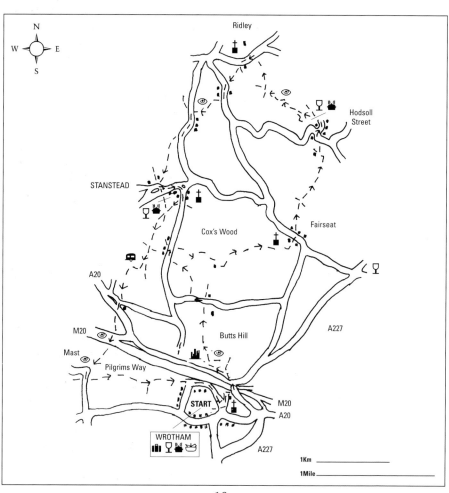

Walk Summary

This is a beautiful walk exploring the hills and valleys north of the North Downs escarpment above Wrotham. It is an area often overlooked by walkers and though close to London, you will rarely see anybody else except perhaps the odd local exercising their dog. Starting from Wrotham, there is a very steep climb to the top of Butts Hill, after which the route drops in and out of several valleys before dropping dramatically down the North Downs escarpment over the M20 and back to Wrotham.

Though not too strenuous, this is by no means a level walk and the ascent at the beginning can be quite difficult, especially in wet weather. Mud can, as usual, be a problem in places - so wear those boots!

Start - GR. 612593 Map 188

The walk starts from Wrotham village which is sandwiched between the M20 and M26. If coming from London along the M20, exit at junction 2. If coming from the east, join the M26 at junction 3 and come off at the next junction, junction 2a. Wrotham is signposted at "Wrotham village only" from a roundabout between the two motorways. The A20 and the A227 also pass beside Wrotham, connecting at the aforementioned roundabout. Street parking at Wrotham is easily possible but preferable is the signposted and free car park off a lane opposite the village church.

The nearest railway station is at Borough Green and from there it is about a two mile walk to Wrotham. There is no obvious alternative start.

THE WRATH OF WROTHAM

The walk starts from in front of Wrotham's majestic church, the tower of which has an arch at its base. This is bound to raise a little curiosity, so before beginning our walk I think it is worth discovering a little about the village first.

Wrotham (GR. 612593 Map 188) is one of those quirky English names, the pronunciation of which bears little resemblance to the spelling. Wrotham is in fact pronounced "Rootum" and it is important to get this right if you want to avoid being unfairly labelled as an ignorant day tripper! The name is probably derived from a Saxon Chieftain or possibly earlier. It has also been suggested that it could be after a bloody skirmish between the Saxons and the Danes, though there is little evidence of this.

The village, considering its position close to so many main roads, is surprisingly tranquil and has a distinct rural feel. It is no stranger to passing traffic and for centuries, before the intrusion of the M20, was a major staging post for coaches travelling between London, Canterbury and the coast. The old London to Dover road dates from pre-Norman times and Wrotham rose in importance as the road became busier. The Archbishop of Canterbury built a palace here to rest at whilst travelling to and from Canterbury, but it was pulled down by Archbishop Simon Islip in 1349 and the rubble used to construct his own palace at Maidstone. The arch beneath the tower of the village church once led to the palace. The palace explains why Wrotham has such a fine church, a truly English church, for it was dedicated to St. George long before he was adopted as the Patron Saint of England.

17

Wrotham, like so many Kentish villages, had a turbulent time during the Tudor period. Henry VIII stayed at "Wrotham Place", opposite "The Bull", whilst waiting for confirmation that Anne Boleyn had been beheaded. "Wrotham Place" still stands but has been much altered since Henry VIII stayed there. Just seventeen years later, Wrotham was involved in another crisis created by the Tudors. By this time Mary Tudor (Bloody Mary) was on the throne and busy wreaking vengeance on all those who had brought about the Protestant Reformation. Kent was particularly hard hit. In England, three hundred people were burned at the stake, seventyfour of them from Kent. The last unfortunate soul, John Corneford, was in fact a son of Wrotham. As a result of her bloody slaughter, Mary's popularity waned and when she announced her marriage to King Philip of Spain, England's arch enemy, some people cracked.

Rebellion was inevitable and it is hardly surprising that the most dangerous started in Kent. The rebellion was led by Sir Thomas Wyatt and almost succeeded. His army marched right up to the walls of the old City of London where Mary is said to have strengthened the resolve of her own army by her cool determination not to give in. The rebellion was crushed and as a result, the unfortunate Lady Jane Grey, the reluctant nine day Queen, was executed along with her husband. Lady Jane had hastily been proclaimed Queen, against her will, after the death of Edward VI, by the ruling Council to avoid Mary, a Catholic, claiming the throne. Mary, the rightful heir, quickly gathered an army and with little opposition, took the throne by force and imprisoned Jane in the Tower. There she would have stayed indefinitely had not her father joined the rebellion during which he was killed. With the involvement of Lady Jane's father, under Tudor politics, Mary had little choice but to have Jane and her husband executed, ending one of the most shameful episodes of the Tudor reign. There is a moving painting of Lady Jane's execution by Paul Delaroche at the National Gallery in London.

After their defeat, supporters of the rebellion fled along what is now the A20 back to Kent, where they were intercepted at Wrotham by soldiers loyal to Mary, led by Lord Bergavenny. A bloody skirmish ensued and the rebels were massacred at an area once known as Blacksole Field (now partly covered by houses and passed at the end of our walk).

After the rebellion, the village saw relative peace for over two hundred years until 1799, when it witnessed the chase and capture of two more rebels, better described as deserters. These two men were deserting from an army put together to fend off Napoleon. The two men were intercepted at Wrotham and after a short battle, captured, but not before one of them had shot and killed Colonel Shadwell, the officer in charge of detaining them. A plaque outside "The Bull" inn recalls the event and his ghost is said to haunt the pub, the current landlady even claims to have seen it!

This brings me nicely onto the village's hostelries. "The Bull", a freehouse with its old AA sign, is the oldest pub in the village. Dating from the 14th century, it was built as a coaching inn and to this day offers accommodation. It is an atmospheric place (if you can ignore the ridiculous bulls head above the fireplace) and probably the best of the pubs in which to celebrate the completion (I hope) of your day's adventure. It also has a superb restaurant on which it stakes its reputation. The most prominent pub in the village however, facing the tiny village *square and church, is "The Three Post Boys", Greene King. At weekends it tends to fill up with day trippers and has lost that warm local atmosphere. The two most local pubs are situated in the part of the High Street which leads east to west from "The Bull". They are "The George and Dragon", Courage, and "The Rose and Crown", Shepherd Neame. The latter is in my opinion, the better of the two and is also the home of the local Morris Men. Along the same street are most of Wrotham's shops, including a general stores and Post Office, should you need to stock up.*

To start, facing the church tower, turn left along the road to walk uphill and when the road forks, keep right to follow a road which is marked as a dead end. You should now be walking between the village cricket green on your right and a graveyard on your left. Further on, after passing the cricket ground and just as the road begins to bend left, leave the road and turn right onto a signposted public bridleway, also marked as the North Downs Way. This takes the form of a tarmac path and leads up to the main road, the A227. Turn left along the main road to cross over the M20 motorway and at the other side, on reaching a roundabout, continue straight ahead and cross the A20 which is signposted to West Kingsdown and Brands Hatch. Do not make the mistake of crossing the road on your right.

At the other side of the A20, join a signposted public footpath leading left uphill, running parallel with the A20. The footpath soon leads out to a dead end road and parking area where you should turn right passing in front of the entrance to a house and in the direction of a yellow footpath arrow, leading directly uphill. After approximately ten metres, take another marked footpath (yellow arrow) on your left to now walk diagonally up the side of Butts hill (take care not to miss it). Although you are, at this point, very close to both the M20 and A20 which are within earshot below, this path is extremely pleasant, indeed, where gaps in the vegetation on your left allow there are fine views to be enjoyed across to the Greensand Ridge and through the Bourne valley to the Weald.

The path you are on follows a fence on your left before, after some distance, turning sharp right to lead directly up the side of the hill. This part of the climb is particularly steep and care is needed, especially in wet weather, if you are to avoid slipping - you will definitely need those boots. Almost upon reaching the top of the hill, go over a crossing path and carry straight on, to now walk along the edge of some pleasant woodland with a field on your right. Keep to the path, ignoring all minor turnings off, to later enter the field ahead where, as before, you should continue straight on, now walking across the centre of the field with the added satisfaction that already, you have conquered the highest point on today's walk.

At the far side of the field, pass through a gap in the hedge to carry straight on across the centre of the next field heading for a point just to the left of a house. On a clear day here, there are very different views ahead to the industrial river Thames and to Grays in Essex. In contrast to the previous views enjoyed, the industrial scene does not destroy the view but tends to make it more interesting. If you are a keen map reader it is a good place from which to identify landmarks. To your left at this point also, is the BBC mast in Cooper's Wood, something which will remain a landmark and navigational point throughout our walk.

At the far side of the field, pass through a gap in the hedge to reach a lane **(GR. 609606)** in front of a house. Turn left along the lane, ignoring a footpath the other side, and keep to the lane to shortly after ignore another signposted footpath on the left. Continue instead, until you meet a signposted footpath on your right which you should take, passing through a gap in the hedge beside a field gate to do so (there could be a stile here later). Carry straight on across the field, heading just to the left of a wood ahead, to meet and follow the left hand perimeter of the wood. This is a particularly attractive part of the walk, the wood having some fine old beech trees with their branches spreading majestically over the edge of the field. The wood is also home to much wildlife from rabbits and squirrels to pheasants and grouse, which scatter from your path as you approach.

At the far side of the field, go over a stile ahead into another field where you should continue across the field, in the direction of a yellow arrow, dipping in and out of a lush green valley, the first of many valleys we shall cross today. At the far side of the field, go over a stile beside a field gate and continue straight on, still going uphill, along the left hand perimeter of another field. At the far side of this field, cross another stile and bear diagonally right across the centre of the next field to reach and cross a stile beside a field gate and reach a lane **(GR. 604612)**.

Turn right along the lane and follow it for approximately one hundred metres to pass "Standsted Lodge Farm" and soon after, go over a stile on your right into a field to join a signposted footpath (stone post). Continue along the right hand field perimeter and as the field meets Cox's wood on your right, go over a stile on your right and thereafter, follow the path through the wood. If you are walking this way in spring, then you will be rewarded with one of the prettiest bluebell displays in Kent.

i **Bluebells** *in late spring are an attractive feature on any Kent walk. They are one of the few flowers which can survive under the canopy of the wood. The reason for their success is that they bloom before the trees get their leaves and block out the light. They are virtually the only flower that does this, the reason why they have such a monopoly on the woodland floor. Bluebells struggle to survive close to other plants and because of this are only usually found in woodland environments.*

The old term for bluebells is "crowtoes". Their bulbs contain starch and were used by the Elizabethans to stiffen their elaborate ruffs. Over the years, the bulbs have also been crushed to make glue.

After a short distance, the path begins to descend, in places aided by steps, to eventually arrive at the far side of the wood. Go over a stile here to enter a field at the bottom of the valley crossed earlier and continue, bearing very slightly diagonally left across the centre to commence your climb of the other side of the valley.

At the far side of the field, pass through a gap in the fence (there could be a stile or gate here later) and thereafter, follow a track ahead, still going uphill. After a few paces the track turns left into a field and you should leave it here to continue straight on along a path ahead which soon brings you out into a small field. Once again, you should continue ahead, keeping a rather loose hedgerow on your right. Take care not to pass through any of the gaps in the hedgerow, but continue to reach and cross a stile at the far side of the field and at this point, ignore a yellow arrow pointing right.

After the stile, ignore another stile on your left and carry straight on across the centre of a field, passing to the left of a beautiful half timbered house. At the far side of the field, go over a stile ahead and bear diagonally right across the next field, heading for a stile at the far right hand corner which you should cross. (At the time of writing, work was being done on the fencing and field perimeters here could change. As long as you pass to the left of the house, making for the main field's right hand corner, you will not go wrong). Thereafter, go diagonally across the centre of the next field, now descending into a valley.

At the bottom of the field, pass through a gap in the hedge and continue straight across the next field, going uphill, where as you climb you should bear left in the direction of a yellow arrow on a wooden post. You will shortly reach the top of the field where you should carry straight on along the perimeter, with a fence on your right. The field naturally comes to an end as it meets Wessells wood and here you should follow the path right, into the wood. The path twists and turns through the wood and sometime later, runs alongside the perimeter of a field on your right before suddenly bending sharp left to pass through the centre of the wood, before arriving at a stile to a field the other side. In the distance ahead, on a clear day, the village of Fairseat, our next destination, is visible.

Go over the stile and continue ahead along the left hand perimeter of the field, going downhill and when the perimeter gives way, carry straight on across the centre of the field to reach a stile at the bottom of a valley. Go over the stile and then a second stile into another field and continue ahead across the centre of the field, going uphill, heading for a stile beside a gate the other side. As you progress, if you look to your left down the valley you will see the tiny village of Stansted, a destination on the return leg of our walk.

At the far side, go over the stile and carry straight on, still going uphill, now following a track through a field. At the far side, pass through a gate ahead and continue ahead, still following the track, taking time here to stop for a break and take in the lovely view behind. As you near the far side of the field, the first buildings of the village of Fairseat once again come into view. Keep to the track to arrive at a pair of gates at the far left hand corner of the field through which you should pass to follow a fenced track the other side. The track takes you into a farmyard. Carry straight on through the farmyard where many of the farm buildings have been converted into dwellings, and pass through another gate ahead at the far side. Thereafter, continue ahead along a tarmac drive to soon arrive at a lane at the centre of Fairseat village, in front of the village pond and beside a small modern church on your left.

Fairseat (GR.622613 Map 188) is a quite rural farming village little changed over the centuries. The old village Post Office (right of the pond) has now closed but still receives letters in its postbox, set in the wall. Opposite the pond is a fine Georgian manor house. The one institution that still survives is the village pub though this is about a mile right along the lane. The hostelry, "The Vigo" inn, started as a drovers stop. It now finds itself on the busy A227 but stubbornly refuses to alter its ways. Inside, you will not hear the sound of piped music or fruit machines, instead just the contented conversation of drinkers enjoying some of the best kept beer in Kent.

To continue, cross the lane and pass to the left of the pond to go through an old iron kissing gate, beside a gate, into a field. Go diagonally left across the centre of the field, heading for the far left hand corner, and on reaching the corner, go over a stile and continue in the same direction across the centre of the next field. As you walk there are excellent views to your left across rolling green fields to the Thames and to your right, an imposing communications tower. At the far side of the field, go over a stile and maintain your direction across the centre of the next field, heading for Hall Wood.

At the far side, cross over a stile to enter Hall Wood and immediately arrive at a "T" junction in the form of a path. Turn right along the path and after a few paces, ignore two paths off to your right in quick succession, keeping to the main path as it bends left. Thereafter, ignore all other turnings off and follow the path until it eventually bends right into a field on your right. You should turn left here and follow the field perimeter, with a tall hedgerow on your left, and at the far side of the field, continue ahead to re-enter Hall Wood. At the other side of the wood, ensure you do not enter the field on your right but carry straight on, now following a hedged track, often used by horses in wet weather so I hope you are wearing those boots!

The track leads to a "T" junction where you should turn left onto another track to shortly pass through a metal gate and enter a concreted yard lined by farm buildings. Continue ahead for approximately twenty metres and then turn right to pass through another metal gate and thereafter, follow another track ahead, passing a rather murky pond on your right as you do so. Later, after passing to the left of "Home Farm House", the track arrives at a road **(GR. 625628)** where you should continue to follow the road ahead (do not turn right). Keep to the road, passing some houses, and as it bends sharp left leave it to continue straight ahead along another road, following the very important sign for "The Green Man" pub and, should you need it, the public telephone. This road is also marked as a dead end.

The road you are now following leads past "Hodsoll Street Village Hall" before arriving at Hodsoll Street's beautiful village green and the excellent "Green Man" pub (Whitbread). This really is an idyllic scene, especially with the pub included! A warm welcome indeed to Hodsoll Street.

Hodsoll Street (GR. 625630 Map 188) centre is a pleasant and surprising site after the rather ordinary approach. The pub looks onto the green, along with a number of cottages, all differing in style but all typical of Kent. The village pub was once the cottage at the opposite side of the green and the cottage beside this used to be the village Post Office. At this time, the pub's present building housed the servants to "Holywell Park". In later years the Lord of the manor objected to having to look out on a noisy pub and moved the hostelry to its present position! On the pub wall a notice briefly explains the history of "The Green Man" and I will try to expand on it here.

The celebration or play of the Mummers dates back to Pagan times. The Green Man represents the mysterious spirits of the trees that apparently deserted them in mid-winter. The ceremony was to encourage the spirits back for regrowth and a new season. To achieve this, the Pagans offered up a human sacrifice and this was

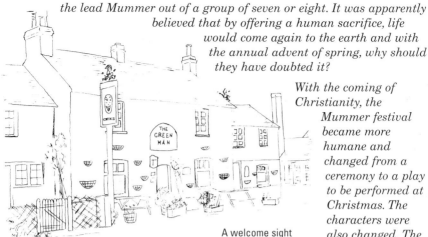

the lead Mummer out of a group of seven or eight. It was apparently believed that by offering a human sacrifice, life would come again to the earth and with the annual advent of spring, why should they have doubted it?

With the coming of Christianity, the Mummer festival became more humane and changed from a ceremony to a play to be performed at Christmas. The characters were also changed. The

A welcome sight

sacrificial victim (winter) became a Turkish knight, Saladin, and the slayer (representing summer), King or St. George. In later plays the slain was always brought back to life by a doctors magic potion, representing the birth of spring. The traditional costume of a Mummer is a bell shaped wicker basket covered in green leaves, though with the few existing plays today, green paper is normally used instead. In later years, Mummer groups would travel from manor to manor or from pub to pub, much like Morris Dancers. Later still, around the 18th century, the Mummer became a key figure at May Day celebrations. By this time he was usually a lone Mummer, not part of a group, and was normally led around the village or town before being symbolically killed. A May Day poem,

"Green George we bring,
Green George we accompany,
May he feed our herds well,
If not, to the water with him"

was often chanted during the procession. The water in the last line refers to him being drowned as a manner of sacrifice. With the Mummer's role changing, so did the name and future Mummer's were frequently called, Green George, May King, Jack-in-the-Green or simply Green Man.

The original words to the Mummer's play have also virtually been forgotten, though Thomas Hardy wrote his own version from memory after having seen a Mummer play during his childhood. Hardy also involves Mummers in his novel "The Return of the Native".

The Green Man referred to by the pub sign was a local chimney sweep who acted as the village's main Mummer in the late 18th century. Looking at the size of the village it is hard to believe there were enough people to hold a Mummer's play let alone watch it! In fact, so small is the village that in a census in 1931, the village was missed and hence is often referred to as "The Forgotten Village".

Forget the village maybe, but one could never forget the village hostelry. "The Green Man" is a fine English pub, selling good honest pub grub with a smattering

23

of international dishes. The green at the front is beautiful but the pub garden, complete with aviary and goats, is equal to it. Whatever the season, you will enjoy a drink at "The Green Man".

To continue, carry straight on past the pub, with the green on your right to then turn left in front of the gates to "Holywell Park", in the direction of a stone footpath sign. This takes you past the beautiful "Holywell Farmhouse", complete with a huge crocked chimney. After a short distance, pass through a couple of gateways and follow a fenced tarmac driveway, passing to the right of a wooden tiled bungalow. Thereafter, pass through another gateway into a field and cross the field, bearing diagonally left in the direction of a yellow arrow. Do not carry straight on in the direction of another yellow arrow. As a guide, you should be heading for the field's far left hand corner, beside a small copse.

On reaching the field corner, go over a stile and continue ahead along the left hand perimeter of the next field and after approximately fifty metres, cross another stile on your left onto a fenced path. Turn right along the path and sometime later, after passing through a gate, follow the fenced path right, ignoring the stile ahead. After approximately forty metres, go straight across a concrete drive and through a gate the other side into a field. Thereafter, you should walk diagonally left across the field, in the direction of a bridleway sign and heading for a gate the other side. N.B. The field through which you are now walking - fencing is temporary and could easily be removed in the future. Please bear this in mind when route finding.

Pass through the gate and continue in the same direction across the next field, heading for a footpath sign and gate at the far right hand corner of the field. Pass through the gate at the field corner and carry straight on along a fenced path, which runs along the edge of a valley on your right, complete with views across to the hamlet of Ridley and Ridley church, our next destination. Sometime later, pass through another gate to soon arrive at a "T" junction. Turn right here, now going downhill, to follow a sunken path through Job's Hill Wood. After a short distance, the path bends left and you should leave it at this point (take care not to miss it) and bear right to follow a narrower path, still going downhill. A few metres on, you will arrive at a stile at the perimeter of the wood which you should cross into a field.

Carry straight on across the field, crossing the bottom of the valley, to soon join and follow the right hand perimeter which is made up of a small copse, at the same time climbing the other side of the valley. When the copse on your right ends, bear diagonally left across the field and head for a small church, just visible, the other side. As you progress, there are fine views left across rolling fields to the BBC mast at Cooper's Wood, seen at the beginning of the walk. At the far side of the field, you will arrive at a lane and at the small hamlet of Ridley. Ahead of you is the beautiful church of St. Peter's, and to your right, an unusual thatched well.

i **Ridley (GR. 616639 Map 188)** *is a truly lovely place. It has a church, a well and yet only a farm and one house to speak of, to take advantage of these amenities. The church is most charming and rare these days, normally unlocked. I had reason to be grateful for this for when researching this walk, I was caught in a* *summer storm and St. Peter's made a welcome shelter. The thatched well is particularly unusual. Council records date it around 1810, though it almost certainly in reality pre-dates the church.*

When Christianity first came to Britain, churches tended to be built close to Pagan religious sites. Water was particularly important to the Celts who worshipped streams, pools and springs and from this sprang (please excuse the pun) Holy Wells. Today, many churches encompass a holy well in their churchyard and some even use the water for baptism. It is quite likely that Ridley's well once had a religious significance and hence the peculiar position of the church.

The Holy Well

You may be interested to know that the modern practices of throwing coins into a fountain and making a wish at a wishing well, stem from the old Celtic practice of throwing jewellery or weaponry into water as a gift to their Gods.

After perhaps making a wish, turn left along the lane, going downhill, and after approximately three hundred metres, shortly after passing a house, turn left onto a signposted public bridleway. The bridleway which is in the form of a track, almost takes you back on yourself, still going downhill. Follow it for approximately thirty metres until you see a path on your right, which at the time of writing is unmarked (take care not to miss it). Take the path right to go down a bank and cross a stile into a field. Go straight across the centre of the field, in the direction of a yellow arrow, dipping in and out of a shallow valley and at the far side, pass through a gap in a hedge to reach a lane, onto which you should turn left. Do not at this point be startled by the sound of roaring engines. It will simply be motor racing at nearby Brands Hatch.

The lane passes through a virtual tunnel of holly and past several attractive properties, immediately after which, you should leave it to join a signposted public footpath on your right (take care not to miss.it), beside the drive to "Haven Manor". The footpath which is fenced, at first follows the perimeter of the garden to the manor and when the garden ends, bear diagonally left across the centre of a field. On a clear day, the BBC mast at Cooper's Wood is again easily visible and to help you, you should be heading for this. On nearing the far side of the field, the path begins to descend into yet another valley and at the far side, pass through a gap in the hedge ahead into another field and turn immediately right to descend directly into the valley, along the right hand field perimeter.

At the bottom of the field, pass through a gap in the hedge to meet a lane running along the bottom of the valley, onto which you should turn left. Follow the lane along the valley bottom, ignoring a signposted footpath on your right soon after and continue to pass the magnificent old thatched "Malthouse" and thereafter, keep to the lane for approximately one hundred metres before turning right over a stile, between two gates. This takes you into a field where you should walk diagonally left, uphill, across the centre, in the direction of the yellow arrow, heading for the field's far left hand corner. Once again, as a further guide, you should be walking roughly in the direction of the BBC mast in Cooper's Wood.

As you near the corner of the field there is a good view to your left over some of the buildings which make up the village of Stansted and beyond to the valley we crossed at the early stages of our walk approaching the village of Fairseat. You should also at this point, see a stile which is approximately twenty metres to the left of the field corner. Make for this, go over it and continue across the centre of the next field, heading for another stile just visible beside a tree stump the other side. At the far side of the field, go over the stile and carry straight on along the left hand perimeter of the next field to meet and cross another stile at the far side. Continue ahead to shortly arrive at a drive and turn left to immediately cross a stile beside a pair of gates to reach a lane and the village of Stansted.

Turn left along the lane, going downhill and ignore a signposted footpath on your right to soon after meet another lane, Plaxdale Green Road. Turn left, still going downhill and on reaching the bottom of the valley and after passing a white weatherboarded cottage on your right, leave the lane and follow a path across a small green on your right, going uphill, to arrive at the entrance to the village church, St. Mary the Virgin. Beside the church there is another beautiful white weatherboarded cottage which looks as though it is only half finished, with the left half still to complete. It is a pretty picture and a good point at which to tell you a little about Stansted village.

Stansted (GR. 607622 Map 188) derives its name from the Saxon era and literally means, "stony ground". The pretty village church looks over most of the village and is beautifully sited. It dates from the 14th century, though it is believed there was originally a Saxon church on the site and some say, a pile of rubble in the churchyard is the remains of this church. Also in the churchyard is a fine old yew,

Half a cottage!

26

said to be over one thousand years old. An old yew tree is always a sign that there was a previous place of worship before a church. Yew trees were revered in Pagan times when it was believed they protected the village from evil spirits and were planted at most sacred sites. Today, yew trees still tend to be planted in churchyards, even if the church is new.

Stansted unwittingly rose to fame recently, with the double theft of its bronze war memorial. It was first stolen in 1964, but found again in a quarry although somewhat damaged. The villagers had it restored only to see it stolen for a second time in October 1995. This time, sadly, to date it has not been recovered. A new memorial is planned and I doubt if the council will risk another made of bronze.

The one village hostelry is "The Black Horse", a freehouse. It is a good honest local, serving a good range of ales and bar food. Walkers are welcome. There is a danger though that the present landlord may retire shortly and if this is the case, I hope the pub lives on and does not go the same way as so many other country pubs.

To continue, keep turning right to arrive at the village pub, "The Black Horse". Thereafter, follow the lane past the pub uphill and continue until just before you reach a small parking area on your left in front of a signposted footpath. Turn right here (not left) to join a somewhat concealed footpath, marked by a low stone post, and follow it between gardens before crossing a stile into a field. Turn left and follow the field perimeter to later meet and cross a stile ahead and thereafter follow a path downhill through woodland.

After a short distance, go over a crossing path and carry straight on in the direction of a yellow arrow (do not make the mistake of taking the path left marked by a red arrow). In spring this area is alive with bluebells. After a short distance, cross another stile ahead and continue along the edge of a very narrow field, at the far side of which you should go over a stile beside a field gate to carry straight on along the left hand perimeter of the next field. Further on, the field begins to rise and as you progress ignore a footpath on your left but continue ahead keeping to the field perimeter to eventually reach the field's far left hand corner.

Go over a stile into another field where you should continue across the field, bearing very gently right, heading for a stile marked by two yellow topped wooden poles at the edge of a wood, Thrift Wood. Cross the stile into the wood and carry straight on, ignoring almost immediately after, a path off to your left and right. Soon after, turn right in the direction of a yellow arrow on a wooden post and keep to the path which now winds uphill through attractive woodland to reach a Caravan and Camping park (recommended accommodation) and turn right here along a track.

The track soon bends left to pass beneath some electricity pylons. After passing beneath the pylons, follow the track round as it bends left again and stay on it to later pass to the right of some washrooms and toilets. Shortly after, at a "T" junction, carry straight on to go over a stile ahead into a field. Do not make the common mistake of following the cow trail across the centre of the field, but cross the field, heading for the far right hand corner.

On reaching the field corner, cross a stile beside a gate to meet a lane **(GR. 598606)**. A short detour - right for a few paces will bring you to "The Hilltop Hotel" (recommended accommodation). Our way however, is to cross the lane and follow another lane ahead. As this ends, continue ahead between some posts to arrive at the noisy A20. Cross the A20 with care to join and follow a track, signposted as a public bridleway the other side. The track, at first, runs alongside Cooper's Wood before ending at a gate, through which you should pass into a field. Thereafter, continue ahead across the centre, following a line of oak trees. To your right now and quite close, is the BBC mast in Cooper's Wood and from here you can really begin to gauge its size. The field is often used for country shows and if you are lucky, you may well encounter just such a pleasant distraction when walking this way.

As the oak trees curve gently left you should carry straight on to pass through a gate at the far side and thereafter, cross over, by way of a bridge, the busy M20. Being a walker like anybody else I am not a lover of main roads. However, there is definitely something about standing over the top of a motorway and this bridge in particular, must afford one of the best motorway bridge views in England, with a fine panorama over the Kentish countryside.

At the other side of the motorway, ignore a path forking off to the right and carry straight on, to start your descent of the North Downs. As the path descends you can enjoy many good views, when breaks in the scrub allow, to your left across to Wrotham our finishing point. Eventually, near the bottom, the path meets a parking area where you should continue ahead to soon cross a second parking area, before coming out at a lane **(GR. 594597)**.

Turn left along the lane, thereby maintaining your direction, still going downhill, and after approximately fifty metres turn left onto a signposted byway. This takes the form of a hedged track which runs between fields and is also marked as the North Downs Way. It is also supposedly the route once taken by pilgrims on their way to Canterbury (see "In Celtic Footsteps"), though this track is much older than that and was probably in use as far back as the Neolithic period, around 4000 BC. It is almost impossible to imagine the many different feet which have walked this way over the centuries. If only tracks could talk ....

From the track there are good views to your left of the North Downs and of course, our old friend the BBC mast. To your right the views are deep into Kent to the Greensand Ridge. Ahead of you now, is the less attractive new development of our final destination, Wrotham. The track later passes under an electricity pylon and later still, meets a track leading off to the right which you should ignore to continue straight on. After this, the track soon draws level with the first houses of Wrotham where the field on the right, just before the houses, is Blacksole field, where the massacre of rebels against Mary Tudor took place (described earlier). Then the field stretched further east where modern housing now stands. On meeting a lane, continue ahead (do not turn right), thereby keeping to the North Downs Way and further on, ignore another signposted footpath off to the right down Blacksole Lane. A short time after this, at a crossroads in front of the beautiful "Pilgrims Cottage", turn right passing the village school and follow the road into Wrotham centre. Though it is hard to imagine today, this road was once the main road, the equivalent of the modern A20.

As you approach the village centre you will arrive at a "T" junction and the village High Street. Turn right here and retrace your steps to the church and the start of our walk. You may wish to celebrate your return by raising a glass in one of Wrotham's friendly pubs and as you mellow, contemplate on a village with such a bloody past, a past it hides so well.

ACCOMMODATION

The Bull Hotel, Wrotham. Tel: 01732 885522

Virtually on the walk, this is a lovely 14th century coaching inn full of charm and character. All rooms have colour TV and most are en suite. They are all well decorated. The hotel also has a restaurant which is locally renowned.

The Old Post House, Fairseat. Tel: 01732 822444

Virtually on the walk, this is the ideal place if you want peace and tranquillity. Accommodation is in a lovely 18th century house with a cottage style garden. All rooms have TV and tea and coffee making facilities. A lovely place to stay.

Youth Hostel, Kemsing YHA, Kemsing. Tel: 01732 761341

Approximately five miles form the walk, the hostel was once a vicarage in an attractive village at the foot of the North Downs. Quite a large hostel with fiftyeight beds, it can be busy in summer with school parties, so be warned and book ahead.

Camping and Caravanning, Thriftwood Park. Tel: 01732 822261
On the walk (the walk virtually passes through it), this is a pleasant site set in several acres of woodland. The camp also has purpose-built barbecues allowing you to continue to enjoy that "outdoor experience". Very well run, but make sure you take your muddy boots off before entering the shop.

THE SOAR FEAT

Distance: 10 miles (16km)

Time: Allow approximately 4¹/₂ hours

Map: Ordnance Survey Landranger Map 188

| START OFFHAM 50M | KEEPERS COTTAGE 165M | BASTED 75M | FINISH OFFHAM 50M |

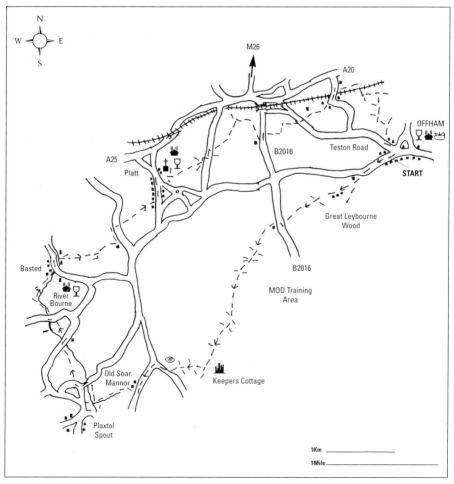

Walk Summary

With at least one walk in every book I try and explore footpaths away from the more popular areas covered by other walking books. This is just such a walk. Do not expect dramatic views and fairytale castles. Instead, you will discover rural Kent at work, the real Kent and at the end you will be a person richer in experience for it. Starting from Offham the first few miles explore Mereworth Woods before following lanes and paths through the fruit growing areas of Kent. After following the river Bourne and visiting the tranquil village of Brasted (good pub), the route then explores some beautiful Greensand woodland before returning to the start. Being an area not well known to walkers, some of the paths can become overgrown in summer and if you only bring shorts you will probably quickly regret it. Having said that, none of the paths are impassable and you are more than rewarded by the wildlife you are likely to encounter. The only other possible difficulty on this relatively easy walk is mud, but then that is hardly unusual. Come prepared and you will have a highly satisfying day out.

Start - GR. 657573 Map 188

The walk starts from the famous village green at Offham. Offham though not on a main road is easy to find, being well signposted locally. If coming via the M20, exit at junction 4 or via the M26 junction 2a. From junction 4 (M20), follow the signs to West Malling and just south of the town, turn onto the lane signposted to Offham and follow it to the village. From the M26, follow the A20 in the direction of the signs for Paddock Wood and after a short distance, turn right at the B2016, again in the direction of Paddock Wood. Almost immediately after, go under a railway line and then turn left in the direction of the sign for Offham and follow the lane into the village. If coming from the south, it is easiest to join to B2016 and then the A228 which passes close to the village from where Offham is signposted.

Parking at Offham is possible at the village green or there is a small car park on the road leading out, west of the village. If you park here, simply turn left to walk along the road and shortly arrive at the village green, our starting point. The nearest railway station is at West Malling from where it is possible to walk to Offham or alternatively, catch a bus or taxi. There is no obvious alternative start.

THE SOAR FEAT

Starting at Offham's famous green, your curiosity is immediately aroused by the unusual white pole with a revolving bar. A good reason to pause and find out a little about the village before we start.

Offham (GR. 657573 Map 188) started as a few houses straddling a Roman road. The Saxons were the first people to build a permanent settlement here and gave the village its name, Offham, meaning "homestead of a man called Offa". Offa could refer to the famous King Offa (see "The Darent Dare"), the first king of England, though Offa was a common Saxon name and could simply remember a local Chieftain or even a farmer.

31

Today, the village has a pleasant mixture of houses, with examples from virtually every century back to the 15th century. The prettiest part of the village is its centre where olde worlde cottages and fine Georgian houses cluster round the green, including one of the village pubs, "The Kings Arms". Above the rooftops, the white caps of oasthouses remind you that this is a Kentish scene.

It is the unusual white pole on the green, however, which commands your attention. The pole, which has a revolving paddle-shaped bar at the top with a weight hanging on a chain at one end, is a Tilting Pole or to use the Roman name, a Quintain. Developed, it is believed, by the Romans to train legionnaires, it became very popular in the Middle Ages to train knights in the art of jousting. Later, it became part of the May Day fun and games and by this time, most villages and towns would have had one. The idea was to ride "full tilt" (as fast as one could - this is where the expression originated), at the pole and strike the flat end of the revolving pole with a lance. A hit resulted in the arm spinning round at the rider's head who in turn had to be extremely nimble to avoid being knocked off his horse by the hanging weight, usually a bag of sand.

During May Day celebrations, huge crowds would gather to watch the tilting competition and where winning would go a long way to help one's climb up the social ladder of village life. No doubt, many competitors gathered at "The Kings Arms" for some "Dutch courage", but whether this affected or helped their performance one can only guess! Offham's tilting pole is the only remaining, working example in the country and occasionally, during May Day celebrations, the odd rider will still try his or her luck at tilting.

To start, at the green, take the lane signposted to Platt and Mereworth, which is the lane cutting across the centre of the green and follow it out of the village passing along the way, a number of pretty cottages and then a very murky pond. After the pond, stay on the lane for approximately a quarter of a mile, (in summer here, the roadside banks are a mass of wild strawberries - and very good they are too!) until you meet a track leading off to the left, signposted as a footpath to Seven Mile Lane. At the time of writing, the sign is in a pretty sorry state and so to be clear, the track which is semi tarmacced, is just before a house on the left with a corrugated roof. Take the track and after a few metres, as the track you are on bears left, leave it to follow another track ahead, this one not being tarmacced. As you continue, you should now have fields on your right with Offham Wood on your left. A short time later, ignore a path on your left to almost immediately after, pass to the right of a house, "Battle Cross". After the house, keep to the track passing several more properties on your left, with open fields to your right where there are good views to the North Downs escarpment. After the last property as the track bends left into a small holding, leave it to continue along a footpath ahead which follows the left hand perimeter of a field, with Great Leybourne Wood, part of Mereworth Woods, on your left. Sometime on, the field on your right ends and the path continues ahead through Great Leybourne Wood.

i **Great Leybourne Wood** *like so many other woods in this part of Kent, started life as a coppice, later to be abandoned. The wood therefore consists mainly of the popular coppice trees of sweet chestnut and hazel.*

Keep to the main path through the wood ignoring all turnings off and on meeting a crossing track ("Lords Walk"), carry straight on to a few paces after, arrive at a

32

crossing path. Again, carry straight on, going over the crossing path, to now follow a path which narrows quite considerably though it is still fairly easy to follow. After running in a straight line for some distance, the path twists through a dip after which it continues through the wood before finally arriving at the far side of the wood at a stile. Cross the stile into what is, at the time of writing, a strawberry field and continue straight on (avoiding the temptation of the strawberries) across the field, heading for a stile the other side.

It may interest you to know that the name "strawberry" is not, as many believe, ***i*** *because strawberries are grown on a bed of straw. It is in fact, derived from the Saxon word "streawberige", "Streaw" meaning "to strew or spread across the ground". The name "strawberry" therefore, literally means berries which spread across the ground, a very accurate description.*

At the far side of the field, go over the stile and turn right along a road, the B2016, for approximately twenty metres to then turn left onto the drive for "Leybourne Wood House". The drive is also marked by a low stone public footpath sign beneath a Scots pine.

Follow the drive passing to the right of the house and continue through a pair of gates to walk through the garden and thereafter, through one of the few traditional timber yards left in the South of England. The fencing here is still made using the old coppicing method.

Coppicing *dates back to when records began. The art of coppicing is to cut the* ***i*** *tree at the stump, encouraging new growth in the form of many slender branches. Depending on the use of the wood, the trees would be cut or coppiced between every seven and fifteen years. To avoid a cash flow crises, coppicing had to be strictly rotated to ensure there was always a fresh supply of timber to cut. The main use for coppicing in Kent was (and still is) for hop poles, which require approximately a thirteen year growth cycle. Every acre of hop field requires around 3,000 poles and one can immediately see why coppicing continues to be part of the Kent economy today (keep drinking that ale!). The main types of trees used in coppicing are sweet chestnut and hazel. Sweet chestnut are ideal for hop poles whereas hazel is more suitable for fencing. Ash, oak and birch are also sometimes coppiced.*

Though coppicing requires initial investment, the management is quite cheap thereafter. By coppicing a tree regularly one can keep it alive indefinitely - it will literally never die. To judge the age of a coppiced tree, you need to measure the width of its stump, or stool as it is known within the industry. A coppiced tree grows one foot in diameter roughly every one hundred years. A coppice always gives the impression of being young but by looking at the width of the stump, you will find that many of the trees are several hundred years old.

After the timber yard carry straight on, following a track through Leybourne Wood. Approximately one hundred metres on, the track forks and here you should take the left hand fork, more a path (take care not to miss it), and follow it through the wood ignoring any minor turnings off. This is a real woodland path with close standing trees virtually surrounding you at all times. Though at any one time you know you are only a short distance from open fields and human habitation, the wood can be very disorientating and your imagination can run wild. You may not expect to see wild boar but in stormy weather in particular, you cannot begin to wonder what lurks either side of the path and suddenly, it is all too easy to believe in the woodland spirits your grandparents used to speak about! After approximately one third of a mile, you will arrive (safely) at a "T" junction in front of a fence. Here, you should turn right for a few paces, before turning left through a gap in the fence, in the direction of a yellow arrow, to enter an area of woodland owned by the Ministry of Defence. This is also used as a training area and there are numerous signs warning you not to stray from the path. Undaunted, cross a track ahead and follow another track the other side, marked by roughly painted blue and yellow patches on the trees. Sometime on, on meeting a junction of tracks, carry straight on ignoring all turnings off to shortly join and follow a semi-tarmacced track ahead. This too is well marked by the blue and yellow paint marks on the trees.

Keep to the semi-tarmacced track, again ignoring any turnings off, until it bends sharp left at which point you should leave it to continue straight on, along another track, this one not being tarmacced. (If you meet a sign stating "Warning Dogs Patrolling - Keep Clear", you will know you have missed the track and should retrace your steps - approximately ten paces back). The track you have just joined is, as before, well marked by blue and yellow paint marks on the trees. The track leads to a "T" junction with another, more prominent track and here you should turn left to, after approximately twenty paces, turn right onto a path marked by a yellow footpath arrow. Pass through a gate, thereby leaving the Ministry of Defence area, and thereafter follow another wide track ahead, ignoring a crossing path. Follow the track for approximately two thirds of a mile, ignoring all turnings off, until you approach a large stone cottage, "Keeper's Cottage", a welcome landmark. Take care here, do not actually pass the cottage, but just as you approach the corner of the garden on your left, turn right onto a narrow path.

The path you have joined runs in a straight line through what is very much a working coppice and soon begins to descend to arrive at a crossing track, part of the Weald Way. Go over the crossing track and follow a now wider path ahead where after a short distance, the path descends ever more steeply. Go over another crossing path and continue straight on, still descending, through an area of coppice which in early summer has a beautiful ground covering of bluebells. Eventually, you will arrive at a fork at the edge of the wood with marvellous views ahead (if the undergrowth is not too high), across to Plaxtol and Rooks Hill, part of the Greensand Ridge. Take the left hand fork, in the direction of a yellow arrow (sometimes hidden), still descending to, after approximately thirty metres, come out at a lane **(GR. 624544)**.

Turn right along the lane which is quite a pleasant change after several miles of woodland walking, and follow it until you meet a lane which leads downhill to your left, signposted to Old Soar and "Old Soar Manor". Take this (Old Soar Road), to go even more steeply downhill now walking between high banks which protect the fruit trees of "Fairlawn Estate". Continue to later pass "Old Soar Oast" which at the time of writing, has its own small shop in the form of a small cart with an honesty box, selling jam, apple chutney and pure apple juice. Immediately after "Old Soar Oast", you will arrive at "Old Soar Manor", a National Trust property.

Old Soar Manor (GR. 619541 Map 188) *is a 13th century solar chapel, all that remains of a Medieval knights' dwelling, a stirring place and well worth a visit. In the place of the old house and attached to the chapel is a fine Georgian farmhouse (private). The name "soar" is extremely old and believed to be Celtic, or perhaps even older. It literally means, "free flowing stream or river" and probably refers to a small stream from a nearby spring, which passes close to the manor.*

i

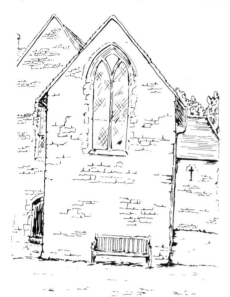

Haunted Soar Chapel

The ghost of a servant girl, Jenny, is said to haunt the chapel. The story goes that in 1775, whilst preparing a Christmas feast, a priest, somewhat the worse for wear from drink, seduced the poor girl and left her with child. On asking the priest for advice on what to do about her pregnancy, he simply instructed her to marry her boyfriend. The shock of hearing this caused Jenny to faint and as she fell she hit her head on the font, knocking her unconscious and as a consequence, she drowned in the font water. The priest kept quiet about the event, leaving Jenny's family to assume she had committed suicide. Jenny therefore, was buried in unconsecrated ground.

Jenny's ghost is said to frequently return to the chapel, determined to reveal the truth and have her body given a Christian burial. The trouble is, nobody knows where her body was buried, though there is a "white post corner" close by, indicating that a suicide victim may have been buried there (see "The Leopard's Loop"). If the story is true, let's hope that one day Jenny will find peace.

"Old Soar Manor" is open to the public from April to September from 10.00 a.m. to 6.00 p.m. At the time writing, admission is free.

After "Old Soar Manor", continue along the lane for another forty metres and then pass through a small gate on your right at the end of a long stone barn. Once through the gate, keep right along the edge of a field with farm buildings on your right and at the far side, go over a stile into another field, with good views to your left over Plaxtol village. To continue, go straight ahead, downhill, across the centre of a field. At the time of writing, the footpath has recently been redirected to the route you are walking now and therefore, an easy to follow path has yet to be established. You will simply have to make the best of it and at the bottom and the far side of the field, turn left to go over a crossing track and shortly after (a few paces), a second to thereafter, continue along the right hand perimeter of the field. As a guide, there should be an orchard in the field on the other side of the hedge on your right. A short distance on, the path joins another narrower path coming in from the left, where you should continue ahead with a stream, often overgrown, running between deep banks on your left. Eventually, you will meet a stile ahead which you should cross to go over a wooden plank bridge into another field.

Continue ahead along the left hand perimeter of the field to, at the far side, arrive at a particularly pleasant spot with the river Bourne bubbling around some tiny wooded islets, it is a tempting place to rest. Though the footbridge ahead is not part of the route, it is a good place from where to survey the scene.

i *A short detour can also be made by going over the bridge and following the path the other side, to a lane and then left along the lane to arrive at the pretty village green of Plaxtol Spout. I hope I have not misled you, for there is no pub here (it's another half a mile!), but there are some of the best preserved period cottages in Kent to be seen as well as Kent's oldest working forge. You will need to retrace your steps to rejoin the walk.*

To continue, our way is not over the footbridge, but right thereby continuing along the field perimeter, following the River Bourne on your left. You can in fact, if you prefer, at points, take a path which follows the river bank.

i *"Bourne", incidentally, is another Saxon name and means "intermittent stream" and normally refers to streams or rivers which regularly dry up.*

At the far side of the field you will meet a lane, onto which you should turn left to cross the River Bourne. After approximately thirty metres, turn right into Dux Lane and follow this uphill until you meet a signposted public footpath to Borough Green, on your right, this is just as you meet the first house on your right. Take this, noting as you turn the old cottage with its supported chimney.

The footpath, in the form of a track, leads across the centre of a field with views ahead to the North Downs and to your right, across typical Kent farmland to Mereworth Woods traversed during the earlier stages of our walk. In summer the track can become fairly overgrown, though there is usually a passage forged by other adventurous walkers! As you approach the far side of the field, the footpath meets and follows the right hand field perimeter ahead to the field corner, where you should exit by descending a bank through some scrub to come out at a lane **(GR. 608546)**. Turn right along the lane passing over the river Bourne once more and follow the lane up the other side of the valley for approximately fifty metres, before turning left onto a signposted public footpath opposite a corrugated barn. The footpath follows the left hand perimeter of a field with the shallow valley of the river Bourne sloping away to your left. At the far side of the field, continue ahead to descend a steep bank and meet yet another lane.

At the lane, ignore another footpath the other side and turn left instead to follow the lane and meet the river Bourne, for the third time, with the haunting ruins of an old mill on your right. Just before the bridge over the river, turn right onto a footpath and follow it with the river Bourne on your left.

Y *A short detour (approximately half a mile there and back), by continuing along the lane, will bring you to, in my opinion, one of the best pubs in Kent, "The Golding Hop". A very traditional and old country pub, it has an idyllic setting and inside, has an unusual gallery seating area. The name incidentally, is after a type of hop first grown by a W.M. Golding of Plaxtol. If the detour is too much now, then I recommend you visit perhaps by car on another day.*

Returning to our walk, after a few metres, go over a footbridge (with care) on your left (take care not to miss it), crossing the river Bourne yet again and at the other side, turn right along another path. Keep to the path ignoring all turnings off, as it twists and turns through the Bourne valley, rich in vegetation, the river itself meandering on your right. In late spring the valley is particularly pretty with the valley floor a carpet of ramsons and lily of the valley. Further on, the path passes to the left of some old dis-used watercress beds, now a haven for moorhens and frogs and almost immediately after this, the path forks where you should take the right hand path which keeps to the bottom of the valley. After this, continue to follow the path along the bottom of the valley, ignoring all further turnings off, to eventually arrive at a track beside a house on your left.

Follow the track ahead, later passing more beautiful houses, before arriving at a lane at the centre of Basted village, with a low stone bridge on your right and a miniature waterfall cascading down the bank beside it, a lovely scene.

Basted (GR. 607558 Map 188) is a pretty village once famous for making paper. *Numerous springs rise in the valley here and you can hear the sound of running* *water wherever you go. Many of the houses have springs rising in their gardens,* *which have been made into garden ponds. There is also a covered spring along the* *lane on your right. A short detour right, along the lane and uphill for a few* *metres, passing the small covered spring on the left, brings you to a traditional* *and very local pub, "The Plough", a tiled building with a long low bar. The pub* *sign is quite interesting showing the stars of The Plough as opposed to the* *traditional farming tool, the name though is actually taken from farming origins* *as the pub sits on Plough Hill. The pub is a freehouse and makes for a pleasant* *stop. You will have to retrace your steps to rejoin our walk.*

Returning to our walk, our way is left along Mill Lane which you should follow , passing a large office building on your right. After approximately thirty metres, fork right leaving the lane to follow the private road to the office complex (you should ignore the "No Public Right of Way" sign - this is meant for motor vehicles). After a few paces, turn first right to go over the river Bourne for the last time and continue to walk between the office block on your right and a warehouse on your left, to thereafter join a narrow path ahead marked as a public bridleway. Almost immediately after joining, ignore a narrow path on the left and carry straight on. The path runs through some lush woodland at the bottom of a valley, known as Long Bottom Wood and much further on, passes to the left of a disused waterworks. If you have children with you, make sure you take care here as there are no railings or protection to prevent a fall. Immediately after the waterworks, the path twists left to climb the valley side and at the top comes out at the edge of some fields.

Follow the footpath as it bends right here to run between the fields on your left and woodland on your right. The path later meets a field ahead where the path bends right along the field perimeter, going downhill. Keep to the field perimeter which twists left and right before arriving opposite a very pretty traditional tiled cottage. Do not make the mistake of joining the cottage drive, but instead turn left along a fenced path, going uphill and still following the field perimeter. After leaving the field behind the fenced path continues in a straight line, running parallel with a lane (often hidden) on your right. As the path goes over a rise, you are afforded lovely views ahead to the North Downs. Later, ignore a gate on your right and approximately fifty metres after the gate, take a path on your right (take care not to miss it) and cross the lane to join a public bridleway the other side, in the form of a tarmac drive. Follow the drive until it bends left, where you should leave it to carry straight on along a well walked path, with the remnants of an orchard on your left.

After this, the path runs along the right hand side of a large field, with good views to your left of Platt village. Keep to the field perimeter, ignoring all paths leading off to the left and at the far side, pass between some metal posts and continue to follow a path between houses before coming out at a road in the village. Turn left along the road, passing a pleasant mixture of modern and old houses, each with individual character, and keep to the road until you arrive at a "T" junction in front of St. Mary's church (GR. 623570). A short detour left here will take you to the village pub, "The Blue Anchor", a Greene King pub which also offers a range of food. Our way however, is straight across the road to walk up a drive the other side and after a few paces, left into the church yard. Unless you want to visit the church (normally locked), turn sharp right onto a path alongside the churchyard wall and follow the path through the churchyard, taking time at points to admire the view back to the church. Shortly after, exit the churchyard via some wooden posts, after which you should follow a narrow path through the beautiful Platt Wood.

Keep to the main path through the wood, ignoring all minor turnings off, to soon start climbing, being aided by steps and passing a conveniently situated bench. Ignore a crossing path immediately after the bench and continue to climb with the path slowly levelling out, passing between a scattering of rhododendrum bushes which in late spring give a tremendous display. As before, you should ignore all minor turnings off, keeping straight on and following the main path at all times, to eventually meet and join another wide path coming in from the right. Continue ahead for a few paces until the path forks and fork left here, to go straight across another path and continue in the direction of a yellow "WW" arrow, indicating that you are now on the Weald Way. Pass between a wooden rail and follow a narrow path between fences and thick rhododendrums almost forming a continuous tunnel to soon arrive at a lane (GR. 630573).

Turn left along the lane, ignoring a footpath the other side and follow the lane for approximately twenty metres, before turning right onto a marked (low stone post) public footpath. Walk across a clearing to follow a track the other side which descends, crossing a fairway, which is part of Wrotham Heath Golf Club. After this, the track continues through a particularly beautiful stretch of Greensand woodland, before crossing and passing two more fairways. The track then, once again, enters woodland and a few metres on, you should turn right onto a marked (yellow arrow) footpath. (Take care not to miss it). The path leads uphill to cross another fairway before entering more woodland.

Approximately ten metres after entering the woodland, leave the main path as it bends right, to continue ahead along a narrower path in the direction of the yellow arrow. The path continues through woodland, later passing a large house on your left, before coming out at an area of open scrub and wide grass fairways, predominantly used for practice. Here, the path is undefined - you should simply continue in the same direction, following the well placed yellow arrows. If you've taken heed of the yellow arrows you will find yourself passing through another short stretch of woodland, before coming out at the golf club overflow car park. Cross the tarmac drive here and follow a path the other side, marked by a yellow arrow. After climbing a short sharp rise, the path arrives at the B2016.

Cross the road and turn left along the B2016, taking great care of the traffic, and after approximately thirty metres of walking downhill, take a signposted footpath (low stone post) on your right which runs through woodland. After approximately thirty metres, the footpath arrives at an old corrugated iron shelter. Turn right beside the shelter to, after a few metres, come out at another fairway. Bear right to skirt around a green, where there are good views left to the North Downs and at the other side, go over a stile into an orchard. Continue straight ahead through the centre of the orchard, following a wide grass track with a line of trees acting as a windbreak on your left and after approximately one hundred metres and as the line of trees (windbreak) ends, turn left onto another wide grass track, keeping another line of trees acting as a windbreak on your left. Again, after approximately one hundred metres, on meeting another wide grass track, turn right to follow the edge of the orchard, keeping a hedge on your left, the other side of which is a field and continue until you arrive at a road. Do not join the road, but turn right instead to continue around the edge of the orchard and after approximately forty metres, pass through a gap in the hedge on your left (there was a stile here at one point which may return in time) to join the road **(GR. 644577)**.

Cross the road and join a signposted public footpath the other side, going over a stile into a field to do so. Go straight across the field passing to the right of a large house and at the far side of the field, go over a stile and bear diagonally right across the centre of the next field passing some stables on your left. Go over a stile in the far right hand corner of the field (N.B. At the time of writing, there are several temporary fences here and the field boundaries may change slightly), and thereafter, follow a narrow path ahead through some scrub and along the edge of a garden. After a short distance, pass through a kissing gate and turn left along a track to come out onto the driveway for "The Old Rectory". Turn left along the drive for a few paces to arrive at a lane at a bend in front of another attractive property.

Turn left along the lane to carry straight on, passing some neatly converted oasthouses on your right, and continue to, a short time later, pass over a railway line, immediately after which you should turn right onto a signposted footpath. The path follows the line of the railway and passes a rather ramshackle property on your left. You will shortly meet and cross a stile to follow the path thereafter along the right hand perimeter of a field, with the railway line still on your right. At the far side of the field, cross a stile into another field and carry straight on to meet and cross another stile at the far side. After the stile, turn right to walk under the railway line into a field the other side, with good views to the your left across to "Church Farm" and Offham church.

Offham church is approximately one mile from the village centre. It is essentially Norman and there are still several traces of the original building. When built, it was attached to a manor, "Church Farm", the house standing beside it today, built around 1650. It is possible to detour a little later and visit the church, though it is nearly always locked.

i

Continue straight on, keeping to the field perimeter and follow it round, ignoring another path soon after off to your right. When I last walked this way, I sat here for a rest to reflect on the day's adventure. After a couple of minutes two deer stepped gingerly into the field and proceeded to graze, unaware of my presence. Suddenly, the peace was shattered by a bright silver and yellow Eurostar train thundering past on its way to London from the Continent. The deer did nothing more than look up out of idle curiosity. I saw a number of passengers hurriedly point their cameras roughly in my direction and then the train was gone and the peace returned. I've since often wondered if I appear in any of the photos with the deer. A few seconds later, the deer re-entered the wood and I was left alone to reflect on the most recent addition to my adventure.

Continue to follow the field perimeter round until sometime later, you see a fairly prominent marked footpath on your right (take care not to miss it). At the time of writing the footpath sign has fallen over, so maybe hidden by undergrowth - therefore, to ensure the instructions are clear, this path is the second path entering Moorlands Wood on your right from the point of joining the field from the railway bridge.

Follow the path through Moorlands Wood, an old coppice, which in spring like so many other woods on this walk is a carpet of bluebells. After a short distance, the path joins another path coming in from the right. Here you should continue ahead, now following a much more prominent path. Carry straight on through the wood, ignoring all turnings off, including sometime later a quite prominent path on your left (although this appears well used it is private and could therefore be blocked off at any time) and continue until you arrive at a prominent crossing path with a bench on your right. Turn left here onto the crossing path and continue, as before, keeping to the main path and ignoring any minor turnings off to later arrive at a "T" junction with another path. Turn right to almost immediately follow a fenced path between gardens. This takes you to a road at the edge of Offham village, which you should follow ahead to soon arrive at another road, onto which you should turn left. This takes you past the village hostelry, "The Kings Arms", a pleasant freehouse and hard to resist! Thereafter, follow the road to the village green and our starting point.

i N.B. Since researching this walk, I've learned that Mereworth Wood is one of a very small number of woods in the U.K. where wild boar roam once more, though not in great numbers. The boars apparently escaped from a park and now breed successfully in the wood. I decided not to change the text of the walk, believing that the average adventurer may better appreciate this update over a calming drink at the end of the day. Cheers!

ACCOMMODATION
The Royal Travelodge Hotel, Wrotham Heath. Tel: 01732 883489
Under a quarter of a mile from the walk, accommodation is in one of the new Travelodge hotels. The rooms are excellently furnished, even if they lack character and represent extremely good value. The Royal Oak is part of the Beefeater chain.

Jordans, Street Hill, Plaxtol. Tel: 01732 810379

Approximately three quarters of a mile from the walk, I cannot praise this accommodation enough. Jordans is a beautifully maintained Tudor house set in a lovingly cared for garden and as if this isn't enough, it is only a few minutes walk to one of the best pubs in Kent, "The Golding Hop"!

Youth Hostel, Kemsing YHA, Kemsing. Tel: 01732 761341

Approximately six miles from the walk, the hostel was once a vicarage in an attractive village at the foot of the North Downs. Quite a large hostel with fiftyeight beds, it can be busy in summer with school parties, so be warned and book ahead.

Camping and Caravanning, Oldbury Hill. Tel: 01732 762728

Approximately three miles from the walk, this is a Camping and Caravanning Club site open to non-members. It has an idyllic location surrounded by National Trust woodland. The facilities are also very good.

THE LEOPARDS LOOP

Distance: 10³/₄ miles (17.5km)

Time: Allow approximately 5 hours

Map: Ordnance Survey Landranger Map 188

START FORDCOMBE 110M	KENT WATER 50M	HOATH CORNER 115M	FINISH FORDCOMBE 110M

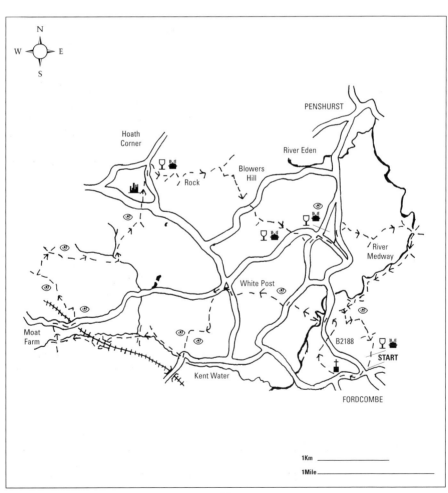

Walk Summary

This is a glorious walk and one for all seasons. Seldom are you without a view and even when not, there is always something else to catch your eye. Water too is a constant feature, the route following in places a number of rivers and streams. Throw in some seductive woodland, majestic sandstone rocks - oh, and of course, a leopard and you have an adventure befitting any Tolkein novel. Leopards apart, the only real difficulties you are likely to encounter is mud and a couple of fairly steep climbs, a small price to pay for a wonderful day out. I must also just mention the pubs encountered en route, for I cannot think of any other walk with such a quality selection of hostelries. There are four altogether and all come highly recommended. Virtually all are on our walk which may be a little risky, but choosing which ones to ignore is much more difficult. It's your choice! Like a number of other walks in this book, I also recommend you try the Leopard's Loop in reverse. This way you will be walking with the views, the route taking on a completely new complexion.

Start - GR. 527402 Map 188

The walk starts in front of the village Post Office and general stores at Fordcombe, on the B2188. Unless you know the locality, the easiest way to approach Fordcombe is:- from the north, follow the B2176 to Penshurst from where Fordcombe is signposted. From the south, join the B2188 from the A264 East Grinstead to Tunbrdige Wells road. A hidden sign points the way from the A264 to Fordcombe, though much easier is to look out for the sign to "Penshurst Place". In case in these modern times the Post Office closes, it can still be recognised by the brick post box outside. The shop is also opposite the village school. Roadside parking is easily possible, though please respect local residents. The nearest railway station is at Ashurst, though much more viable is Royal Tunbridge Wells from where it is possible to catch a bus, or if money is no object, a taxi. There is no obvious alternative start.

THE LEOPARD'S LOOP

Before starting on our adventure, I believe it is worth finding out a little about the village from where we commence.

Fordcombe (GR. 527402 Map 188) is a scattered village on the southern slopes of the river Medway. The centre is virtually the village's highest point where a school, general stores and a cluster of cottages surround a small green. The scene is typically English and looks a lot older than it actually is, for virtually none of the buildings were constructed earlier than the 19th century. The name "Fordcombe" as it suggests, means "a ford in a valley". This was at Chafford Bridge at the western end of the village. "Chafford" is a much older name and means literally, "a ford at the bend of a river". The excellent village hostelry, "The Chafford Arms", proudly recalls the original name and the pub sign depicts a horse crossing the ford.

The pub is an attractive ivy clad building with a beautiful award winning garden. To enter the lounge bar in particular, you will have to pass through a virtual jungle of colour which at night is lit by white fairy lights, creating a truly magical spectacle. The comfortable lounge bar also has a restaurant which tends to specialise in fish. The public bar is a very relaxed and local affair and very welcoming. It is easy to lose oneself in here, though take care not to overdo it or you could just be the subject of the next verse of the pub's poem!

One other building of note is the village church, though this too like most of the village, only dates from 1848. Inside, is interred Sir Henry Hardinge, who lay the foundation stone of the church. He was once the Governor General of India and whilst there, started the construction of India's famous railway network. There is not much more to see at Fordcombe. Perhaps the village's biggest asset is its warmth and vitality. This is no museum village but a thriving community served by a church, a school and a pub, all determined to put village life first.

To start, from the village Post Office, cross the B2188 and walk down Chafford Lane in the direction of the sign for Walter's Green and Ashurst. Follow the lane for approximately a quarter of a mile and then turn right onto a track, signposted as a footpath and also to "Chafford Farm" as well as a number of other dwellings, including "Lockerbie" which offers B&B. As a further guide, this is just before a lane leads left and if you meet this turning, you have missed the track and should retrace your steps. Follow the track to its end (approximately two hundred metres) at the brick gateway to "Chafford Farm", and here go over a stile on your right to then turn immediately left and follow the left hand perimeter of a market garden called "The Orchard". As you progress, you are afforded a taste of what is to come with a lovely view ahead across the Medway valley to Hobbs Hill. On reaching the corner of "The Orchard", go over a stile ahead and thereafter, follow an enclosed path right. Later, the path descends as it approaches some houses and crosses a lively stream, before climbing to reach the B2188. Turn left along the B2188 for a few paces, before crossing the road to join a driveway the other side, signposted as a footpath. Follow the driveway, which after passing between some idyllic properties continues between fields, before arriving at the gateway to the magnificent "Fordcombe Manor". Do not pass through the gateway, but turn left instead to follow another drive and descend to meet the B2188 once more **(GR. 522409 Map 188).**

Cross the B2188 for a third time and go over a stile to join a signposted footpath the other side. Follow the footpath, gently bearing left, to shortly cross the river Medway via a bridge. At the other side you will be greeted with a choice of four different paths, each marked by a yellow arrow. Our route is path number 463, which is the second yellow arrow in from the right (or if you want to be awkward the third from the left!). From the footbridge, the path bears very gently diagonally right across the centre of a field (it does not follow the river) where, as a guide, you should head for a point approximately thirty metres to the left of a brick pill box (gun emplacement) visible at the far side. As you approach the pill box you should be able to make out (if the river mist stays away) a stile in the distance, for which you should head.

Go over the stile and cross a footbridge into a field the other side where you should carry straight on, now going uphill, along the left hand perimeter of the field. As the field perimeter gives way you should continue straight on, following a line of old oaks and heading for a point just to the left of a brick bungalow. At the top of the field, go over a stile and turn left to follow a lane. After approximately forty metres, just as you approach some houses, take a signposted public footpath on your right up a tarmac drive. Shortly after, go over a stile and continue along the right hand perimeter of a well kept garden to quickly go over a second stile beneath an arch of climbing rose to enter a field.

Once in the field, turn immediately left and after a few paces, right to follow the right hand perimeter of the field, climbing steeply. Note a sunken path on your right, now overgrown. This was once the original path and denotes the age of this route, which has seen use for over six hundred years. At the top of the field, go over a stile and maintain your climb along the right hand perimeter of the next field. You will probably have to pause at least once to catch your breath and take this opportunity to appreciate the glorious views behind across the Medway ◉ valley and deep into East Sussex. At the far side of the field, cross a stile and continue ahead along the right hand perimeter of another field where the gradient now begins to level. At the field end, go over a stile and continue ahead, passing to the right of a wooded hollow to cross another stile into a field. Bear very gently diagonally left across the centre of the field and as you approach the top of a rise, head to the right of Blacklands Wood in front of you.

At the far side of the field, pass through a gap in the fence (there may be a stile here later) and continue ahead along a well walked path with Blacklands Wood on your left. After a few paces, pass through a gate ahead and turn left up a bank to arrive at the left hand corner of a field. Go straight across the centre of the field (if the way is unclear, keep approximately thirty metres between you and the woodland on your left) and at the far side of the field, pass through a gate to arrive at a lane **(GR. 508414)**. Turn right along the lane and follow it until just after passing a house on your left, turn left onto a much narrower lane which at first looks as though it is a private drive, to pass between gardens on your right and a couple of houses on your left.

This junction of roads is known as White Post. Though not certain, this is ***i*** *probably due to a suicide victim being buried at the crossroads just the other side of the gardens on your right. During the Middle Ages, people who committed suicide were not allowed to be buried on consecrated ground and were often buried at crossroads as a sort of symbolism to indicate that they could not cope with the crossroads of life. These graves (some containing more than one body), were often marked by a white post or if the parish was a generous one, a white cross, the white signifying that the deceased took a cowardly way out. If you study an Ordnance Survey map, you will often find crossroads marked with a person's name or simply as "White Post" or "White Cross". Where there is a name it is generally the name of the poor suicide victim who is buried there.*

After a few paces, turn left along another lane and follow it for approximately one hundred metres before turning left onto a track which is in fact a byway, though at the time of writing, it is unmarked. The track (which can be muddy), was once a fairly major thoroughfare and leads over the top of Hobbs Hill. Just before the track starts its descent into the Kent Water valley, it turns sharp right where on your left you will see a gateway from where you can enjoy some superb views over the valley. After the viewpoint, keep to the track as it bends right to ◉ run along the valley side and sometime later, as the track bends sharp left to re-commence its steep descent into the Kent Water valley, you are privileged to meet a second equally good viewpoint by taking a small detour along a narrow path ahead to another gateway, from where there is a magnificent vista. You will ◉

need to retrace your steps to rejoin our walk. After bending left, the track descends steeply and becomes narrower, turning into more of a path and running between steep banks. In wet weather this sometimes doubles as a stream and can be fairly treacherous so care is needed.

As you walk it is hard to believe that years ago people would have driven their horse and carts up and down this track. Quite often, steep hills like this would have been too much for a normal horse and cart and a few enterprising peasants therefore used to gather at the bottom of the hill with their donkeys or cock horses (see "The Churchill Challenge") to assist for a small fee in pulling the load to the top. At the busier hills, small hostelries sprang up to cater for the travellers waiting to have their loads pulled up. Many of these hostelries still survive today and recall their origin by their names, such as "The Donkey" or "The Cock" . Next time you see a pub or inn called "The Donkey" or "The Cock", see if it is situated on, below or near a hill.

Near the bottom of the hill, pass through a gate and continue ahead, still descending, to arrive at a tarmac drive to "Hobbs Hill Farm and Oast" on your right. Turn left along the drive, descending to the bottom of the Kent Water valley, to arrive at a lane beside a house. Continue straight ahead along the lane to shortly arrive at a bridge over Kent Water. Do not go over the bridge, but take a signposted footpath on your right, to follow the river upstream whilst walking through a field. You are now following the Sussex Border Path with Kent Water on your left acting as the boundary between Kent and East Sussex. In case you need reminding, you are in Kent. At the far side of the field, go over a footbridge crossing a small tributary to the river, and bear diagonally right thereafter across the next field to later meet and follow the right hand field perimeter. Kent Water continues to twist and turn on your left, on occasion virtually meeting your path.

Your route continues in a similar fashion through a succession of fields with Kent Water leaving you at points, but always returning. Sometime later, you will arrive at a bridge which crosses the river on your left into East Sussex. Our way from here is over the bridge, but it is worth mentioning at this point the path which leads across the field on your right. This, if you wish to take a detour, leads to a beautiful hamlet known as Bassett's set in a steep valley with several ponds. It is a lovely setting and has some of the best examples of Wealden half timbered housing in Kent. If you choose not to take this detour, I recommend a visit another time or perhaps on your way home in the car.

Returning to our route, as mentioned, our way is left over the bridge, into East Sussex, at the other side of which you should turn right to continue following the river, though now on the opposite bank. After a short distance, go over a stile and carry straight on, still with the river on your right. As you progress, you will see the Croydon to Uckfield railway line running close to your route on the left, along an embankment. As you near the end of the field, look out for a bridge taking the railway line over a track connecting your field with the one adjacent and pass under this to turn right the other side, along the field perimeter.

At the far side of the field, go over a footbridge and stile and continue across the next field along the right hand perimeter and at the field corner, cross a footbridge at what is a particularly pleasant spot, to continue ahead, once again following Kent Water on your right. After passing a newly landscaped lake, go over a stile to arrive at a junction of paths and two bridges. Our route is across the bridge on your right, re-entering Kent, to thereafter continue along the left hand perimeter of a field. Continue in the same direction through a second field, passing to the right of a house and pond (the pond is one of several and all that remains of a moat), to eventually go over a stile beside a gate onto a lane, Moat Lane **(GR. 484409)**. Turn right along the lane, crossing over the Croydon to Uckfield railway line and immediately after the railway line, leave the lane and turn left into "Sandfields Farm", which also offers B&B - a tempting thought! Follow a track through the farmyard, passing to the right of the farmhouse and shortly after, ignore another track leading off to the right to carry straight on, now going uphill, to shortly continue along the right hand perimeter of a field.

At the far side of the field, do not be tempted to follow the track which continues ahead uphill between banks, but turn left instead and continue to follow the field perimeter round, with some wonderful views over Kent Water which leads into the Medway over to your left. The view makes an ideal stop for an early break. As you continue, if you can take your eyes off the view, look for some low sandstone cliffs, which form the field perimeter on your right. This part of Kent is famous for its sandstone formations, though the cliffs passed on "The Toads Terror" are far more spectacular. Later, cross a stile ahead and continue along the right hand perimeter of the next field with an equally good but completely different view to your left across patchwork fields to Cowden village.

Approximately twenty metres into the field, bear very gently diagonally left down the side of the hill, making for a small wooden stile just visible in the fence ahead. Go over the stile and carry straight on along the right hand perimeter of the next field where again there are good and different views to your left. At the far side, go over a stile beside a metal gate and after approximately twenty paces turn left along a track. The track soon becomes concrete and passes to the right of the beautiful "Wickens Farm", complete with a rustic sandstone barn. After the farm the concrete graduates into tarmac to become a pretty narrow lane winding between fields, a classic English scene. Follow the lane until you see a track signposted as a

footpath on your right. Take this and follow it uphill to sometime on go over a stile beside a gate. After the stile keep to the track and as it meets a picturesque tile hung cottage ahead, bear right around the perimeter of the property.

When directly in front of the cottage bear diagonally right across a field, passing to the right of an electricity pole and thereafter heading for a stile visible the other side. Go over the stile into another field and cross the field in the direction of a yellow arrow which points diagonally right (do not make the mistake of taking the route in the direction of an arrow pointing directly ahead). At the time of writing, to help guide you, the farmer here has kindly erected a post at the centre of the field as a marker for the footpath. In case this disappears in future (cows like to use it as a scratching pole and one day may flatten it!), as a further guide, as you reach the centre of the field (at the top of a rise), head for a stile at the edge of a strip of woodland directly ahead and approximately fifty metres to the left of a gate at the top of the field. Do not make the mistake of heading for the stile beside the gate, the stile is purely for farm use and is not a public right of way. As you progress, if searching for the stile doesn't take up all your attention, take time to admire the panorama the field affords. To your right is Kent Water valley, behind you is "Horseshoe Green Farm" and to your left a small wood with the lovely name of Bilton's Gill.

i *"Gill" is an old name for a brook or wooded valley. At around the same period, it was also commonly the name given to beer made with an infusion of ground ivy. I've often wondered whether in this case "Gill" describes the wooded valley or was it a place where Bilton secretly brewed and enjoyed his Gill away from prying eyes!*

On reaching the far side of the field, go over the stile and follow a beautiful path through a mature coppice, where in late spring the floor is a sea of bluebells. Sometime later, cross a stile ahead and continue thereafter, straight on across the centre of a field. After approximately fifty metres, you will pass what looks like a newly created pond on your left. The pond is in fact very old and has only recently been restored. It is fed by a spring producing cool fresh water throughout the year.

After the pond, maintain your direction following what is a fairly well walked track with sandstone cliffs bordering the field on your right. We have, in fact, from "Sandhills" almost circled the hill, which above the cliffs levels to a virtual plateau. Follow the track for approximately two hundred metres and look out for a stile on your left (take care not to miss it). When you spot the stile, leave the track to descend across the field and go over the stile to continue your descent through woodland to shortly meet a bridge crossing a stream at the bottom of the valley. This is another of those idyllic spots thankfully hidden from the maddening crowds. In spring the floor is covered with the delicate greens and white of wild garlic and with the blue bubbling stream in between, it is a picture that will stay with you for a long time to come. Cross the bridge and thereafter, follow a prominent path up the other side of the valley, ignoring a path initially off to your right and soon after, another off to your left. Further up, another path joins from the right which you should ignore to carry straight on to soon pass through an area of mixed woodland with a sprinkling of hand-planted conifers.

Eventually the path arrives at a stile which you should cross to enter a field. Once in the field, maintain your route ahead, along the right hand field perimeter, continuing to climb! At the top of the field make for a stile approximately ten metres to the left of a gate. Here, it is worth pausing for a breather and to take time to look back across rolling fields to "Horseshoe Green Farm". Go over the stile and immediately after, turn left to follow a narrow path along the edge of a wood. A short time later, cross another stile ahead to continue in the same direction along the right hand perimeter of a field. Ignore a gate and stile on your right and continue your route along the field perimeter to arrive at the far side of the field and another stile, which you should cross to meet a lane (**GR 496425**).

Cross the lane to join a signposted public footpath the other side and follow it along the edge of some more attractive woodland to eventually reach a stile (ignore a path off to your right just before the stile). Go over the stile and follow a well walked path ahead between fields. Ahead in the distance, on a clear day, you can just make out the line of the North Downs. It is also a time for celebration, for this is the highest point on the walk. At the far side of the field, turn right along a track to meet a lane, onto which you should turn left. Follow the lane which quickly descends Rock Hill, appropriately between low rocky sandstone cliffs, to later arrive at the pretty tile hung hamlet of Hoath Corner.

Hoath Corner (GR. 496431 Map 188) is a magical place. As you descend Rock Hill with majestic sandstone cliffs bordering your way, you cannot help but sense that such a dramatic approach is going to lead to something special. Hoath Corner does not disappoint. As you approach the hamlet, to your left a hedged garden shelters in the curve of a high sandstone cliff. Facing tile hung cottages welcome you. Following the lane past these leads past more idyllic cottages to one of Kent's best kept secrets, "The Rock", a pub which is almost irresistible.

As you enter the hamlet, our way is right along a track, signposted as a public footpath to Penshurst. First however, you will almost definitely wish to stay on the lane for a few more metres to pay homage to "The Rock".

Returning to our route, follow the track passing some beautiful tile hung cottages on your left and when these end, continue ahead along a well marked path which leads downhill through a field. After approximately thirty metres, the path descends a bank and twists right (ignore a path to your left here) and you should keep to it (if in doubt, follow the yellow arrows) to continue through picturesque mixed and open woodland. After a further twenty metres, the path forks and you should take the right hand fork (take care not to miss it), to climb gently uphill through the wood and later meet a fence and field on your left. Ignore a stile in the fence at this point and continue by following the path with the fence on your left.

The path soon leads to a "T" junction where you should turn left to immediately arrive at an outcrop of sandstone rock. This is the rock from which the pub takes its name. *There are many legends surrounding the rock but perhaps the most common is that it was once used as a Druids' sacrificial alter.* Take care! Climbing the rock (also with care), affords some wonderful views across to the North Downs and Bough Beech reservoir. After the rock, continue along the path still keeping the fencing on your left, to shortly come out into another field ahead where you will enjoy yet more views. Once in the field, turn right along the right hand perimeter and go over another stile at the field corner onto a track, in front of a beautiful Wealden cottage. Turn left along the track and when this ends continue by following a path to the right of a garage and then another beautiful tiled cottage, before going over a stile into a field. Continue straight ahead along the left hand perimeter of the large field and as you progress, look out for views on your right to "Stonewell Park". Just before reaching the far side of the field you will pass a number of ponds which, like the earlier pond passed, are fed by natural springs.

On reaching the far side of the field, go over a stile and continue ahead along a track which, after a short distance, bends right. You should keep to the track, ignoring a path ahead and a few paces on, ignore also a marked path on the left. After a few more paces however, when the track bends left, you should leave it to follow a path ahead which, as a guide, runs gently downhill with field perimeter fencing on your right (take care not to miss it). Sometime later, the path takes you over a footbridge to arrive at the edge of Penshurst Vineyard. Tours of the vineyard are possible by appointment, though perhaps much more enjoyable is to try the wine which is available at most of the local pubs. Continue ahead along the right hand edge of the vineyard, with Courtlands Wood on your right and when the woodland ends, turn right to continue following its perimeter and then at a corner, as the vineyard ends, carry straight on now along a path which passes to the right of a pond. After the pond, cross two more footbridges in quick succession and continue across the centre of a field to meet and cross yet another footbridge into a second field.

Before crossing the next field, I should point out that the yellow arrow points slightly too far to the right. Instead, cross the field by continuing straight ahead (slightly to the left of the arrow's direction), at the same time starting your ascent of Blower's Hill. Approximately half way across the field, you will walk through a line of trees, passing to the left of a hollow, after which you should make for a stile, now visible at the far side. Cross the stile and follow a path along the edge of some woodland to shortly arrive at a road (GR. 511425). Cross the road, ascend some sandstone steps the other side and then follow a narrow path through brambles to arrive at a field. Continue straight ahead across the centre of the field, passing to the left of a group of trees which surround a pond and, after the pond, maintain your direction, carrying straight on, making for a point just to the right of a fenced garden to a house ahead. The path soon meets and follows the perimeter fencing to the property where ahead now, are wonderful views to the slopes either side of the Medway valley. Shortly after, go over a stile on your left, just prior to meeting a triangulation point marking the summit of Blower's Hill (103 metres).

Bear diagonally right across a small field to soon go over a stile and maintain your direction to meet and cross yet another stile and arrive at a track. Turn right along the track and follow it, passing a number of houses, before arriving at a road beside the excellent "Bottle House Inn", a freehouse. To complete the scene, on the other side of the pub are some lovely, typical Kentish weatherboarded cottages.

The inn always has a choice of at least three real ales, including the locally brewed Larkins. However, it is more famous for its food which is said to be the best in the area (I can particularly recommend the game). If you enjoy wine, you are in for a treat for the landlord has carefully selected over fortyeight for the drinker to choose from. The building was originally a 15th century barn, which was later converted into cottages, only becoming an inn in the 1930's. If whilst enjoying the local brew you see an object apparently moving on its own, don't worry it will simply be the pub ghost, Elizabeth. Of course, such a startling happening could be the effect of the local brew and to blame it on a ghost makes for a most original and convenient story!

To continue, on arriving at the inn, turn left along the road for a few paces and then right onto a signposted public footpath. This is an enclosed path which leads to a lane, onto which you should turn left. After passing a couple of houses, the lane arrives at a "T" junction where you should turn right (take care of the traffic here as it can, at times, be busy). A few paces on, ignore a road on the left signposted to Tonbridge and continue instead to follow the much more appealing sign to "The Spotted Dog" - yes, yet another pub! It is only a few metres before you arrive at the pub and what a delight it is.

Hugging the side of Smarts Hill, from the pub garden or terrace you are afforded the best views from any pub in Kent, perhaps even in the South of England. Certainly, on a summer's day there can be few better ways of passing time than supping a cold drink whilst soaking in the panorama. The front of the pub is an attractive weatherboarded affair, reached by a series of steps. Inside, there are plenty of cosy corners and an inglenook fireplace which still burns logs in cold weather. There is usually an excellent range of real ales on offer, including one of my favourites, Royal Oak and Old Spotty (after the dog and not because it puts spots in front of your eyes!), which is brewed specially for the pub. There is an interesting story regarding the pub's name. In 1520, when it became a pub, the Sidney family, Earls of Leicester from Penshurst (see "The Chiding Challenge") ordered a pub sign of a leopard, the family crest. The sign painter unfortunately, was a little short sighted and mistook a rough sketch for a Talbot (the fore-runner to the Dalmatian) and painted the dog instead of a leopard! No-one could be bothered to change it and the pub has been called "The Spotted Dog" every since!

After the pub, continue along the road passing a converted chapel and after the last house on your left, take a signposted public footpath left which leads down the side of Smart Hill. Go over a stile and continue your descent along a well walked path, taking in as you go the tremendous views across the Medway valley. At the bottom left hand corner of the field, go over a stile and down some steps to arrive at a road, the B2188. Turn left along the road for approximately fifteen metres and then join a signposted public footpath on your right, going over a stile to do so which takes you into a field. Carry straight on, following the left hand field perimeter and at the far side, turn right along a farm track. The track continues between fields with views to your left of "Swaylands School", a large house just visible through the trees.

The track leads to "Nashes Farm" and on entering the farmyard you should follow the track as it bends round to the left, passing to the left of the farmhouse itself. As the hedge to the farmhouse garden ends on your right, continue straight ahead between fields and at the far side, do not make the mistake of following a track *i* ahead to your left into a field, but follow the main track ahead instead which runs between hedges. The track later passes a pond on your right, opposite which there used to be a cottage known as "Wild Boar". This has long since disappeared though the name lives on as a reminder of the wildlife that used to roam this valley.

Eventually, the track enters a field ahead. At this point you should turn right, keeping to the right hand perimeter of the field where to your left now, there are good views across to the hamlet of Swaylands and ahead, the small church at Poundsbridge, visited on "Toad's Terror". On reaching the corner of the field, ignore a stile on your right and continue ahead across a bridge over the river Medway. If you haven't eaten at any of the pubs but have come prepared with a picnic, then this is a lovely place to stop and a good place to learn about the river.

i ***The River Medway*** *rises from a spring just above Turners Hill in East Sussex. From there, it winds its way across the Weald before carving a way through the North Downs to join the river Thames. The river over the centuries has helped shape the landscape in more ways than one. It brought the first invaders into Kent. First there were the Celts, then the Romans, Saxons and Danes, all of whom used the river for safe navigation into the then densely forested Weald. In fact, "Weald" is derived from the German word for a wood, "Wald". The Celts called the river "Medu", meaning possibly "sweet water". This description later led to the name of that sweet English drink, Mead, "sweet water", a good description for those who have never tried it. The Romans named the river, "Fluminus Meduwaeis" and then the Saxons, "Medwaeg", which is close to today's name.*

The River Medway

In 1740, it was planned to open the Medway for navigation, virtually to its source. The work progressed and succeeded up to Tonbridge where it stopped, the planners having run out of money. Nearly one hundred years later, another attempt was made (see "The Chiding Challenge"), but this too was doomed to failure. We must be somewhat thankful for these failures, as today the river acts as a pleasant companion to a walk. Its silent, gentle course through the Weald gives additional interest without the help of man.

Once over the bridge, turn right and walk along the river bank. Pass through a couple of fields, keeping to the riverbank, and at the end of the second field ignore a marked footpath (yellow arrow) on your left and continue, following the river, now walking through a third field. As the banks of the river at the other side begin to grow steeper, you will see a brick pill box, the first in a series of pill boxes (gun emplacements) and if you are an obsessive map reader you will notice on the Ordnance Survey map that the path runs in a straight line across the fields and not along the river bank. The stiles for this route have virtually disappeared and my suggestion therefore is to ignore the map and (like everybody else) keep to the river bank, even if following the twists and turns makes your walk slightly longer. If however, at the far side of the third field, you find the way into the next field a little difficult, there is a footbridge which you can use approximately fifteen metres in from the river. You will have to look for it as it can be quite hidden though easily accessible.

Sometime later, both the river and our route pass beneath electricity cables. After this, continue to follow the river to the far side of the field and after crossing a footbridge into another field, turn left to follow the left hand perimeter of the field, at first walking away from the Medway. Keep to the field perimeter, with a ditch on your left (see how many frogs you can spot), and approximately two thirds of the way across the field, look for a single plank bridge crossing the ditch and a yellow arrow on a tree the other side. (Take care not to miss it, for at the time of writing, this footpath is not marked on the maps). If you find yourself arriving at the far left hand corner of the field with a stile ahead, you will know you have missed the bridge and should retrace your steps.

Go over the bridge and squeeze through a gap in the hedge into the field adjacent and then proceed to climb out of the valley along the right hand perimeter of the field. On reaching the top right hand corner of the field, turn left to continue following the field perimeter enjoying marvellous views left and ahead over the Medway valley. Incidentally, the large brick building in the valley below is a water museum. Continue from the field corner for approximately fifty metres, after which you should look out for a narrow path on your right, entering a copse. This is marked by a yellow topped post and is just after a gap leading to another field on your right (there could be a gate here later).

The path leads through the centre of the copse passing a number of murky ponds, before coming out at a stile the other side. Do not cross the stile, but turn right instead to follow a path uphill along the edge of the copse. After passing beneath a large beech, you will arrive at the corner of a field. Maintain your direction along the left hand perimeter of the field, still climbing and after approximately two hundred metres, look out for and cross a stile on your left. Immediately after, turn right to continue in the same direction, though now along the right hand perimeter of a field and just before you reach the top right hand corner, go over a stile on your right into another field. First though, it is worth taking one last look back over the Medway valley and see how many routes from other adventures in this book you can spot. Go diagonally left across the centre of the next field heading for the far left hand corner with the welcome houses of Fordcombe now visible. Particularly welcoming is "The Chafford Arms", easily recognisable by its various tall chimneys. How many of you are quickening your pace now? As you progress, befitting to such a classic walk, you finish with marvellous views right across the Kent Water and Medway valleys, to the terrain encountered on most of today's walk.

On reaching the corner of the field, go over a stile and follow an enclosed path between houses to come out beside the village stores, our starting point. In case you need reminding, "The Chafford Arms" is right - cheers!

ACCOMMODATION

The Leicester Arms, Penshurst. Tel: 01892 870551
Approximately one mile from the walk, this is an inn simply oozing with history. It is situated at the centre of Penshurst, just across the road from the famous "Penshurst Place". All the rooms are comfortably furnished and all are en suite. A stay here also allows you to experience Penshurst in the evenings, at its quietest - a memorable experience.

Hoath House, Chiddingstone Hoath. Tel: 01342 850362
Approximately a quarter of mile from the walk, this must be one of the best, if not the grandest, B&B's in west Kent. Accommodation is in a superb medieval house in an area of outstanding beauty and, if this is not enough, the Streatfield family are charming hosts.

Youth Hostel, Kemsing YHA, Kemsing. Tel: 01732 761341
Approximately ten miles from the walk, the hostel was once a vicarage in an attractive village at the foot of the North Downs. Quite a large hostel with fiftyeight beds, it can be busy in summer with school parties, so be warned and book ahead.

Camping and Caravanning, Oldbury Hill, Styants Bottom. Tel: 01732 762728
Approximately nine miles from the walk, this is a Camping and Caravanning Club site which is open to non-members. Quite a small site, it is set in a beautiful location surrounded by National Trust woodland.

THE GREENSAND GRAPPLE

Distance: 11¹/₂ miles (18.5km)

Time: Allow approximately 6 hours

Map: Ordnance Survey Landranger Map 188

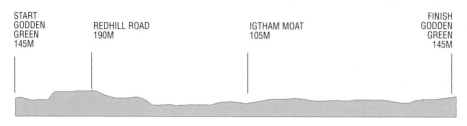

START	REDHILL ROAD	IGTHAM MOAT	FINISH
GODDEN	190M	105M	GODDEN
GREEN			GREEN
145M			145M

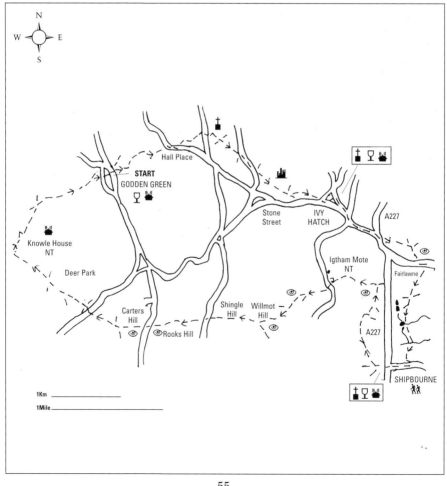

Walk Summary

This is a superb walk which I also recommend you try in reverse. After initially traversing ancient woodland the route dramatically descends the Greensand Ridge, passing the first of three fine country houses, before turning west to follow the Greensand Ridge back to the start. On the second leg, which in places follows the Greensand Ridge, you will pass perhaps two of Kents' best country houses, both in the hands of the National Trust. This is a walk with never a dull moment and one which is definitely open to all seasons. One word of warning though, mud can be a real problem in wet weather and this can make the walk a real grapple. Wear those boots and only attempt the walk in foul weather if you are fit!

Start - GR. 554552 Map 188

The walk starts from in front of "The Bucks Head" pub at the small village of Godden Green. Godden Green is close to Sevenoaks and is signposted from the A25 at Seal. If coming from the south, join the A21 and come off at the Sevenoaks junction. Thereafter, follow the A225 towards Sevenoaks for approximately one mile and then turn right onto a lane. This is the first turning right after joining the A225 and great care is needed if you are not to miss it. Follow a narrow lane for approximately two miles and then turn first left, at the next junction, to shortly arrive at Godden Green.

The nearest railway station is at Sevenoaks and from there it is a delightful short walk to join the route at "Knole House". An alternative start can be made at Shipbourne on the A227 (GR. 592522 Map 188).

THE GREENSAND GRAPPLE

Godden Green is a delightful place from which to start and gives a hint of the treasures to come. A number of large houses surround a triangular green with "The Bucks Head" pub, Courage, at the western edge, beside a pond. A Union Jack normally flies proudly at the northern tip of the green. The pub is a good place to start or finish and welcomes walkers. It is famous for its Sunday roast, something worth trying as long as you don't mind carrying the weight!

To start, with your back to "The Buck's Head", from the opposite side of the road beside a red phone box and bus stop, walk directly across the green, following the telegraph poles, to the point of the triangle the other side. At the far side, continue ahead along a track to at first pass between a golf course on your left and an imposing large brick house on your right. Follow the track alongside a wood and thereafter, past a small farmhouse on your left to almost immediately after the farm, as the track bends left, leave it to continue straight on, now following another track. After approximately twenty metres when this track also bends left, leave it to continue ahead along a wide path going downhill, marked by a yellow footpath arrow (take care not to miss it).

The path dips in and out of a valley before passing through a gate ahead into a field, where you should carry straight on, along the right hand perimeter of the field, at one point passing the tall stone perimeter wall and watch tower of "Hall Place" on your right. At the far side of the field, pass through a kissing gate to arrive at a lane, beside the entrance to "Hall Place". Turn right along the lane (do not make the mistake of turning right into "Hall Place") and follow it for

56

approximately fifty metres to then join a signposted public footpath, the other side of the road, on your left. The footpath which is almost big enough to be described as a track, runs through Hanger Wood, an ancient and still working coppice (See "The Soar Feat" for point of interest on coppices), with the floor of the wood in spring a carpet of bluebells.

Keep to the main path or track, which later bends right and then left to pass through the centre of a wood, ignoring all turnings off including, at one point, a narrow crossing path, to later arrive at a major crossing path beside a huge beech tree. Turn right here (take care not to miss it), thereby leaving the official marked (yellow arrow) footpath to shortly, approximately twenty metres, arrive at a lane. (If by chance you miss the crossing path and arrive at a lane anyway, simply turn right until you meet a footpath on your left, to arrive at the same point). Cross the lane to follow a signposted footpath the other side, which runs steeply uphill through Redhill Wood. This time, the woodland is ancient oak. At the top, on meeting a "T" junction in the form of a straight path running between banks (an indication of its old age), turn right to follow the path. The path though often muddy, is a delight in all seasons with ancient oaks and a floor of moss, bracken and hurtleberries combining to produce a wonderful array of colours.

Later, another path closes in from the left on the path you are following. Do not join this, as it later leads away again, but keep to the path you are on. A short time later, ignore a marked (yellow arrow) path leading downhill to your right to again carry straight on. After this there can be what at first seems a confusing array of paths to follow. However, if you keep straight ahead at all times along the main path, which virtually runs close to the top of a slope on your right, all the way, you will not go wrong. Eventually, after approximately half a mile, if you haven't deviated, the path arrives at a lane **(GR. 572553)**. Turn right along the lane to soon pass St. Lawrence church and school, both of which serve the parish of Seal. Immediately after the school, leave the lane to join a signposted public bridleway on your left, which once again takes you through ancient woodland. After a short distance, ignore a marked bridleway on your left and continue straight on, with your route later running parallel with a tree covered gully on your right, a disused sandpit (take care here if you have children or dogs, as the sides of the pit are particularly steep). In winter in particular, there are good views across the wooded pit to the small village of Stone Street, complete with oasthouses and surrounded by Kentish orchards. Apart from enjoying the views, you can also take satisfaction in the fact that we are now at the highest point of our walk.

Keep to the main path at all times, continuing straight ahead and ignore all turnings off, including at one point a marked bridleway (blue arrow).

The bridleway, not part of our walk, leads over Raspit Hill to Oldbury Wood which conceals a large Celtic hill fort dating from around 100BC. There is also evidence of a battle having taken place here with the Romans.

The main path is usually clearly distinguishable as being the most muddy. There is however, a slight danger of forking off to the right and if you find yourself going sharply downhill with the sandpit on your right, you will have wandered off the main path and will need to retrace your steps. The main path does eventually descend, though gradually, between banks to arrive at a lane between houses **(GR. 584546)**. Turn right along the lane to, after a few paces, arrive at Stone Street Road and turn left along the road to, after approximately fifty metres, take a footpath on your left, signposted to Bewley. After a short distance, the footpath arrives at another lane which you should cross to join a marked footpath the other side. A few paces on, pass through a gate ahead and thereafter, follow a fenced footpath through a nursery.

The footpath soon arrives at yet another lane onto which you should turn right to follow it until you arrive at a "T" junction at the centre of Ivy Hatch village, beside the excellent "Plough" pub, a freehouse famous for its cooking. To continue, at the "T" junction, turn left along another lane and a few metres on, ignore a lane right by a small green to continue in the direction of the sign for Plaxtol. Continue to follow the lane out of the village and just after passing a national speed limit sign (a diagonal black line in a white circle), look out for and join a path running parallel with the lane on your right. The path twists and turns through a line of beech trees, always with the lane close to your left, and eventually arrives, with the lane, at the A227 **(GR. 592541)**.

Cross the A227 to join a track directly the other side, signposted as a public bridleway (low stone post) and follow it to shortly pass through a small gate beside a larger one, with a sign announcing your arrival at the Fairlawne Estate. After the gates, the track continues in a straight line with High Beeches, a small copse on your right and an orchard on your left. A little further on, look out for a field gate on your right from where you can enjoy some fabulous views over the Weald. Do not pass through the gate, but continue to follow the track to later come out at a field, where you should continue ahead along the right hand perimeter, with a narrow strip of woodland on your right. As you progress, there are lovely views ahead across the Bourne valley to Mereworth Wood, part of "The Soar Feat" walk. If you know the area or are a good map reader, you will also be able to pick out the National Trust's "Soar Manor", while on your left there are excellent views to the North Downs.

Keep to the field perimeter until the woodland on your right is replaced by a fence and here, go over a stile on your right into a field adjacent. To continue, cross the field bearing gently left and heading for the field's far left hand corner, at the same time starting your descent into the Weald. This is a superb part of the walk with tremendous views ahead across the Weald to the South Downs. As you progress, to your right, there are also good views of the imposing "Fairlawne House". At the corner of the field, go over a stile and turn left along a lane and keep to the lane for approximately seventyfive metres, until you see a signposted footpath and stile on your right. Our route is right, taking the footpath. First however, you may wish to make a short detour by following the lane ahead for a few more metres to reach the lovely village of Plaxtol and its unusual hostelry, "The Rorty Crankle". You will have to retrace your steps to rejoin the route.

Returning to our route, go over the stile and cross an area of open landscaped parkland, in the direction of the footpath sign, heading for a yellow post and passing to the left of some magnificent ornamental gates. These gates are purely for decoration and simply there to give a pleasant outlook from the house, now just visible on your right.

"Fairlawne House" (GR. 593535 Map 188) *was built around 1720 on the site of an old moated manor house. This house used to be called "Fair Lane", suggesting that at one time a large fair (probably Medieval) was held here. The original house was once home to Sir Henry Vane, Secretary to Charles I. Vane, although a Parliamentarian was also a severe critic of Cromwell. Indeed, Cromwell is famous for once having exclaimed, in a moment of anger, "The Lord deliver me from Sir Henry Vane!". In 1635, Sir Henry was appointed Governor of Massachusetts but quickly made himself unpopular and sailed back to England just two years later. In 1640, he entered the House of Commons and was active in promoting Parliament over the King. In 1641, he was also one of the main architects in bringing about the death of Charles I's Chief Advisor, Thomas*

Look out for the ghost!

Wentworth, 1st Earl of Strafford. After this success, Vane quickly rose in power and from 1643 to 1653 was effectively the civilian head of Parliament. It was after Cromwell dissolved Parliament in 1653 that Sir Henry Vane became his severest critic, though even this did not save him from the Royalists. In 1660, Charles II was restored as King and there followed a bloody persecution and vengeance of all those who had opposed the monarchy and the church during the Parliamentary period. Sir Henry, despite his open criticism of Cromwell was never forgiven for his hand in Wentworth's death and in June 1662 he too was beheaded. Sir Henry Vane's ghost is said to walk the park on the anniversary of his death. He is accompanied by his wife and carries his head under his arm!

In 1872, Edward Cazalet purchased "Fairlawne" and in the early 20th century, Major Peter Cazalet formed a famous racing stables here. Major Peter went on to become the personal trainer for horses owned by H.M. The Queen Mother. In 1932, Peter Cazalet married the daughter of P.G. Woodhouse and it is believed "Fairlawne House" was used by Woodhouse as a model for "Shipley Hall". Today, the estate is owned by an international investment company, something that would never happen to "Shipley Hall"!

After passing the gates bear diagonally right, at first following the line of a bank on your right. After approximately fifty metres, just after passing a small circle of horse chestnut trees on your left, bear gently left away from the bank heading for another yellow post in the distance. As you near a fence the other side, head for a stile which should, by now, be visible. The estate have put up several yellow poles as markers for the path, but if the weather is misty or if it is a day with poor visibility these may be difficult to see. If this is the case, as you near the fence look out and head for the stile.

Cross the stile and continue directly ahead, across another wide open field, once again following the yellow posts. As you cross the field, to your right are possibly the best views of "Fairlawne House" and gardens. On nearing the far side of the field, your way begins to descend and you should continue to the very far right hand corner of the field, ignoring a stile and marked footpath on your right, to arrive at a small gate beside a field gate, actually at the field corner itself (this is, once again, distinguishable by a yellow post). Pass through the small gate to then descend to meet a tarmac drive in front of an ornamental pond. The pond is one of a chain fed by a large spring known as the Lady Vane Spring, which rises

i   incredibly from 1,200 ft below the surface. The ponds are a favourite place, it is said, for Sir Henry Vane's ghost. Cross over the drive to follow another drive the other side, which passes to the left of the ornamental pond with an intricate bridge connecting to an island at the centre.

After the pond, carry straight on, passing to the left of some renovated outbuildings and pass through a small gate beside a field gate ahead. Walk straight on across the centre of a field, following a slightly raised track, and at the far side go over a stile and cross a footbridge over a stream, into another field. Cross the centre of the field, heading for some houses the other side with some fine views right along the Greensand Ridge, the route of our adventure later. At the far side, after following a beech hedge on your left, pass through a gate and follow a fenced path between gardens before arriving at a lane. Carry straight on along the lane which quickly bends left and then right, and ignore a lane on your left to pass to the left of the village hall and soon after, arrive at a "T" junction at the open green of Shipbourne Common. Turn right to follow a lane across the centre of the common, heading for a church the other side. You are now following the Greensand Way, a long distance walk which we shall meet and follow again before the day it out. The common doubles as Shipbourne village green.

i   ***Shipbourne (GR. 594523 Map 188)*** *is actually pronounced "Shibbon". The name stems from the 13th century and literally means, "sheep stream". "Ship" is an old Kentish word for "sheep" (you will still hear the old pronunciation in the more rural areas) and "Bourne" is a Saxon word meaning "a stream that dries up or with an intermittent flow". The stream the name refers to is actually called the Bourne and is followed for some distance on another walk, "The Soar Feat". The spring rises close to the village and until recently, the stream was dammed for use as a sheep dip, though this is now in ruin.*

At the far side of the common you will arrive at the A227 with the welcome sight the other side of "The Chaser Inn", a freehouse and hotel. The hotel was built by Edward Cazalet of "Fairlawne House" around 1880 and continues to serve the traveller good ales (usually Harveys) and food to this day. Cross the road, the A227, and take the driveway to the church in the direction of the sign for the Greensand Way. Pass through the gateway into the churchyard and fork right to follow the main path round to the church entrance, which is unfortunately normally locked.

i   ***Shipbourne Church (GR. 595522 Map 188)****, dedicated to St. Giles, is originally Saxon but was heavily restored in 1771 and again in 1880, the latter by Edward Cazalet, at the same time as "The Chaser Inn" was built. The foundation stone at the foot of the tower was laid by Mrs. Edward Cazalet on 24th October, 1879.*

The church is famous for its huge gargoyles which stare down from the tower. The gargoyle, like so many features in traditional style characters, originates from the Celts. The Celts venerated the head and often kept the heads of notable enemies preserved in Cedar oil to show off to visitors. Heads of less important victims were displayed on poles around their camps, not only to ward off future enemies but also, they believed, to give them power. Other forms of Celtic art are also based around the head. The Church followed suit, though for traditions' sake only and many older English churches have heads carved above the door or on the font. (Wotton church in Surrey [see "10 Adventurous Walks in Surrey"] has a carved head of a pope above the door which is also the first known carving of a pope in this country). The heads later became more grotesque and surreal and over the centuries, the gargoyle was born. When admiring these heads I wonder how many people today realise their grotesque origin, very few I suspect - and perhaps it's better that way!

To continue, walk past the entrance, pass through a kissing gate in the church wall the other side and thereafter, on meeting a choice of three paths, take the right hand path to go immediately over a stile into a field. Cross the field, keeping roughly to the right hand perimeter and at the far corner, go over a stile and cross a track at the corner of another field to, after a few paces, go over another stile into a third field which you should cross, keeping to the left of some newly planted fenced trees. At the field corner, go over a stile and turn right to follow a track along the right hand perimeter of a field, thereby leaving the signposted Greensand Way. The track follows the field perimeter and later skirts the village cricket pitch on your right which has a bubbling brook acting as a boundary, complete with bridges for the fielders to chase stray balls. In wet weather, the cricket pitch doubles as a haven for local ducks!

A little later on, when the track bends right going over the brook and passing behind the cricket clubhouse, leave the track and continue ahead through a group of trees planted in lines and after approximately twenty metres at a yellow post, turn left going uphill along the left hand perimeter of a field. As you climb, there are good views back to the church at Shipbourne. At the top of the field, go over a stile beside a couple of gates and continue along the left hand perimeter of the next field. To your right now, are good views to "Fairlawne House". At the far side of the field, go over a crossing track, ignoring a gate on your left, and a few paces on, pass through a small gate to the left of a couple of field gates and carry straight on along the left hand perimeter of a third field.

As you near a line of oaks ahead and are almost level with "Fairlawne House" on your right, look out for a gate on your left and go over a stile to the right of the gate, with a couples of old sarsen stones at its base (take care not to miss it). Our way is now along a lovely old hedged path, the hedges concealing some ancient iron railings, indicating that the path was once a coach drive to "Fairlawne House". It leads to the ancient "Igtham Mote", our next destination, and it is not long before you pass a National Trust sign introducing "Igtham Mote".

Stay on the fenced path, ignoring all turnings off and noting the wonderful converted oasthouses which you pass later on your right, to eventually arrive at a tarmac drive and the car park to the National Trust property of "Igtham Mote". Carry straight on along the drive, do not turn right into the car park, to soon pass "Igtham Mote" itself. The National Trust have recently installed an entrance and shop beside your route making it is easy to pause and explore the property. I recommend you take time to do this.

i

Igtham Mote (GR. 584534 Map 188) is an evocative place and in such perfect preservation it easy to imagine a knight riding across one of the lichen-crusted stone bridges over the moat. Built around 1340, it is perhaps the best preserved Medieval manor house in all England. Certainly, its setting is unequalled.

"Igtham Mote" started life as a fortified house for one Sir Thomas Cawne, though before this must have been a building of some importance for "Mote" is Saxon (Mot) for "meeting place". Over the centuries successive owners added to the house and by the 16th century a great hall, a chapel and a crypt with walls over four feet thick, had been added. In the 17th century the house received one of its most impressive features, a beautiful carved Jacobean staircase.

It is the Selby family who lived in the house longest. A Sir William Selby purchased the house in 1591 and the family continued to live here for almost three hundred years. Perhaps the most famous member of the family was Dame Dorothy, a Lady in Waiting to Elizabeth I. It is widely thought that she tipped off authorities about the Gunpowder Plot through a letter sent to her cousin warning him not to attend the Opening of Parliament. A long inscription on her tomb in the church at Igtham village at first appears to confirm her role in thwarting the Gunpowder Plot, but many historians now believe it simply refers to a needlework picture she made of the event. Doubters of the latter theory argue that an inscription on a tomb is hardly likely to remember something as insignificant as a piece of needlework. Dame Dorothy's role in thwarting the Gunpowder Plot will, I fear, be argued over for centuries to come.

The last private owner of the house was an American, Charles Henry Robinson, who in 1985 presented it to the National Trust. When the National Trust started renovating the house they uncovered a woman's body bricked up inside one of the walls. From her skeleton, it would appear that she was walled up alive but for what reason, no-one knows. It was not however, an uncommon practice during the earlier centuries to hide "peasant women" in this way. It usually involved a peasant woman who had been unfortunate enough to fall pregnant by her master or someone in the family. The disappearance of a peasant woman would have caused much less of a stir than the disclosure that she was pregnant by a family of nobility!

Local legend recalls another unfortunate death through affairs of the heart. A Cromwellian soldier on wading through the moat in his armour for a secret rendezvous with one of the daughters of the house, is said to have slipped and (due to the weight of his armour) drowned! Another Civil War story, this one a little more cheerful, recalls how a cavalry of Roundheads searching for Royalists hiding at "Igtham Mote", got lost amongst the maze of lanes and gave up trying to find the house. This could be one of reasons for "Igtham Mote" having survived intact all these centuries. Despite being fortified, there is not one sign that the house ever needed to be defended against an aggressor and the pleasing result is here for us all to enjoy today.

To continue our walk, keep to the driveway as it bends left after the house, going uphill, to arrive at a lane with an old post box set into the barn wall opposite.

Turn right along the lane and after approximately twenty metres, turn left onto a marked bridleway (blue arrow), a track, which leads directly into "Mote Farm", at the same time rejoining the Greensand Way.

Pass to the right of some farm buildings and keep right as the track bends right in front of some old oasthouses. After the oasthouses, the track (an old packhorse route) begins to climb starting your ascent of the Greensand Ridge. As you progress take time to pause and enjoy the wonderful views behind. Further on, the track forks and you should take the right hand fork, in the direction of the blue bridleway arrow. The track eventually levels out and continues between fields before it meets another track leading off to the right marked by a blue arrow. You should ignore this to continue ahead, in the direction of the yellow arrow and the Greensand Way sign. As a further guide, there is now a copse on your left which in late spring/early summer has a floor covering of ramsons creating a heady scent.

The track dips and rises along the side of Wilmot Hill affording marvellous views in places, across the Kentish Weald, before suddenly and quite surprisingly, arriving at a beautiful stone and tile cottage.

Wilmot Cottage (GR. 574529 Map 188) *has an unparalleled position, enjoying* ***i*** *lovely views over the Kentish Weald to the South Downs. The cottage was originally an ale house, built to take advantage of the droving and packhorse trade which passed this way. Ale houses such as these were the forerunners of the popular institution, the inn, though a lot less comfortable. At the time of the drovers and packhorse routes, anybody could set up an ale house, the law did not require a licence. To show that you were selling ale, one simple hung an evergreen bush on the end of a long pole over the road. This is the reason you can still find pubs called "The Bush" today. The most famous must be "Shepherds Bush" in London, the borough's name literally recalling an ale house once popular with shepherds or drovers.*

Many ale houses simply served ale and basic food, though some also offered very basic accommodation, usually in a wooden hut with reeds or grass on the floor for a bed. There would have been no private rooms and people slept dormitory style. As the popularity of the ale house grew so did their notoriety and they were often dangerous places to stay after dark. Smuggling in particular, has long held a close relationship with our country's hostelries. In the 14th century, things got so bad that a law was passed forbidding ale houses to serve after curfew (around 10.00 p.m.), the basis for our unpopular "drinking up" times today. Not long after, another law was passed requiring owners of ale houses to hold a licence to sell liquor. With the new regulations and the decline of drovers and packhorse routes, the old ale house quickly vanished, making way for the more respectable inn which remains an integral part of our transport system today.

Staring wistfully at the cottage, one cannot help feeling that perhaps our ancestors were just a little too hasty in abandoning the ale house, particularly "Wilmot Cottage"!

Ignore the footpath on your left here to carry straight on, past the cottage and a covered spring on your right. The cover which is relatively new, replaced an older one. After the spring, your way is up some steps to go over a stile, before bending left to once again, follow the contours of the hill. After following the line of a field with more superb views left, the path passes through a lovely area of woodland with moss covered boulders strewn across your path. At one point, as you walk, you should ignore a path leading off to the right and continue, still following the contours of the hill. Later, go over a stile and follow the path which descends slightly to sometime on, run along the right hand perimeter of a field, before eventually arriving at another stile. Cross the stile to arrive at a lane **(GR. 566531)** where you should turn left to follow it and after approximately twenty paces, turn right onto a signposted footpath to, as before, follow the contours of the hill through a wood. The path twists and turns rising and dipping through the wood and later passes a wonderful half-timbered house just visible through the trees on your left.

Just after the house, the path soon runs behind some kennels below "One Tree Hill", where you are guaranteed a noisy greeting! After passing the kennels, the path meets a track which you should follow ahead past a house to, not long after, arrive at another track onto which you should turn right, thereby walking straight ahead with lovely open views to the left, before eventually arriving at a lane **(GR. 557529)**. Cross the lane to follow the driveway for "Shepherds Mead" left and after a few paces, in front of a white gate, turn right onto a signposted footpath (yellow arrow), still following the Greensand Way. The path, which is fenced, later affords more superb views across the Weald before arriving at a "T" junction in the form of a bridleway. Turn right onto the bridleway and after approximately ten paces, turn left to go up a bank and cross a stile and thereafter, follow another path, still marked as the Greensand Way. This path initially runs along the perimeter of a field used for riding competitions and passing this way when an event is taking place, provides a good excuse for a pause to watch the proceedings.

The path proceeds to follow the perimeter of the field round and half way along the far side, you should look out for another path leading into the trees on your left. Join this, to shortly go over a stile (take care not to miss it) and thereafter, follow a narrow path through Redlands Wood. The path soon brings you to a lane which you should cross, to pass through a gate in a deer fence the other side. You are now in the ancient "Knole Park" where deer roam freely so please keep any dogs on a lead. Follow a wide path ahead to soon arrive at a driveway, known as Chestnut Walk, which you should cross to follow another drive ahead in the direction of the Greensand Way sign.

Stay on the drive, ignoring all turnings off, to eventually arrive at another prominent crossing drive which runs in a straight line from left to right, also line by trees and known as Broad Walk. As a further guide, to your right the drive runs across an open grass area heading for the roof top of a house. Cross over the drive and join a less prominent path the other side, marked by a low wooden post as the Greensand Way. This soon leads to a crossing track which you should ignore, to follow another track ahead instead which soon runs to the left of the walled garden to "Knole House". (If you find yourself descending into a valley, then you will have turned left at the crossing track in error and should retrace your steps). The steep valley on your left once contained a stream which ran into the river Darent. Its spring dried up several centuries ago and all evidence of the stream has slowly disappeared. As you approach the wall you will see it is divided by iron railings affording a very private view of "Knole House".

Follow the wall round to the front of the house, with good views across the valley on your left to Sevenoaks, to meet the main driveway to the house and the entrance. A good point at which to say - welcome to "Knole House".

Knole House (GR. 540542 Map 188) *protected by the National Trust, is the largest private house in England. It has 365 bedrooms, one for every day of the year and a staircase for every week of the year! One can just picture an unfortunate guest spending hours trying to find his or her bedroom!!*

The house was built by Thomas Bourchier, Archbishop of Canterbury, in the early 15th century. In 1532, Henry VIII took it over, preferring it to the palace at Otford (see "The Darent Dare") and his daughter, Elizabeth I, gave it to Thomas Sackville, 1st Earl of Dorset. The Sackville family have lived at "Knole House" ever since and with the help of the National Trust, maintain one of England's finest houses.

I will not attempt to do justice to the house for that is virtually impossible in a walking guide. Instead, I urge you to visit and buy a local guide book. What I will add however, is that the interior is as impressive as the exterior and houses a renowned collection of historical portraits and one of the finest collections of 17th century furniture in the country. To continue, follow the driveway across the entrance to the house and a few metres on, on arriving at a small parking area, turn right in the direction of a sign for Tea Rooms and then shortly after, left to join another drive, marked at the time of writing by a No Entry sign, a white horizontal line in a red circle, to now walk away from the house. As a further guide, the drive is lined by trees and leads downhill, passing a small walled garden on your right. Keep to the driveway, ignoring any turnings off to the left or right, to later arrive at a golf course. Here, you should follow the drive (now more a track) as it bends right to cross a fairway, ignoring a grass track which leads directly ahead. The fairway sits at the bottom of a shallow valley and as the driveway climbs the other side, you will enjoy good views to your right, back to "Knole House".

Knole House

Keep to the driveway to eventually exit the park via a gate and immediately after, ignore a footpath off to the left to follow a wide track ahead instead. To your left now are views across a field to the suburban areas of Sevenoaks, known as "The Wilderness" and, as a backdrop, the North Downs and the Otford Gap. Stay on the track which passes through a pleasant mixture of scrub, woodland and rhododendrons, ignoring all turnings off, until you sometime later see a wide path forking off to the right. This is just as you can see some houses through the trees ahead. (If you find yourself arriving at a wide gate you will have gone too far and should retrace your steps to find the fork). Take the path which forks right to soon pass through a kissing gate and thereafter, follow a path between gardens, to soon arrive at a lane in front of a pretty stone cottage.

Go straight across the lane and continue ahead along a track the other side, passing some stables, before arriving back at Godden Green. Turn right to arrive at the "Bucks Head" pub, our starting point.

ACCOMMODATION

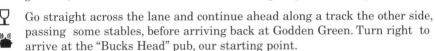

The Chaser Inn, Shipbourne. Tel: 01732 810360
On the walk, this is an unusual inn built in the late 19th century. The rooms are very comfortable and in the relaxed bar one can enjoy a wide range of good food. What more could you want!

Stavecrow Place, Tonbridge. Tel: 01732 365863
Approximately two miles from the walk, this is a luxurious B&B in a large house surrounded by woods. In the grounds is a heated outdoor swimming pool, ideal to soothe those aching muscles.

Youth Hostel, Kemsing YHA, Kemsing. Tel: 01732 761341
Approximately 11 miles from the walk, the hostel was once a vicarage in an attractive village at the foot of the North Downs. Quite a large hostel with fiftyeight beds, it can be busy in summer with school parties, so be warned and book ahead.

Camping and Caravanning, Mabledon Farm, Tonbridge. Tel: 01732 352407
Approximately four miles from the walk, this is a charmingly small site set in an orchard. The site includes a farm shop and, in summer, you can pick your own fruit. Small but good facilities. Particularly good for camping.

THE DARENT DARE

Distance: 12$\frac{1}{2}$ miles (20.5km)

Time: Allow approximately 6$\frac{1}{2}$ hours

Map: Ordnance Survey Landranger Map 177 and 188

START
OTFORD
60M

OTFORD MOUNT
204M

LULLINGSTONE
CASTLE
50M

FINISH
OTFORD
60M

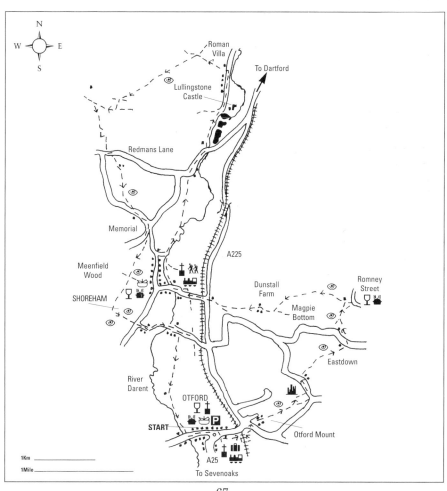

Walk Summary

This is a stunning walk though not for the faint-hearted. Almost immediately, you get a taste of what is to come with a steep climb to the top of Otford Mount before a series of more steep climbs and descents as the route passes from one valley to the next. A welcome half way break can be made at Shoreham where there are a number of hostelries from which to choose, before exploring the main valley en route, the Darent or Darenth as it is commonly known. Although a great deal of effort and stamina are required to complete this walk, you will be well rewarded. There are a number of surprisingly good views, many of which are worth more than a moment's pause and even when there isn't a view, the general landscape is quite enchanting. Add the lovely river Darent, a Tudor castle and Roman villa and some of the largest and oldest oak trees in Europe and you have a very exciting day out on offer. Just two words of warning. Apart from some steep climbs, mud can be a problem in wet weather, sapping that valuable stamina, so make sure you wear those boots. The second is cloud. Cloud and mist tend to congregate above Otford Mount reducing visibility to just a few metres. Remember this if you are looking forward to some wonderful vistas! Good luck!!

Start - GR. 525594 Map 188

The walk starts from the public car park at Otford, opposite "The Bull" pub. Otford is fairly easy to get to, situated on the A225, just north of Sevenoaks and the M26. From the north, the simplest way to join the A225 is either at Dartford or junction 3 of the M25, from where you should follow the A20 to Faringham and then the A225 south to Otford. From the west, if coming along the M25, join the M26 and then come off immediately after, following the signs for Sevenoaks. This takes you on to the A21 where you should almost immediately come off, again following the signs for Sevenoaks. Thereafter, follow the A25 to Riverhead and at a mini roundabout, turn left in the direction of the sign for Maidstone. At the next mini roundabout go straight on in the direction of the sign for Bromley, A224. Stay on the A224 until just after passing over the M26 and take a turning right, signposted to Otford, and follow the road all the way into Otford, where you will see the public car park on your left. From the east, come off the M26 at junction 2a and follow the A25 towards Sevenoaks. The junction with the A225 for Otford is well signposted and controlled by traffic lights. The centre of Otford is a pond in the middle of the A225. To get to the car park which is in the High Street, you need to turn left at the pond (if you are coming from the south) and right at the pond (if you are coming from the north). Otford also has quite a well served railway station.

The one obvious alternative start is at Shoreham village (**GR. 520616 Map 177**) which also has a railway station, though starting here mains leaving the hardest walking to last. It's up to you.

THE DARENT DARE

Before starting the walk, I feel it is worth knowing a little about Otford. This way, you can decide whether to explore the village now, en route, or if you have the energy, at the end of your walk.

Otford (GR. 525594 Map 188), *despite the busy A225 running through its centre* **i**
and the many visitors at weekends, retains a kind of dignity. It still has a local
feel and with its ruined palace, an air of mystery.

Due to its location, at the head of a large gap in the Downs (known as the Otford
gap) and with its plentiful supply of fresh water, Otford has always been a place
of some importance. Bronze Age remains have been discovered and I am sure
older remains simply wait to be, but it was the Romans who truly built a town
here and just east of the railway station the remains of a Roman villa were
recently uncovered. In fact, the Romans found the entire Darent valley a pleasant
place to live and evidence of Roman habitation is to be found all along the valley.
The most important find is that of a well preserved villa at Lullingstone, visited
later on our walk.

After the departure of the Romans, the valley and Otford would have been an
unsettled place. It is probable that the local population revolted against their
overlords, appointed by the Romans, and ransacked the many villages along the
valley. In the 5th century came the gradual invasion of the Saxons. In Otford's
case they were a race or tribe known as the Jutes and hailed from the coastal
areas of modern day Denmark. Contrary to popular belief, the invasion was
generally not a bloody one, but a gradual mixing of races controlled overall by the
Saxons, simply because of their better organisation. Over the next two hundred
years, Saxons, Celts and even many remaining Romans generally lived peacefully
side by side. In some areas, such as the West Country and Wales, the Celts even
regained some of their powerbases and ruled independently. It was only really in
the late 7th and 8th centuries that rivalry between Saxon kingdoms within
England brought war. Out of the rivalry Mercia became the strongest kingdom
and by 670 AD, London was under Mercia's control. In the 8th century, King Offa
inherited the throne of Mercia and was proclaimed the first King of all England -
Rex Totius Anglorum Patrae.

Some modern day historians still argue the fact of Offa's rule of all England,
siting many areas in the country which resisted his rule, one of the most notable
being Kent. Kent had Canterbury as its capital, a town which St. Augustine had
proclaimed to be the head of the Roman church in Britain. This gave Kent a great
deal of importance, an importance which Offa detested and it wasn't long before
he invaded the Kentish kingdom. One of the earliest and fiercest battles was
fought here at Otford at a place now known as Offa's field. Offa went on to defeat
Kent and truly ruled all England until his death in 796 AD. He gave the Otford
estate, presumable in thanks for his victory, to the Archbishops of Canterbury.

Offa's successor, Cenwulf, ruled until 821 AD when Mercia was overthrown by
Wessex and Winchester became the country's capital. In 1016, Otford's Saxons
found themselves defending another invasion, this time by the Danes, a race
ironically from the same region as the original Saxon invaders. This time the
defenders, led by King Edmund Ironside, were successful and the Danish army
slaughtered.

Otford rose in prominence when a manor house was converted to an Archbishops
palace. Thomas a Becket stayed at the palace on more than one occasion and a
tall oak settle (chair) said to have once belonged to Thomas a Becket, now sits in
"The Bull" pub. Several stories are attached to his visits. In one story, it is said

that whilst here he ordered all nightingales to be removed as they disturbed his prayer and in another, that he put a curse on all Otfords' blacksmiths after one of his horses had been badly shod. These stories were penned by a 16th century historian and as this was the time of the Reformation, were probably false, made up to discredit one of England's most revered Catholics. Another story tells of Thomas a Becket striking the ground with his staff in search of water. Legend has it that a spring gushed forth and from there on, the palace was blessed with a continuous supply of fresh water. A well in a private garden close to the palace is said to be the site of this miracle. The well is certainly old enough. It is likely the village pond at the centre of the A225 was also built for the palace. Records of the pond go back as far as the 11th century and today, it is unique in that it is the only pond in the country listed as a protected building - the listing also includes the duck house! The protective listing came about in 1960, after road planners had tried to have the pond destroyed to improve the route of the A225.

In the early 16th century, Archbishop Warham ordered the palace to be modernised and the palace was greatly enlarged and improved. It is the ruin of this palace which remains today. With its modernisation Thomas Cranmer often frequented the palace as did Henry VIII, though the latter complained that it was a "rheumatic" place. Henry VIII once stayed at the palace with over five thousand retainers, on his way to the Field of the Cloth of Gold, the famous meeting with King Francis I of France. The meeting, though a display on both sides of power and wealth, was intended to form a peace between the two nations. It was short-lived however, as within two years Henry VIII had resumed his war with France and rather ungratefully stripped the lead roof at Otford palace for ammunition and sold the remains. Without the roof the palace quickly deteriorated and with it, Otford's importance.

Today, the village, despite its close proximity to London and busy main road, retains many of the buildings from its Tudor heyday, particularly around the palace and church. The village also has four hostelries, three of which are very reasonable. The most famous and definitely one worth a visit, is "The Bull", Courage. "The Bull" was once the refectory for Otford's palace and was granted a licence by Papal Bull in 1538, the reason for the pub's name, though the brewery have, unimaginatively, hung a sign depicting the animal, a bull. Inside the pub are two large Tudor fireplaces and some wooden wall panelling, some of which has the heads of Henry VIII and Catherine of Aragon carved. It is likely that the fireplaces are original features of the pub, though some say they were removed from the palace. In one corner is a tall oak settle, which as mentioned earlier, is said to have once belonged to Thomas a Becket. It is also claimed that any wish you make whilst sitting in the chair will come true. Both claims are dubious and the chair is so uncomfortable that any wish would have to be made pretty quickly! A good test, I believe, is to wish for your next drink to be a free one - it didn't work for me!! The pub also has a large pleasant garden and conservatory and serves good honest pub food.

Undoubtedly Otford's prettiest pub is "The Horns", a freehouse, passed at the end of our walk. The pub is converted from three Tudor cottages with a pretty tile hung exterior, added in the 18th century. It has two bars, both of which are very cosy and serves a good selection of real ales. My only criticism is that like so many pubs, it is virtually becoming a restaurant and at weekends especially, stopping for just a drink can almost seem unsociable to the attentive diners.

Probably my favourite hostelry is "The Crown", facing the village pond. This is the undoubted local and as such always has a lovely relaxed atmosphere. The lounge bar has a fine bay window and a jumble of cartoons and photographs reflect the landlord's great sense of humour. The pub serves a good range of real ales and some good food, though this is first and foremost a pub and not a restaurant. Otford's fourth pub is "The Woodman", also facing the duck pond. The pub is one of Shepherd Neame's and as such is the village's only pub tied to a local brewery. The beer is cheap and the only other reason to visit is the curious dÇcor.

Pubs apart, Otford has a number of interesting cafés and restaurants along its High Street, as well as a General Stores allowing you to stock up.

To start the walk, facing "The Bull", turn left and walk up the village High Street to soon arrive at a roundabout with the famous village pond at its centre, in front of "The Crown" pub. Continue straight on, past "The Crown", until you reach another pub, "The Woodman". Cross the road, the A225, here and at the other side, continue straight on along a narrow tarmac path across a small green, passing to the left of a copper beech and war memorial. After this, pass through a gateway beside a superb tiled cottage into the churchyard of St. Bartholomew.

The cottage, apart from the church, is the oldest building in the village. Dating from the 14th century, it used to be a Court House and sometimes doubled as a prison. The huge chimneybrest was added during the Tudor period. Before that there would simply have been a hole in the roof. This particular Tudor chimney is quite rare today, as on the inside it divides into two flues and one of the flues remains unaltered. This would have been used to cure meat. On entering the churchyard, you are immediately struck by the size of the church's stout 12th century tower with its unusual 17th century wooden porch. The walls of the tower, in places, are nearly five feet thick, though the most interesting wall for historians is that of the nave. This wall was built around 1050 AD and is entirely Saxon. Included in the materials for construction were bricks from a Roman villa and a mill stone, also Roman. Inside the church, one charming feature is that it is still mainly lit by candles and the effect can be quite moving.

i
✝
■

Follow the path through the churchyard passing to the right of the church and as you progress, look right where you will see the remains of the Bishop's Palace, now inhabited only by pigeons and rooks - and perhaps the odd ghost. A short time on, ignore a path to your right and follow a path beside a long red brick wall to the far side of the churchyard and pass through a gate to thereafter, follow an enclosed path which leads to the car park for Otford railway station. Do not enter the car park, but turn right to continue following an enclosed path and when this turns right again, leave it to go over a stile on your left. Cross the railway line with care and at the other side, go over another stile and then follow another enclosed path which shortly arrives at a road between houses.

Turn left along the road for approximately ten metres and then left onto a tarmac path. Follow the path until you come to a metal gate and footpath sign on your right. (Take care not to miss it). If you find yourself approaching Otford railway station you will know you have missed the footpath and should retrace your steps.

After passing through a gap beside the gate, follow a wide path through a copse into an area known as "the chalkpit". The path soon leads to a grass area at the centre of the old chalk workings. Turn left at the grass area following its perimeter and at the next corner, continue straight ahead along a path leading uphill through the trees via a series of steps. After a short distance, the path leads out to a road, Pilgrims Way East, part of the old Pilgrims Way (See "In Celtic Footsteps"). Turn right along the road, following in the steps of pilgrims for just a few paces, until you come to a North Downs Way information sign. Cross the road at this point to join the more modern long distance route, the North Downs Way, also signposted as a public footpath.

Your route now immediately starts to climb, running between gardens, and if you are unfit the climb can be somewhat of a shock and certainly prepares you for the rest of the walk! As you climb, you soon leave the gardens behind to arrive at the more natural hillside of Otford Mount with the path flanked by bushes. The going now becomes much steeper and for some it will feel as though you have already completed several miles! Do not worry, help is at hand for further up you will pass a thoughtfully located memorial seat, a good place to recover and if the clouds are kind, a good opportunity to take in the rewarding views of Otford below and beyond to the North Downs in Surrey. Your way from the seat is onwards and upwards, ignoring any minor turnings off.

Eventually the path levels out and passes through an area of mature woodland before going over a stile into a field. Once in the field, the path forks and you should take the left hand fork to follow the left hand edge of the field, thereby leaving the North Downs Way. As the field perimeter bears sharp left, leave it to carry straight on heading for a point just to the left of a white triangulation point (204 metres - and the highest point on the walk), visible ahead. On rejoining the field perimeter continue straight on to follow the perimeter, a line of trees on your left, to soon reach the field's far left hand corner. Go over a stile and turn left along a lane to shortly pass a number of properties on your right. After the last property, "The Granary", (note the clock beside the drive opposite - there is a story here somewhere), go over a stile on your right to join a signposted footpath. Follow the path to soon cross two more stiles, after which you should continue ahead, now walking along the right hand perimeter of a field, descending gently.

At the far side of the field, go over another stile and follow a narrow path downhill through the delightful Great Wood. At times the path can be almost tunnel like with vines, in places, connecting the trees overhead.

On one occasion when walking this way, the wood was shrouded in dense cloud which gave the woodland a distinct air of mystery, with each tree appearing as a moving shadow. On another occasion, on a hot summer's day, a fox appeared on the path ahead delighting in the dappled shade from the myriad of greens in the canopy above. It casually turned to look at me and then trotted along the path ahead as though intending to by my guide, but it was alas, going far too fast.

The wood ends only too soon and after going over a stile, you will come out at a field. Carry straight on, across the centre of the field, to shortly start climbing a steep hillside, Eastdown, ignoring a newly created footpath on your left, no matter how tempting.

The climb, although tough brings its rewards, especially in summer when the hillside is a mass of chalkland flowers and higher up, there are some very good views, particularly down the valley to the barns at Magpie Bottom. Near the top, go over a stile under a beech tree into another field and carry straight on across the centre, as though heading for the far left hand corner. On going over a rise, roughly at the centre of the field, aim just to the right of a garden fence ahead and on meeting the fence, follow it ahead to soon arrive at a stile beside a gate. Go over the stile and turn left along a lane and after approximately twenty paces, turn right onto another signposted footpath, to follow a narrow path up a bank and over another stile. This takes you into a field where you should carry straight on, along the left hand perimeter. At the far side, cross another stile and continue ahead, this time along the right hand perimeter of the next field. Be warned, the heavy clay soil here can, in wet weather, make the going quite tough.

At the far side of the field, go over a stile beside a gate and continue ahead to then immediately pass through a gate on your right (do not make the mistake of going through the field gate directly ahead). You will now follow a wide path which is fenced, running between fields and heading for a large house at the hamlet of Romney Street in front. A short way on, look out for a stile on your right with a footpath running diagonally across a field the other side. Our way here is straight on, but if you want to visit "The Fox and Hounds" pub, a freehouse, at Romney Street, our next destination, then the stile and footpath on your right is a short cut. To rejoin the route from the pub, standing with your back to the pub, turn right and follow a signposted public bridleway to another stile where you will rejoin the official route **(GR. 549615 Map 177)**. As mentioned, to continue our route, ignore the stile on the right and carry straight on, with superb views ahead to your left across rolling hills to the Thames at Dartford. On arriving at a "T" junction in front of a garden fence **(GR. 549615 Map 177)**, turn left over a stile in the direction of a footpath sign for Shoreham, to enter a field. However, if you want to visit "The Fox and Hounds" pub at Romney Street, your second opportunity, then turn right instead. The pub is less than a minute's walk and after, you will need to retrace your steps to rejoin our walk.

To continue, carry straight across the field, keeping the garden fence on your right and at the far side, go over another stile into the next field, where you should continue ahead, now going downhill, with more superb views ahead and to your right. As you descend, the path passes to the right of some trees surrounding a small hollow and after a short steep descent rises gently to arrive at a stile at the far side of the field. Cross the stile and go over a crossing track before climbing another stile into a field. Here you are immediately rewarded with more fine views across a valley with a golf course at the bottom. The only dampener on this idyllic scene is the recognition that our route leads up the steep slope the other side! It is a good time to pause to fully appreciate your surroundings and contemplate the mentality of the author of this guide! When you are ready, descend to the bottom of the field, keeping to the right hand perimeter and at the bottom, go over a stile which at the time of writing, is cleverly carved out of a log, to thereafter follow a hedged path across the golf course. At the end of the hedged path, go over a stile to immediately start your ascent of the steep valley slope.

The climb is quite a test and I recommend you take some stops along the way to catch your breath, if not to enjoy the views back. Whilst looking back, if you look right you may recognise the steep slope of Eastdown, climbed earlier. Further up, go over a stile and follow a narrow path which twists uphill through woodland, at the other side of which you should cross another stile into a field. Bear diagonally left across the corner of the field, heading for another stile visible at the left hand perimeter. Cross the stile (currently a redundant stile as there is a gap in the fence here), and continue in the same direction across the centre of the next field. At the far side, go over a stile beside a gate and turn right onto a track which dips in and out of a valley before entering the farmyard of "Dunstall Farm" with the attractive flint farmhouse on the left.

Carry straight on through the farmyard and as the track forks, bear right and then left around a corrugated barn, in the direction of a footpath sign. As the barn ends and the track bends right, leave it to carry straight on across the centre of a field, at the far side of which you should continue ahead following a narrow path which starts to descend the steep slope of White Hill through woodland. After a short distance, go over a crossing path to continue your descent along what can at times be a slippery path, though in places your way is helped by steps. The descent suddenly eases and virtually levels out, the path now being much wider, and at this point you should ignore several minor paths leading off at either side to continue your route ahead. Sometime on, the path you are on meets a bridleway (Fackenden Lane) descending from the left. You should join this, bearing right, to continue your descent and shortly after, pass the attractive "White Hill Cottage" on your right, before arriving at the main road, the A225 **(GR. 526615 Map 177)**.

Cross the main road and follow another road the other side, signposted to Shoreham. The road passes beneath a railway line where there are steps to your right leading to Shoreham station (alternative start). Later, the road passes the entrance to Darenth Valley Golf Course and soon after this, you should ignore a signposted public footpath (part of the Darenth Valley path) on the left to continue ahead along the road. As you approach the first houses of Shoreham village, leave the road to join a signposted footpath, also the Darenth Valley path, on your right. Do this by passing through a gap beside a field gate and continue ahead, along the left hand perimeter of a field, for approximately ten metres, to then turn left passing through a kissing gate into the village churchyard. Thereafter, follow a quite majestic brick path lined by a procession of neatly cut yews through the churchyard, taking time out to visit the church before coming out at the other side of the churchyard at a road in front of "The Olde George Inne", a Courage pub. A good time to say, welcome to Shoreham and a good halfway stop.

__Shoreham (GR. 522616 Map 177)__ is a delightful village and considering its position, incredibly peaceful. The magnificent entrance, via the yew lined church path, is only the first of many delights.

The church itself dates from the 13th century, though the majority of the current building was constructed around 1755. Probably the most striking feature inside is an oil painting depicting the return from Africa to Shoreham of Lieutenant Verney Lovett Cameron, RN, whose father was, at the time, vicar at the church.

74

Verney Cameron became the first European to cross Africa from coast to coast, whilst leading an expedition to relieve David Livingstone. In 1878, he headed another expedition overland from Constantinople to Baghdad, to test the feasibility of a continuous railway. Ironically, he died not on one of these daring expeditions, but in England where he was thrown from his horse whilst out hunting. The painting depicts a joyous village celebration with Cameron's father waiting for his son at the church porch.

Another former vicar at the church was the Reverend Vincent Perronet, who was a good friend of John Wesley. Wesley frequently preached at Shoreham and it is reported that on one occasion his friend, the vicar and his family had to rescue him from a hostile crowd whilst preaching at the bridge over the Darent. Other famous sons of Shoreham are the artist, Samuel Palmer, who lived at "The Water House", overlooking the river Darent, and the writer Lord Dunsany.

From "The Olde George Inne" the village's main street continues, straddled by chocolate box cottages, to cross the river Darent via a low stone bridge. A short distance the other side is a lovely pub, "The Kings Arms", a picturesque weatherboarded affair with the only remaining Ostlers Box in the country. I'll leave you to discover what an Ostlers Box is and you'll thank me for this, for you will have to visit the pub to find out! Inside "The Kings Arms" has a curious mixture of dÇcor which somehow works. It has a very cosy feel, more like a home than a pub. There is a wide selection of real ales on offer, including Ruddles, as well as good basic pub food. For real ale lovers though, the best pub is "The Royal Oak", but this is even further up the road from "The Kings Arms" and quite a detour from our route. You may just wish to content yourself with one pub, "The Olde George Inne" - and a welcoming place it is too.

To continue, carry straight on along the road passing to the right of "The Olde George Inne" and thereafter, past numerous attractive cottages, to soon meet and follow the river Darent which flows with vigour at the other side of the road. A few paces on, just before the road crosses the river via a pretty bridge, turn right onto a lane, Darenth Way.

Darent and Darenth. It can seem peculiar that the valley apparently has two *i* names, Darent and Darenth. The long distance footpath following the valley from Riverhead to Dartford is called the Darenth Valley Path and yet the same Council produces leaflets on the valley headed "The Darent Valley". Which is it and why the confusion? The answer is quite simple - both terms are correct and the choice is yours.

The word "Darent" is Celtic for "river where oaks trees grow". Apart from some notable exceptions later on our walk, most of the oak trees to which this once referred have been felled for use in the shipbuilding industry. "Darenth" is a corruption of the Saxon word, "Daerintan", and literally means "estate on the river Darent". The estate was probably originally Roman and ran from one of the many villas along the valley. The word "Daerintan" is a good example of how Celtic, Roman and Saxon cultures and words mixed. The Celtic "Darent" is obviously there, the later "a" and "e" together after the initial "D", is typically Saxon and the ending in "an" is Roman or Latin. The two curious terms for the valley therefore, probably originated with the forming of a Roman estate and have continued ever since.

As you join the Darenth Way, note the old ford on your left. Even after the bridge was built the ford was popular with cart drivers who used the ford to rid their wheels of mud. Note also the war memorial which asks you to look out for the cross on the hill, something we shall do more than once before the day is out. It is a beautiful spot for a rest, even so soon after the pub. Try to imagine John Wesley preaching on the bridge, surrounded by a hostile crowd. Listening only to the pleasant gurgle of the river Darent, perhaps it was Wesley's disturbance of the peace that the villagers objected to and not the content of his preaching?

To continue, follow the lane alongside the river and when it ends continue ahead through a gate, your way now running between a wall on your right and the river Darent on your left, and following a drive to some houses. As the drive twists right to serve the houses, leave it to carry straight on, keeping to the left of a hedge and still following the river. If you look left now, you will see the large white cross cut out of the hill side, referred to by the war memorial at Shoreham bridge. The cross was cut in remembrance of those men from Shoreham who died in World War I. It is one of only three turf cut crosses in the country. (The other two are in the Chilterns and featured in two walks respectively in "10 Adventurous Walks in the South Chilterns"). From here on, the path simply follows the river to eventually arrive at a footbridge, where on the opposite bank there are some lovely Victorian terraced cottages with gardens leading down to the river. Ignore a path on your right here and turn left instead over the footbridge and at the other side, follow the path as it immediately bends right and shortly after, left, where it becomes a narrow lane. To your right at this point is a lovely half-weatherboarded old mill.

Follow the lane for approximately twenty paces before turning right onto a marked footpath (yellow arrow), beside a Kent County Council sign detailing the Darenth Valley Path. From here, your way, once again, follows the river Darent, though this time along the western bank. A short time later, pass through a kissing gate and continue ahead along the right hand perimeter of a field, with the river meandering away to your right. At the far side of the field, pass through a gap in a hedge, to then follow a path diagonally left across the centre of the next field (do not make the mistake of following the right hand field perimeter). This is another lovely part of the walk. To the east the valley side rises steeply, whilst in contrast, to the west the valley is protected by a gentle range of hills set in a curve to form a natural bowl. Admiring all this beauty it is hard to imagine that the landscape is squeezed between the M25 and the A225 with London no more than a few miles away.

At the far side of the field, pass through a gap in a hedge and go over a concrete drive and across another field thereafter. At the field end, go over a stile into another field and continue ahead, now between fields, with the field on your right, at the time of writing, being given over to the beer drinkers' favourite crop, hops! At the far side of the fields, you will arrive at a lane onto which you should turn right, thereby carrying straight on. After passing a number of houses and a farm on your right, the lane passes "The Hop Shop". This is a farm shop specialising in dried flowers and hops. It is well worth taking a look, even if only to smile at the model windmill at the entrance, operated by the river Darent. Continue to follow the lane until it bends right where you should leave it to enter the car park for Lullingstone Visitors Centre. Unless you wish to visit the Visitors Centre which also has a small café and shop, at the car park entrance join a footpath signposted to Lullingstone Castle.

We are now entering Lullingstone Park, an estate consisting of 690 acres. Incredibly, the estate was formed by the Romans (perhaps the estate which confused the valley's name?) and has been managed as an estate ever since. During the Roman period, it would have been much larger and the immense area of remaining estate lane allows a unique insight to land management over the centuries.

The path now once again follows the river Darent and after approximately one kilometre arrives at a lake. Carry straight on across a small car park and thereafter, follow a lane ahead, passing to the left of Lullingstone Castle. The castle is open to visitors from April to September and offers a Tea Room at the castle gateway.

***Lullingstone Castle (GR. 529644 Map 177)** is in fact a Tudor mansion and has never been a castle. You will be immediately impressed by the huge brick gatehouse, added in 1497 and one of the best examples in the country. The main house was built by one, Sir John Peche. In the same century, Sir John once served at the court of Henry VII.*

The castle later passed into the hands of the Hart family (who still live at the castle today) and it was Sir Percival Hart who was responsible for much of the current interior. Sir Percival was a great friend of Queen Anne and revelled in his importance from the relationship. Queen Anne became a frequent visitor to the park and much of the modernisation of the house was for her benefit. Some of the modernisation, though, was for practical purposes and not just to impress. Queen Anne was a very large lady and found it difficult to walk far or climb stairs. Sir Percival, being ever attentive, had a completely new staircase built with shallow treads to compensate. The ancient St. Botolphs church, "the church on the lawn" was also restored for Queen Anne's benefit and at the other side of the river, Sir Percival built a bath house exclusively for the Queen's use. The bath house was built over a spring and the waters are said to have therapeutic qualities.

Gateway to Lullingstone Castle

Queen Anne was often in poor health and no doubt appreciated the waters' effect, though her doctors advised that if she cut down on the brandy, this would improve her health faster than bathing in spring water! The bath house was once fully tiled with a thatched roof - alas now all that remains are a few ruined walls.

Sir Percival's influence over Queen Anne apparently did not extend to his daughter. On the eve of her wedding to Sir Thomas Dyke she escaped by knotting together sheets from her bed and climbed down from her bedroom to elope with a young naval officer called Bluet. Sir Thomas swore he would never marry anyone else and when Bluet died nine years later, he kept his promise and married the girl who had once so cruelly jilted him. The family name has been Hart-Dyke ever since.

In 1875, it was a later member of the family, Sir William Hart-Dyke, and two colleagues who first laid down the rules for lawn tennis and it was in the castle grounds that the first lawn tennis court was laid out, with a ladder between two barrels instead of a net.

A silk farm was started in part of the house and silk produced by the farm was used to make Queen Elizabeth's Coronation dress. In 1957, the farm was moved to Dorset and the silk produced today is still favoured by the Royals - indeed, Diana, Princess of Wales, used it for her wedding dress.

The castle, once in danger of ruin from World War II bombing as well as a lack of funds, has now been restored to its former glory. Part of the house has been converted to private apartments but the state rooms, still recognisable to Queen Anne, are open to the public in summer. The little church, a virtual historical record of the families that have lived here, can be visited at any time - something which I recommend.

To proceed, continue ahead along the lane. The top of the hill to your left is believed to be the site of a Celtic fort, the first real settlers in the valley. Keeping to the lane, you will later pass "Park Farm" on your left and then some attractive houses, after which you should continue until just after passing a white posted gateway (approximately one third of a mile from the castle), you should turn left onto a signposted footpath, also marked as a circular walk **(GR. 529650 Map 177)**. First however, you may wish to continue for a few paces more to view Lullingstone Roman Villa (ú2.00 admission fee) which has a number of fine mosaics.

i ***Lullingstone Roman Villa (GR. 530651 Map 177)*** *is the best of several excavated villas in the valley and arguably one of the most important Roman discoveries in the country. The villa started life as a simple farm, before being extended to a villa of some grandeur around 350 AD. This is when most of the five existing mosaics were laid. The villa was apparently quickly abandoned at the beginning of the 5th century, roughly the time when the Roman Legions were called back to Rome and soon after, was razed to the ground by fire. The fire could well have been started deliberately. As mentioned under "Otford", with the departure of the Romans, many villas were ransacked by the local population and it looks as though this was the case at Lullingstone. The surviving mosaics are well worth viewing and the villa is one of a handful that when excavated, was found to have housed a Christian chapel.*

Religion during the Roman occupation was a confused affair. The Romans brought with them their classic gods and built in their honour, great temples. They could not however, convert the Pagans who continued to worship their own gods under the guidance of the Druids. Over the years, the two extreme brands of religion became entwined and Celtic-Romano temples became common. In Europe, two new religions also grew in popularity, Mythraism from Persia and Christianity from Palestine. Mythraism became popular with the elite Roman classes, whilst Christianity was banned, with followers punishable by dealth because of the religion's refusal to swear loyalty to the Emperor. This did not stop the spread of

Christianity and by the 2nd century, there were Christian sects in Britain.

It was not until 313 AD, two centuries later, that Rome finally gave in and Emperor Constantine the Great officially recognised Christianity on behalf of Rome. This was not without some concessions, one of which was that all biblical figures in future had to be shown with a light above their heads. The light was to represent the God of Light, Mithras and made acceptance of Christianity easier for the Romans. Holy figures are still represented in this way today, the light now commonly known as a halo.

Not all Romans, even after Rome's acceptance of Christianity, abandoned their old faith and this could well have been the case at Lullingstone. The chapel is a conversion of a large room and evidence suggests that this was during the late 4th or early 5th century, just at the time when the Legions were leaving the country. It could well have been (but only a theory) that the resident family rapidly changed their beliefs to appease the local population. If this was the case, they were misguided, for Britons only truly accepted Christianity centuries after the Romans had left.

Returning to our route, as stated, turn left onto a signposted footpath and follow it up some steps through woodland to shortly go over a stile and thereafter, continue between fields. You will now find yourself climbing steadily out of the valley. The climb is quite a long one and this may be one of the points you regret buying this book. By way of compensation however, there are some lovely views right along the Darenth valley, where a Victorian railway viaduct crosses the valley. As you climb, ignore a stile and footpath on your right and continue for approximately forty paces more to take a path forking left, thereby leaving the official footpath and following a designated path through Lullingstone Park. The path runs between fields affording beautiful views left over the Darenth valley and Lullingstone Castle. At one point it passes a lone sycamore tree planted in 1871 to celebrate the birth of Sir William Hart-Dyke's eldest son, Percyvall. After the tree, the path continues over a rise before descending into a dry valley, with more views ahead across Lullingstone Park Golf Course.

The path descends (ignore a path left) passing to the right of a green at the bottom of the valley and as you commence to climb the other side of the valley, take care to avoid making the mistake of following a muddy horse track ahead. Instead, ensure you take the path ahead on the left, passing between some wooden rails, to thereafter walk uphill via a series of steps. Later, after passing between some more wooden rails you will arrive at an open field, still part of the golf course, where you should continue ahead, keeping approximately ten metres distance between you and a line of small oak trees on your right. As you near the woodland the other side, head for a red ringed post just to the right of a horse chestnut tree, to then pass between some wooden rails and follow a winding path the other side through woodland. (Do not make the mistake of following the more prominent muddy path to your right. This is extremely muddy during most times of the year and used primarily by horses).

The path twists and turns through the wood always with the golf course just visible on your left. Do not make the mistake of joining the wide path running parallel on your right. Sometime later, after approximately one third of a mile, you will meet a crossing path. As a guide, to your left here is a huge old pollard oak and beyond, a modern outbuilding on the golf course.

i *The Pollard Oak is one of several hundred in the park. They are the oldest living things in Kent and outside of the New Forest and the Forest of Nottingham are the greatest collection of Pollard oaks in the country. (Tell that to the doubters of Kent who believe the country is no more than a suburb of London). Although it is hard to tell exactly, it is estimated that some of the trees date back to the 11th century and perhaps even before. It is almost impossible to imagine that some of these trees may have witnessed Norman knights riding through the park.*

All the Pollard oaks are impressive and some have a circumference of over 10 m (33 ft), an incredible size. The largest oak in Europe is in Denmark and measures 13.9 m. It is the continuous Pollarding which creates the trees' huge girth. The trunk is allowed to grow to a height of between seven and fifteen feet and then it is cut. After this the branches are harvested every twenty years. This way, there is a constant harvest of wood and the branches stay above the reach of the deer whilst affording some shelter. Probably the most famous Pollard oaks are in Windsor Great Park, but take it from me, the ones at Lullingstone are far more impressive.

To continue, go over the crossing path continuing straight on, following a narrow path, to shortly pass another Pollard oak, before eventually coming out at a wide crossing path with another path joining from the right. Carry straight on over the crossing path to follow a path the other side, marked by a blue ringed post and passing between a golf tee on your right and a green and some bunkers on your left. The path then widens and continues through woodland, going over another crossing path before arriving at a tarmac drive (**GR. 512645 Map 177**).

Turn right onto the tarmac drive and follow it across the golf course, where ahead to your right the club house is visible. Follow the drive for approximately one hundred and fifty metres until you see a footpath sign pointing left, also signposted as a circular walk (take care not to miss it). Turn left onto the footpath, passing between a tee and a practice green before descending through the beautiful Upper Beechen Wood. The path then traverses a fairway at the bottom of a shallow valley and continues up the other side where you should keep to the main path, ignoring any turnings off to the left or right. At the top, follow the path as it bends round to the left to, after a few paces, arrive at a crossing path with a tall wooden signpost. Turn right here, in the direction of the sign for "Public Footpath 206", to almost immediately meet a ladder stile and gate. The stile is left over from the days when Lullingstone was a deer park.

After the stile and gate, we say goodbye to Lullingstone Park and continue by following a fenced path which runs alongside some farm buildings, to shortly meet and cross another stile into a field. Carry straight on along the right hand field perimeter and at the far side, go over another stile and down some steps to join Redmans Lane.

i *The name "Redmans" is probably after a reddleman, who once lived close by and used the lane to visit his clients. A reddleman was a man who made a kind of red ochre dye for marking sheep and would often pass from farm to farm marking the sheep as part of the service. The dye would often stain the marker's skin, hence the name Reddleman or Redman. A reddleman is one of the main characters in Thomas Hardy's novel, "Return of the Native".*

Turn left along the lane and after approximately fifty metres, turn right onto a driveway to "Greenacre", also signposted as a public footpath. Follow the driveway to the house, the latter being in the form of a low bungalow, and walk to the right of the house, thereby leaving the driveway, to follow a fenced path ahead. The path soon passes another property, after which it bends right into a field. Continue ahead, along the right hand perimeter of the field and as you approach the far side, ignore a path leading off to your right and carry straight on to cross a stile ahead into another field. Here you are immediately rewarded with fine views across Timberden Bottom and up the Darenth valley, a good place to take a breather before the last stretch of the walk.

Once in the field, bear left along the left hand perimeter, descending gradually into a valley with a scattering of hawthorn and dog rose on your left, which act as good cover for rabbits. The path eventually arrives at a lane in front of a large brick bungalow with an excellent flowerpot man in its garden - do you remember them? Turn left along the lane, continuing your descent, to soon be welcomed by two elegant lines of beech trees protecting the lane. Continue until you arrive at a "T" junction where you should turn right. *First however, take time to ascend some steps on your right to view a small stone memorial with a heart felt message which reads, "Behold therefore I will allure her and will lead her into the wilderness and there I will speak to her heart".*

Returning to our walk, follow the lane uphill and ignore another road leading off to the left and continue for approximately thirty metres, before turning left onto a signposted footpath in front of an ornate Victorian cottage. The path immediately splits into two and you should take the right hand path, not the sunken path and a few paces on, turn right to follow a wide path along the side of the Darenth valley. Later the path forks and you should take the left hand fork, marked as a public footpath (yellow arrow). Do not take the bridleway. The footpath runs along the edge of Meenfield Wood and affords tremendous view across the Darenth valley and the village of Shoreham which lies immediately below. If you have a good eye, you can trace the early part of our walk. On a clear day, Otford Mount is also visible, a welcome reminder that the most strenuous part of the walk has been completed.

As you progress, look out for the Shoreham Cross on the hillside below. After passing the cross, ignore a marked crossing path and carry straight on for approximately another half a mile, to meet and cross a stile beside a field gate which takes you into a field. Turn left to commence your final descent to the bottom of the Darenth valley where to your right now the welcome sight of Otford village, our finishing point is in view.

At the bottom of the field, go over a stile and continue ahead along a track between fields, to eventually arrive at a lane. Cross the lane to join a No Through road marked as a footpath (yellow arrow), the other side. The lane ends beside the beautiful tile hung "Kennel Cottage" and here you should carry straight on along a narrow footpath which follows a delightful arm of the river Darent. As you join the footpath, note the newly planted woodland on your left, Robin's Wood, which was planted for and dedicated to a previous owner of "Kennel Cottage". The footpath leads to a footbridge over the stream beside a ford, a delightful spot to stop for a rest and perhaps cool your feet.

Go over the bridge and continue ahead along a track to soon pass a number of attractive buildings, including a beautiful old weatherboarded mill, complete with mill pond and weir. After the mill, you should follow a narrow tarmac lane, going gently uphill (this is the last climb - I promise!) to soon meet a golf course where the lane levels out. Turn right here onto a marked footpath (yellow arrow), also marked with the letter "D" , indicating that you are now back on the Darenth Valley Path. The path which is fenced, runs across the golf course with good views across the valley on your right and continues for approximately half a mile, at one point going over a crossing track, before arriving at a stile. Go over the stile and maintain your direction thereafter, following the left hand perimeter of a large field.

At the far side of the field, go over a stile and across a crossing track and over a second stile into another field. Maintain your direction, following the right hand field perimeter with your final destination, the village of Otford, now in view ahead. At the far side of the field, go over another stile into the next field, where you should continue ahead and for the last time, following the river Darent. At the far side of the field, cross yet another stile and follow a path ahead, noting as you walk the pretty property which is actually built over the river, to soon arrive at a lane between an old oasthouse and a 17th century mill house. Follow the lane ahead to arrive at Otford High Street. Turn left along the road to immediately pass the welcoming inn, "The Horns". If you can take your eyes off "The Horns", note the old timbered Tudor building opposite and the chapel beside it. From here, if you can resist the temptation to stop at "The Horns" (I rarely can!), then continue to follow the road back to "The Bull" pub and our starting point. The only thing left to do now is to decide on the venue for a celebration and a chance perhaps to ponder over an English valley which, with a little digging, provides so many clues to our early history.

ACCOMMODATION

The Royal Oak Hotel, Sevenoaks. Tel: 01732 451109

Approximately six miles from the walk, this is a lovely 17th century coaching inn, still with the coaching inn feel. All the bedrooms are individually styled and the hotel is famous for its good food. Just the thing after a strenuous day out.

The Hop Barn, Otford. Tel: 01959 523509

Virtually on the walk, this is a lovely place set in a tranquil country lane just off Otford's High Street. As the name suggests, accommodation is in a converted hop barn with oast house. To complete the picture, the barn is set in a beautiful cottage-style garden. Only minutes walk from Otford's High Street, the Hop Barn is ideally situated for an idyllic stay.

YHA, Kemsing YHA, Kemsing. Tel: 01732 761341

Approximately two miles from the walk, the hostel was once a vicarage in an attractive village at the foot of the North Downs. Quite a large hostel with fiftyeight beds, it can be busy in summer with school parties, so be warned and book ahead.

Camping and Caravanning, Thriftwood Park. Tel: 01732 822261

Approximately six miles from the walk, this is a pleasant site set in several acres of woodland. The camp also has purpose-built barbecues allowing you to continue to enjoy that "outdoor experience". Very well run, but make sure you take your muddy boots off before entering the shop!

THE CHURCHILL CHALLENGE

Distance: 12¹/₂ miles (20.5km)

Time: Allow approximately 6¹/₂ hours

Map: Ordnance Survey Landranger Map 187 and 188

START
CROCKHAM
HILL
115M

IDE HILL
216M

FINISH
CROCKHAM
HILL
115M

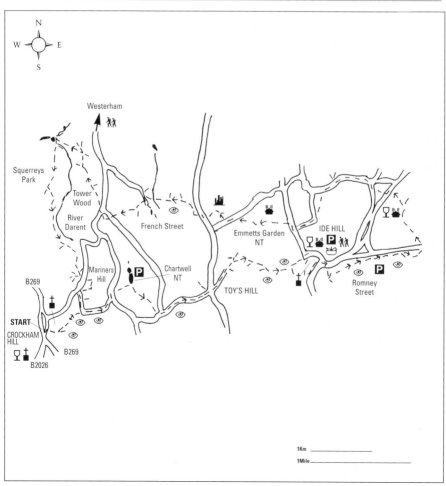

Walk Summary

This is one of my favourite walks combining some dramatic scenery with numerous points of interest. Indeed, there is so much to stop and admire it is all too easy to lose track of time and return after dark - take care! The walk involves a certain amount of lane walking, but to take nearly all footpaths would mean missing some superb scenery and you would be extremely unlucky to meet more than a couple of cars. There are quite a few ups and downs and mud, in places, can be difficult. Combine this with all the interest on the walk and I suggest you make an early start to ensure an enjoyable and full day out. Lastly and perhaps most importantly, there are at least three hostelries on or close to the route, plus one at the start or end. A short detour into Westerham also allows a wide choice of venues at which to recover or enjoy a drink.

Start - GR. 443506 Map 187

The walk starts from the village of Crockham Hill, close to Kent's border with Surrey. Crockham Hill is easily reached, being on the B2026 just north of Edenbridge. If joining from the A25, you can either take the B269 at Limpsfield which later turns into the B2026, or join the B2026 itself at Westerham. The nearest M25 junction is the Godstone junction (junction 6). From the south, the B2026 connects with the A264 between Tunbridge Wells and East Grinstead. If coming from deep within Kent, there is an intricate number of roads which can be taken, though perhaps the easiest is the B2027 from Tonbridge. Street parking is possible at Crockham Hill, though I do not recommend parking along the main road. There are a couple of side roads opposite the Post Office which are ideal. The nearest railway station is at Edenbridge from where there is an infrequent bus service or, if money is no object, a choice of taxis.

Alternative starts can be made at the villages of Ide Hill or Westerham, though doing this makes a visit to Crockham Hill an optional extra and tiredness may tempt you to miss what is an extremely pleasant part of the walk.

THE CHURCHILL CHALLENGE

Before starting the walk, I believe it is worth finding out a little more about Crockham Hill.

Crockham Hill (GR. 442506 Map 187) has an idyllic setting in a majestic fold on the Greensand Ridge. The village has a special place in my heart for apart from school trips, it was at Crockham Hill that I first discovered youth hostelling. Sadly, the Youth Hostel has now closed (a controversial decision) and with it, the General Stores. Happily the village pub, "The Royal Oak", Shepherd Neame, still survives and although modernised, still retains some charm. It is a good place at which to end a day out and regulars will be only too keen to talk about past landlords and, in particular, one who used to fry and deliver fish and chips to one's door every Friday.

With the B2026 running through the village centre, Crockham Hill can be a little off-putting. However, take time to explore and you will be pleasantly surprised. The original road that ran through the village still exists and contains some majestic properties. At the junction of this road and the modern-day road and opposite the Post Office, is a small memorial garden known as the Sundial

Garden, donated to the village in 1955. The garden is planted with cherry and apple trees and in spring is a sight to behold. In summer blooms a very special rose, the Octavia Hill rose, after one of the three original founders of the National Trust. Octavia Hill lived in a cottage at the edge of Crockham Hill Common at the top of Crockham Hill. Today, she would be pleased to find her favourite viewpoint at the top of Mariners Hill (passed later) has changed little since the days when she campaigned so hard to preserve our heritage.

To start the walk, facing the Post Office (which also doubles as an antique shop), turn left and walk up the main road, to shortly turn right onto a narrow lane signposted to the Holy Trinity church.

The Ragstone cottage (number 2) on your left as you join the lane, in the mid-19th *i* *century belonged to a family of builders, Thomas Horseman and Son. In 1842, they were employed by Charles Warde of "Squerryes Court" (passed near the end of the walk), to build the village church. The stone for the church came from Chiddingstone (see "The Chiding Challenge") and was cut in the builder's yard, now the cottage garden.*

Follow the lane downhill, past the school, until it bends left to meet the church. Our way from here is straight on through a small kissing gate ahead, though first you may wish to visit the church.

Crockham Hill Church (GR. 444507 Map 187), *dedicated to the Holy Trinity,* *i* *was donated to the village by Charles Warde of "Squerryes Court". Inside the* *✝* *church is a fine grey marble effigy of Octavia Hill, as well as a memorial window.* *■* *Her grave is under a yew tree to the right of the path as you enter the churchyard. In recognition of her work she was offered a tomb at Westminster Abbey, but preferred to be buried at her beloved Crockham Hill.*

Returning to our walk, as mentioned, as the lane bends left to meet the church, carry straight on

to pass through a small kissing gate ahead into a field, marked as footpath 376. Go straight across the field bearing slightly left (do not make the mistake of taking the footpath which runs along the field's right hand perimeter), to pass a small picnic area with several benches. At the far side go over a stile and continue straight across the centre of the next field, gradually veering away from a track visible on your right. You should now be heading for a small hamlet, Froghole, perched on the site of Mariners Hill. The oasthouses and farm to the *i* left of the hamlet are famous for being part of a painting, copies of which you may see on many a pub wall.

As you reach the centre of the field you will find yourself at the top of a small rise with lovely views to your right. From here you should continue straight *◎* across the field, heading for a small footbridge visible ahead, roughly thirty metres to the right of a field gate. You will at the same time, pass a spring on your left which in winter or wet weather can form a small pool. In dry weather it may only be recognisable by the reeds growing here.

The numerous springs which rise quickly in wet weather and dry when the rain *i* *stops, coupled with the local Atherfield clay, create a somewhat unstable environment and landslips here are common. If you look around, you will see the many bumps and hollows created by previous earth movement, the most famous of these being the great landslide of 1596. Over a period of three days, the land is said to have moved by over one hundred and forty feet! Two ponds on the hillside disappeared and in their place were mounds of earth. In one field, a crater over thirty feet deep also appeared. Today, all is peaceful but a serious spell of wet weather could mean a repeat of 1596. Take care, especially if it is raining.*

Safely at the far side of the field, go over a stile and cross the footbridge mentioned, to enter another field where you should continue ahead along the left hand perimeter and commencing your climb of Mariners Hill.

Shortly after passing a field gate on your left, go over a stile on the same side and follow a fenced path through a well tended garden, to soon continue your climb of Mariners Hill via a series of steps, known as the Buttles Steps, after their founder.

i *The steps and garden from which bubble numerous springs, is a truly magical scene. The springs run into the stream below and on to the river Eden. Before piped water came to the hill earlier this century, locals came to these springs for water, which was the main reason for building the steps. It is said that whilst collecting water you had to be careful not to tread on the numerous frogs which delighted in the damp, rocky environment - perhaps the origin for the hamlet's name of Froghole.*

After passing an idyllic thatched cottage the steps (134 in total) bring you to a narrow lane in front of a converted oasthouse. Turn right along the lane which at first runs along the edge of Mariners Hill, affording excellent views to your right over the Weald. Apart from the view, take time also to admire some picturesque properties passed along the way.

i *A couple of these houses still have (not visible from the lane) plague troughs in their gardens. A plague trough was a hollowed out stone where charitable residents left food for victims of the plague. A bottle of vinegar would also be left and the victims would wash coins in this as a disinfectant and leave the coins in payment for the food and provisions.*

The lane slowly begins to descend and you should ignore all turnings off to later arrive at a gate ahead, beside the entrance to "Little Court" on your right. Pass through the small gate ahead and continue along the lane, which now bends left, with yet more good views to your right and another converted oasthouse directly ahead.

Just before passing the converted oasthouse, look out for the delightful "Mariners" house on your left, a 16th century listed building. The house has a lovely stepped garden with bronze herons and swans offering added interest. Immediately after the oasthouse, pass through a gate to arrive at a road **(GR. 454512 Map 188)** and note the old post box here on your left. Turn left along the road and after approximately thirty metres, turn right onto a drive, signposted to "Chartwell Farm" and also as a public footpath to Puddledock. If you wish to visit "Chartwell House", the home of Sir Winston Churchill, then a short detour (700 metres), by continuing along the lane, will bring you to the house entrance.

Chartwell House, N.T. (GR. 454513 Map 188) *sits in a lovely location in a* *shallow sloping valley, sheltered by wooded hills and with lovely views across the* *Weald to the South Downs. The original house dates from the 16th century and it* *is said that Henry VIII stayed in the oak panelled bedroom when courting Anne* *Boleyn. Sir Winston Churchill bought the house in 1922 from A.J. Campbell* *Colquhoun. Churchill was surprised and amused when he realised the vendor* *had been at Harrow with him and that they had shared bottom place when in the* *4th form.*

Once purchased, Churchill employed the architect Philip Tilden to enlarge and *modernise the house. The work took two years and what you see today is largely* *Tilden's work. Tilden often commented on Churchill's impatience and attention* *to detail and was heard to observe on more than one occasion that despite* *Churchill's busy schedule he had never had a client that "spent more time,* *trouble or interest in the making of a home". It is for this reason primarily, that* *"Chartwell" is really worth a visit, for the house is much as it was at the time of* *Churchill's death in 1965. The following year, 1966, the National Trust opened* *the house to the public under the supervision of Lady Churchill, who was eager* *not to let the house become simply a museum. A visit to the home really does* *allow you to touch on the life of one of our country's most famous leaders and to* *better understand the gentlemanly politics of which he was part. It would be an* *injustice to the man to try and relate a brief history of his life in a walking book.* *Instead, I urge you if not at this moment, to find time on another day to visit* *"Chartwell" and better understand the heritage of the countryside through which* *you are walking.*

"Chartwell" is open to the public from 30th March to November, on Wednesdays, *Saturdays and Sundays. Entrance to the house is via a timed ticket. If you are* *further interested in Churchill, then you can become a member of the Churchill* *Society, details of which are available from ICS, P.O. Box 244, Tunbridge Wells,* *Kent, TN3 OYF.*

Returning to our route, as mentioned, take the drive signposted to Puddledock, with more wonderful views ahead and to your right and on your left the walled kitchen gardens of "Chartwell". The brick wall you can see surrounding the kitchen garden was actually built by Churchill himself. As you progress, you will also begin to see the rooftop of "Chartwell" on your left.

When the drive forks, take the right hand fork to continue straight ahead, ignoring another drive off to the right immediately after. Carry straight on to shortly pass "Chartwell Farm" on your right and ignore all turnings off to almost immediately after, arrive at a wonderful set of old oasthouses, between which there are excellent views behind to your left, particularly in winter when the trees are bare, of "Chartwell". Pass through a kissing gate, beside a field gate, and thereafter continue along a concrete drive ahead, going over a pretty stream which runs from Chartwell Lake, just visible on your left.

Also visible beside the lake on your left is a bronze statue of Churchill and his wife, *Clementine. The statue is by Oscar Neman and was paid for by the Churchill Statue* *Trust to mark the 50th anniversary of Churchill's appointment to the position of Prime* *Minister in 1940. It was unveiled by H.M. the Queen Mother in November, 1990.*

After crossing the stream ignore a path off to your left and go over a stile ahead to carry straight on. Your way is now along a narrow footpath which runs between fields before eventually (after approximately half a mile) arriving at a lane **(GR. 461509 Map 188)**. Go over a stile and turn left along the lane, passing a small cluster of houses on your left, the hamlet of Puddledock, where you should ignore another smaller lane on your left, between the houses, to carry straight on now going uphill. As you continue, though it is difficult to see, look out for a field on your left in which there is a lovely pond, often frequented by a variety of geese.

As you progress the hill becomes steeper but the climb is well worth it, when at the top you arrive at the small and pretty village of Toys Hill, with lovely south-facing views and, on a clear day, a view to the South Downs. On your right, a seating area beside the now covered village well, allows you to enjoy the views in comfort.

A plaque informs us that it is one Frederick Feeney, who died on 26th March, 1897, we must thank for this area of comfort. The well and the small piece of land around it was donated to the National Trust in his memory for "the enjoyment of those who love nature". The well was sunk at the end of the last century to benefit the villagers who, until then, had had to collect their water from the stream at Puddledock at the bottom of the hill. Unfortunately, the well, initially, was not a great success. At a depth of 96 feet, it took two people several minutes to wind up one bucket of water. The villagers, as a result, preferred the stream.

With the arrival of electricity, an electric pump was installed and for a brief period before water was piped to individual homes, the well was a success. It also had the honour of being the highest pump in Kent and the only electric pump protected by the National Trust. Unfortunately, today, as mentioned, the well

The Well – Toys Hill

and pump are covered and not in working order. However, the view is still the same and well worth a few moments' pause.

After admiring the views, continue through the village along the lane to soon arrive at the small village green, with the old County Library on your left. Cross a road ahead here and continue down Scords Lane, marked as a dead end, the other side. As you join the lane, note the house on your left, "Tally-Ho", (private). *i* This was once the village pub and locals tell me that it was a very basic affair with a hole in the garden for a toilet. Even with piped water it appears that the village still had problems, for it was apparently quite common at the pub for the water to stop and the landlord to send out for water from the village pump to allow him to wash his glasses.

Follow the lane, passing some superb properties, until you meet a turning off to the right with a stepped signposted footpath on the left.

If you want to visit the first pub on the route, or close to the route, "The Fox and ♀ *Hounds", which is well worth a visit and if not now is a must for you to experience another time, take the footpath marked on your left, climbing the steps. Thereafter, follow the footpath through woodland to meet another prominent footpath. Turn left here and then right along a road a little later, which you should follow to arrive at the pub. You will need to retrace your steps to rejoin the walk. (The entire detour is approximately half a mile). The lane right (not our* *i* *route) leads to "Scords Farm", famous for its natural spring which rises in the wood close by and is bottled and sold in shops and pubs as "Kentish Spring".*

To continue, our route however, is straight on along the lane ahead, in the direction of a public bridleway sign. After passing to the left of a couple of houses you will later meet a gate ahead and here you must fork left onto a marked (blue arrow) path. Immediately after joining the path, turn right onto a much narrower path which runs alongside a fence on the right (take care not to miss it!). After a short distance, you will arrive at a "T" junction in the form of another path and here you should turn right, going downhill through Scords Wood. You are now also following the Greensand Way which will keep us company for the next few miles. Later, after passing to the left of a house just visible through the trees, the path meets a small clearing with a bench and a path bearing left. Ignore the path left and continue straight on, still going downhill, to shortly arrive at the edge of a field and a stile, with superb views ahead over Bough ◉ Beech Reservoir **(GR. 476518 Map 188)**.

Go over the stile and turn left along the field perimeter to soon arrive at a stile beside a field gate. Cross the stile into another field to immediately bear diagonally right, heading for a field gate and stile below and still following The Greensand Way. At the far side, go over the stile and continue ahead through another field, in the direction of a yellow footpath arrow and on reaching the far right hand corner of the field, cross a stile and then a bridge over a pretty stream and continue uphill, following the left hand perimeter of another field. At the top left hand corner of the field, go over yet another stile and continue uphill along a farm track which runs along the right hand perimeter of a field. As you climb it is worth pausing to look back at the earlier part of our route, in particular, Toys Hill. To your left, there are also good views across to "Emmetts House", passed on the return journey of our walk today. ◉

At the top and at the right hand corner of the field, go over a stile and continue your climb along a hedged track, ignoring a stile and footpath on your right, to continue your climb uphill. (The footpath on your right is a scenic route, an alternative, around the edge of Ide Hill but misses the village and more importantly the pubs!). As you climb, the first houses of Ide Hill will come into view, with the church spire also visible ahead to your right. At the far side of the field, go over a stile and carry straight on along a narrow lane to soon arrive at a road in front of one of the pubs at Ide Hill, "The Crown". Welcome to Ide Hill!

i

Ide Hill (GR. 486517 Map 188) is a pleasant spread out village at one of the highest points on the Greensand Ridge. A jumble of period houses surround a large green, with the village church at the northern tip and shops and the two village hostelries at the southern edge. The shops include a Post Office, General Stores, a traditional butcher and a gift shop which doubles as a tea room. The two village pubs are both worth discovering. "The Crown", recently modernised, dates from the mid-18th century. A sailor boarding here in 1885, is said to have been the cause of an outbreak of small pox in the village. There are no such dangers today and the pub is a welcoming place, serving well kept beer, mainly Courage Best and Directors and some very reasonably priced food. The most picturesque pub is "The Cock", Greene King, facing the green and the village well. It is arguably the oldest building in the village, dating back to at least the 15th century. Facing the pub, one can see how it has been extended over time with equal thirds of the building having completely different styles and yet somehow they all come together as though always having had the intention of merging. Inside, one is not disappointed for the landlord of over twenty years, is determined to keep this a local meeting place and a hubbub of village activity. A large inglenook fire which still burns "real" logs - no room for imitation here - warms a large low beamed ceiling bar, basic but unassumingly comfortable. As with imitation fires, fruit machines are also not welcome, with customers encouraged instead to enjoy the art of conversation. A nice touch is a rope above the bar from which you can hang as though on a tube train, instead of leaning your elbows on the bar itself. Not surprisingly, the pub is reputed to have a ghost, a gentleman blacksmith who is said to occasionally warm himself by the fire. During some recent improvements to the pub, on knocking out some bricks, a small hoard of gold Napoleon III coins were found. Why they were there is a mystery, though Napoleon III spent some of his time in exile at nearby "Brasted Place". Surprisingly, although both Toys Hill and Ide Hill were used as a meeting place for troops during the Napoleonic Wars, there are no tales of ghosts from this activity.

The well opposite the pub was dug about the same time as the one at Toys Hill. It is reputed to be 95 feet deep, as deep as the church is high. The 95 ft tower of the Victorian church, with help from the hill on which it sits, makes it the highest church in all Kent. Though relatively modern, inside it has a splendid blue and gold ceiling, in memory of President Kennedy, donated by an American family who lived in the village.

The village, like the church, gives the appearance of being old but is in fact relatively young when compared to its neighbours. For centuries Ide Hill was nothing more than a den, a place to graze pigs and a stopping point on the drovers road (for pigs) between Brasted and Hever. "The Cock" probably started life as an ale house for this trade. It is known that later the inn stabled horses to help pull carriages up the hill. These were called "cock horses", a common term and the origin of the pub's name. As the road got busier, so the village grew but not to any great extent and even today, it is a modest place with its biggest asset being its glorious location.

To continue, facing "The Crown" pub, turn right and after a few paces do not follow the road round to the left (unless you wish to visit "The Cock"), but carry straight on instead, in the direction of the sign for the Greensand Way, heading for the church and with the village green on your left. Just before reaching the church, turn right onto a tarmac drive, marked by a National Trust sign for Ide Hill and continue to reach the gates for "The Old Vicarage", where you should turn right onto a signposted footpath, still part of the Greensand Way. The footpath runs along the crest of Ide Hill and affords marvellous views to your right along the Greensand Ridge and the earlier parts of our walk.

As the field on your right ends and you arrive at Ide Hill proper, ignore the main path which forks right here and continue ahead in the direction of a yellow arrow and the Greensand Way sign. On reaching a crossing path turn left to almost immediately arrive at a seat dedicated to Octavia Hill, allowing you to take a break and enjoy yet more good views across the Weald in comfort. The dedicated ◎ seat was well earned for it was as a result of great persuasion from Octavia Hill that Ide Hill became one of the National Trust's first acquisitions and looking around, you can appreciate what a great acquisition it was.

Continue along the edge of the hill, ignoring a path off to your right in front of the seat and one to your left behind the seat, still following the yellow arrows and the Greensand Way sign, to now walk very gently downhill with a house on your right. This is another very attractive part of the walk, particularly in mid-spring when Ide Hill woodland is a carpet of bluebells.

Follow the path until you see another signposted footpath leading off to the right [yellow arrow], (take care not to miss it) and take this, as a further guide, still following the Greensand Way signs. The footpath descends quickly to arrive at a road junction with a National Trust picnic field on your left (there are lavatories here also). On meeting the road, turn right to immediately meet and cross the main road

Don't miss Pooh Corner

POOH CORNER

and thereafter, turn left to follow it the other side, in the direction of the road signs for Riverhead and Sevenoaks.

After approximately fifty metres, leave the main road and take a small lane right, still following the Greensand Way signs and immediately upon joining the lane, take a track leading off to the left, signposted by a blue bridleway arrow and, as before, the Greensand Way. The track leads above some pretty houses on your right and beyond these there are lovely views back to Ide Hill and "The Old Vicarage" standing prominent. Incidentally, don't miss "Pooh Corner"!

The track soon arrives at an entrance to a house with its own mini roundabout. You should turn first left here, almost going back on yourself and following a path which goes uphill, marked by a blue bridleway arrow and still as the Greensand Way. The path, at first, runs through an old sweet chestnut coppice and if you are walking this way in autumn you may be rewarded, if you enjoy sweet chestnuts, with quite a feast! After a short distance, turn right, still following the blue bridleway arrow and the signs for the Greensand Way, thereby zig zagging up to the top of the hill (take care not to miss this turning). Soon after, the path bends left and runs along the top of the Greensand Ridge, following a fence on your right. The fence soon finishes and you should continue ahead, keeping to the path along the ridge and ignoring all turnings off. A break in the trees will, on a clear day, allow excellent views across the Weald and to Bough Beach Reservoir. In places, the local Council have provided benches allowing one to enjoy the view in comfort.

Stay on the path, keeping to the edge of the ridge, ignoring all turnings off which at one point includes a marked footpath (yellow arrow), to later arrive at a crossing path. Go straight over this, continuing in the direction of the blue bridleway arrow and the Greensand Way sign. Soon after the crossing track the path bends left to meet another path onto which you should turn right, again following the blue bridleway arrow and the Greensand Way sign. As before, follow the path along the ridge, ignoring all turnings off, to eventually arrive at a car park.

Walk through the car park towards the entrance, cross a narrow lane and join a signposted bridleway the other side. Almost immediately after, the path forks and you should take the left hand fork, still following the now familiar blue bridleway arrow and the Greensand Way sign. Again, keep to the path along the top of the ridge, ignoring any turnings off, to eventually arrive at another small car park, where you should carry straight on to continue to follow the bridleway along the ridge. Shortly after the car park, ignore a signposted footpath on your right which is where we leave the Greensand Way which, from here, descends the Greensand Ridge. Our route instead, is to continue ahead still following the top of the ridge.

Shortly after, pass through some wooden rails and ignore a signposted "Permissive Bridleway" on your left. The path continues to take you along the ridge and eventually comes out at a grass clearing dominated by an old beech tree where you will gain perhaps the best views of Bough Beech Reservoir. Ignore a path off to your left here and carry straight on, in the same direction, still keeping to the edge of the ridge. Soon after, the path arrives at a point on the ridge which is dominated by a lone and very tall pine and, once again, there are marvellous views. The path bends sharply around to the left here and you should follow it, soon after passing through some wooden rails where you should ignore a path leading off to the left to continue straight on. The path eventually leads out to yet another small car park and thereafter a road. Cross the road and join a signposted footpath (low stone post) the other side, leading through Sheephill Wood. The path twists and turns through the wood, crossing old boundaries and works, before reaching a track the other side beside a gate. Turn left along the track with a field on your right and follow it as it begins to descend, going over a crossing track as you continue. You are now entering Hyde's Forest.

The track leads down to the bottom of a valley where you will meet a junction of tracks. Here, you should carry straight on to gently climb the other side of the valley. As you climb through a newly planted fir plantation, looking around you there is not a house, oasthouse or orchard in sight making it very hard to imagine you are actually in the county of Kent. On reaching the top of the valley side, turn left onto a track marked by a yellow footpath arrow (take care not to miss it) and, after approximately thirty metres, look out for and cross a stile on your right. Turn left after the stile along a track, to shortly enter a field and walk straight across the field, heading to the right of a large brick building visible ahead.

At the far side of the field, go over a stile beside a gate and follow a track ahead to arrive at a road beside "Chimneys", a popular restaurant and pub.

"Chimneys" was originally called "The Woodman Inn" and originated from an old ale house. It played a major part in the 19th century, housing men hunting a rogue jackal which was killing local sheep. The jackal was shot nearby and to celebrate, "The Woodman" stayed open until every barrel of beer on the premises was dry! Today, the old inn has been turned into a family-style pub and attracts hoards of visitors from London at weekends, eager to experience a "traditional country pub". It is not my cup of tea, but the real ales (normally Fremlins and Youngs) are well kept and the food is extremely good value.

Turn left along the road, taking great care as the road can at times be quite busy, to soon join a signposted footpath on your right, which runs between fields. To your right as you walk along the footpath, you will enjoy, on a clear day, your first view of the North Downs. At the far side of the fields, go over a stile and along a drive to meet a narrow lane beside a house, "Beech Grove". Turn right along the lane and after approximately twenty metres, fork left and follow the lane past a small triangular green and thereafter, "Mackerels Cottage".

After "Mackerels Cottage" the lane begins to descend and you should ignore a marked footpath on your right whilst at the same time, enjoying views ahead to your left to the church at Ide Hill, visited earlier on our walk. As you descend, look in the fields here for highland cattle, a feature of a farm we will shortly pass. The lane eventually arrives at the bottom of a valley and a very picturesque hamlet known as Brook, the name having been derived from the bubbling brook which runs along the lane here for a short distance. To your right are some lovely terraced cottages and to your left, the farm mentioned specialising in highland cattle, "Brook Place". (Look out for the farm sign as you pass).

"Brook Place" is unashamedly Georgian and has a beam inside with the date 1721. It is known however, that the original house is much older and probably Tudor. The inhabitants of the house during the 18th century were lucky in that they had the only flush toilet in the parish. This was cleverly constructed by using the natural water pressure from a nearby spring to regularly flush the toilet.

Follow the lane through the hamlet to commence the climb the other side and later as the lane begins to level off, look out for a footpath on your left, opposite "Little Norman Fields". Take the footpath, going over a stile to do so, and continue ahead along the right hand perimeter of a field. At the far side, go over another stile and continue along the right hand perimeter of the next field until you are approximately half way across the field, where you should meet and cross a third stile ahead. You will thereafter, follow a fenced footpath, lined by hazel, between fields to soon meet and cross another stile into a third field. After the stile bear left across the centre of the field, passing to the right of a lone hawthorn tree at the centre and thereafter, heading to the left of a farmhouse ahead. As you cross you gain good views right to "Emmetts House", our next destination.

At the far side, before going over a stile, it is worth looking back at a couple of picturesque oasthouses and, as a nice backdrop, the North Downs. Cross the stile and follow a fenced footpath around the edge of a property to come out at a drive beside an appropriately named house, "The Ramblers". Continue ahead along the drive to meet a lane, ignoring a footpath at this point on your left, and carry straight on along the lane, do not turn right, to later ignore another footpath on your left. Keep to the lane to eventually arrive at a "T" junction beside some houses. Turn right at the "T" junction along a road which can be quite busy at times so care is needed and after approximately fifty metres turn left onto a drive to Ide Hill Cricket Club.

Pass through a gate beside a larger one and follow the drive, passing the cricket pitch on your right which must be one of the smallest in the country. Note the small stiles around the perimeter fencing of the cricket pitch for collection of the cricket balls from the adjacent field. After the cricket pitch, follow the drive uphill with good views to your left of Ide Hill, to later arrive at the delightful Emmetts Garden and house which are in the care of the National Trust.

i

***Emmetts Garden and House (GR. 478524 Map 188)** was donated to the National Trust by Mr. and Mrs. Bolle in the early 20th century. The house was once a farm but when the Lubbock family bought it as a summer residence in 1893, they converted it into a rather grand three storey house. The method of*

*doing this is worth relating. The original farm had two storeys and to add the
third storey, the builders detached the roof from the house and lifted it whole,
until a third storey was built onto which they slowly lowered the original roof. The
gardens were laid by Frederick Lubbock, brother of Lord Avebury, and it is the
gardens today which people come to see. In particular, the display of
rhododendrons in spring is a sight not to be missed. The gardens are open daily
(except Mondays and Tuesdays) to the public from April to October.*

Our route follows the drive straight ahead through the gardens (if in doubt,
simply follow the signs for the tea rooms and lavatories), where to your left as
you walk, you will once again enjoy a view to Bow Beech Reservoir visible earlier
on our walk. As you approach the public lavatories, which are housed in the old
stables, leave the drive and continue straight on along the left hand wall of the
lavatories. Take great care NOT to take the more obvious path which forks left.
At the end of the wall, you will notice a low stone footpath marker. Continue
straight on here, following a narrow path uphill through Scords Wood thick with
laurels and rhododendrons. After a short distance, on meeting a stile, cross this
and continue ahead ignoring another path off to your left. Soon after, go over a
crossing track and carry straight on, going over a stile beside a couple of gates,
and keep to the main path ahead ignoring any turnings off, at one point crossing
another stile, to later arrive at a road.

Turn left along the road and after approximately twenty metres and as a wooden
fence ends on your right, join a path which enters the wood on your right,
marked as an unofficial bridleway. Immediately upon joining fork right, thereby
ensuring that you do not take the main path left. The path you have joined is
less distinct and follows some perimeter fencing on your right. Keep to the path
which twists and turns through the wood, ignoring all turnings off, to later meet
a crossing track onto which you should turn left. Follow the track to later meet a
tarmac driveway onto which you should turn left, passing some houses on your
right, before arriving at a road at Brasted Chart **(GR. 468525 Map 188)**.

Turn right along the road and after approximately twenty metres, turn left onto a
signposted public footpath to Westerham. The footpath runs alongside a fence on
your right (do not make the mistake of joining the drive to a house here) and as
you continue, ignore a narrow path off to your left to carry straight on. After a few
paces, bend sharp right beside an old iron fence post, with the path now running
along the wooded edge of a valley, before descending gradually to meet a field on
your left. On meeting the field, leave the path to go over a stile left into the field
(take care not to miss it) and continue diagonally across the centre of the field, in
the direction of a sign to French's Street. To your right now are glorious views to
the North Downs and nestling below them, the village of Westerham.

As you continue, look out for a stile at the left hand perimeter of the field which
you should cross to follow a fenced path quite steeply downhill. Ahead of you now
is a wonderful view to the oasthouses of French Street and as you descend, there
are more unusual oasthouses to your left which are owned by the National Trust.
On meeting a crossing track, go over this and then a stile the other side into a
field. Cross the field, going downhill and heading for a point the other side directly
below the houses of French Street, perched on the other side of the valley. At the
bottom of the field, go over a footbridge across a tiny brook to then commence your

climb, the other side of the valley, following a fenced path. After a short distance, go over two more stiles to then continue to follow a fenced footpath steeply uphill which in wet weather can be particularly muddy and hard-going so take care. Is this a good point to ask how your legs are coping?

Eventually, you will meet and cross a stile to arrive at a lane in front of an old Post Box and the lovely hamlet of French Street **(GR. 459528 Map 188)**. Our way is left along the lane, though first I suggest you turn right to have a look at the hamlet's almost unique private graveyard.

i   **The Berry's Private Burial Ground**. *Set in a dramatic location, this is one of only a few privately owned burial grounds in the country. A sign on the iron entrance gates states that it belongs to one George Berry, St. Thomas Street, London. The burial ground came into the possession of the Berry family early in the 19th century through marriage to the Browne family of Westerham and Brasted. The burial ground holds over four generations of Brownes and as many of the Berrys. The founder of the burial ground, who still has the principle grave, was one Joseph Berry (1644-1721). There has never been a church here but the ground was consecrated in the 17th century. The Berry family are still responsible for its upkeep today. The graveyard is an atmospheric place and must have one of the most striking locations of any graveyard in Kent. If you know of any better, then please let me know!*

Returning to our route, as mentioned, turn left as you arrive at the hamlet along the lane, passing some idyllic cottages until, after a short distance, you see a drive on your right, signposted as a bridleway and also as our old friend, the Greensand Way. Take this to once again join the Greensand Way and after a short distance, when the drive bends left, continue ahead to follow a wide grass track. The grass track soon narrows to become a path and meets a narrow tarmac lane. Turn left along the lane, ignoring a path immediately after on your left, thereby leaving the Greensand Way.

If your legs are flagging it is possible to take a short cut here by following the Greensand Way past "Chartwell" and back to Mariners Hill. From there you can retrace your steps back to the start.

To complete "The Churchill Challenge" proper, follow the lane which bends round to the right in front of a cottage, "The Orchard" and as the lane ends, continue ahead along a narrow footpath which runs through the woodland of Hosey Common. Keep to the main path through the wood, ignoring all turnings off, to later meet a prominent crossing path and go over the crossing path to carry straight on and sometime later arrive at a fork. Take the left hand fork, the less prominent of the paths, to soon after arrive at a lane **(GR. 454524 Map 188)**.

i   *Close to the lane at this point, in 1927, when digging for gravel, a hoard of gold coins were found buried. On examination, they were found to be Celtic gold slaters and extremely rare. The hoard, now with the British Museum, is commonly referred to as the Westerham gold.*

Cross the lane and follow a track ahead the other side, ignoring all turnings off. When the track narrows, after passing through a couple of small clearings, continue straight ahead along a path, continuing to ignore all other paths to the left and right. On arriving at a junction of paths with a small hollow ahead and as a guide a small boulder at its edge, turn right and then right again to walk away from the hollow and boulder, almost going back on yourself. Follow the footpath through the wood until you come to a prominent crossing path, onto which you should turn left to shortly arrive at a road **(GR. 452524 Map 188)**.

Cross the road and join a signposted public footpath to the right of a gate, following it downhill through some pleasant woodland, ignoring all turnings off and keeping a bank and ditch to your left. Sometime later, keep to the path as it twists left through the bank and ditch and thereafter, immediately right to continue downhill, now with a garden to a large house on your right. The garden is quite a feature and you should look out for the miniature grotto within its perimeter. Almost immediately after passing a garden gate on your right, the path arrives at a "T" junction where you should turn right to continue your route downhill along a wide path. Keep to the path with a field on your right and after a short distance, as the path bends left to go uphill, fork right to follow the field fence on your right and arrive at a stile. (Take care not to miss it - if you find yourself going uphill you will have missed the fork).

Go over the stile into a field and turn immediately right to go uphill, keeping to the right hand field perimeter. At the top there are good views left across a valley and also ahead to the North Downs. As you come over the rise, directly ahead and clearly visible are the church spire of Westerham church and the rooftops of houses which make up the rest of village. After approximately two hundred metres, look out for a stile on your right (take care not to miss it). Do not cross the stile but turn left instead and walk directly across the centre of the field, heading for a gate the other side. As a guide, the gate is to the left of a grass mound and just before you reach it you should walk along the right hand edge of a hollow. Do not make the mistake of following the well walked path across the field, in the direction of Westerham and the North Downs. As a further guide if you are unclear, as you walk, the church spire at Westerham should always be on your right.

At the far side of the field, go over a stile beside the gate and continue straight on along the left hand perimeter of another field, with the village of Westerham now clearly laid out before you. As you progress the descent becomes steeper before arriving, at the bottom, beside a small stream, the beginnings of the river Darent. Walk to the left hand corner of the field and pass through a kissing gate to cross the Darent by way of a concrete bridge and arrive at a lane in front of an attractive pond. If you want to detour and visit the village of Westerham, turn right. To continue our walk however, you should turn left.

If visiting Westerham, turn right again on meeting a road (the A25) and follow it into the village centre. You will have to retrace your steps to rejoin the walk.

Westerham (GR. 445540 Map 187) *though still called a village is, in reality, a small town. At the eastern end stand the village church and "Quebec House" (National Trust). At the centre, the famous village green with the statue of Churchill are surrounded by rambling cottages and pubs and at the western edge of the village, "Pitt's Cottage" and the grand "Squerreys Court" are to be found. With so many attractions, it is not surprising that the village (town) has become something of a tourist Mecca and the number of eateries serving this trade is quite* *astonishing. After working up an appetite visiting "Quebec House" and "Squerreys Court" and admiring the statue of Churchill, you can choose between Indian, Thai, Chinese, Turkish Kebab, French cuisine, Fish and Chips or good old pub grub to quell your hunger. There are also numerous pubs to quench the thirst, though in my opinion, the best by a long way is "The Grasshopper", a freehouse, facing the village green. The pub also serves genuine home cooked food.*

Apart from Churchill, Westerham is famous for once having been the home of General Wolfe, who lived at "Quebec House" and William Pitt the Younger, who lived at "Pitt's Cottage", now an Indian restaurant. "Quebec House" is now in the care of the National Trust and is open to the public Tuesday afternoons only, from April through to the end of October. "Squerreys Court", a 17th century manor house at the western tip of the village, is also open to the public between April and September. The house has a famous collection of old masters, including works by Rubens and Van Dyck.

There is much more to tell about Westerham and to explore it properly, I suggest you perhaps visit on another day, equipped with a local guide book. The one I recommend is "Westerham and Crockham Hill Guide", published by the parish council and available from the village bookshop. The bookshop sells a wide range of local publications and the owner, who plays a major part in the Churchill Society, is a wealth of information in terms of the village and local area, though please take care not to waste his time.

Returning to our walk, as mentioned, turn left along the lane to meet a gatehouse, "Park Lodge", and immediately after cross a stile on your right to follow a well walked, fenced footpath uphill. In winter through the trees to your right as you climb you can just make out "Squerryes Court". The footpath we are now following actually runs through the grounds of "Squerryes Court", known as "Squerryes Park".

i   *In the early 19th century, John Warde of "Squerreys Court" often led the local hunt through the park. Today, he is remembered as the father of hunting and is believed to have been the first man to keep a pack of hounds exclusively for fox hunting.*

Near the top of the rise, go over a stile and continue ahead, still following the fenced footpath. To your left now is Tower Wood, so called because of a tower (a folly) at its centre. Later, go over a stile and continue directly across the centre of a field to meet and cross another stile the other side and continue along a well walked path across the centre of the next field. At the far side of the field, go over yet another stile and thereafter, turn left along a wide track (do NOT continue straight ahead). The track later descends into the dramatic and picturesque valley of the river Darent which is dammed in places to form large ponds, used to breed fish.

As the track nears the bottom of the valley you should ignore a crossing track as well as a stile on your left to carry straight on. Shortly after, the track bends right to continue through woodland and you should ignore this to continue ahead instead over a stile beside a gate, in the direction of a yellow footpath arrow, number 356. Your way is now along the right hand perimeter of a field with the river Darent to your left. As a point of interest, to your right at the top of the wooded hill is an Iron Age fort, which when originally built would have been

i

clearly visible with none of the trees we see today. At the far side of the field, go over a stile and continue in the same direction across the centre of the next field, heading for a point to the right of a house and a stile the other side. As you walk, look out for a couple of attractive cottages on your right.

At the far side of the field cross the stile and turn left, ignoring two other footpaths, one directly ahead and another to your right, to follow a path which runs to the right of the beautiful "Crockham House". In the garden of the house rises a spring, the source of the river Darent. Shortly after the house, the footpath begins to climb gently uphill between banks, the latter denoting the antiquity of the path, and then continues through woodland. Later, ignore a marked (yellow arrow) footpath on your left and continue straight on to shortly after ignore a marked bridleway (blue arrow) on your right, to then join and follow a drive ahead to soon arrive at a main road, the B2026 (GR. 449514 Map 187).

Cross the road and join a signposted public bridleway other side, which is to the right of the driveway to "Windmill Bank Cottage" and where we follow the Greensand Way for the last time. The bridleway runs uphill, the last uphill - I promise!, to arrive at another path in front of a fence and holly hedge. Turn right here, thereby saying a final "farewell" to the Greensand Way and follow a narrow path through woodland, ignoring all turnings off, to arrive at another path leading off to your right which is just before reaching a field. The field marks the top of Mariners Hill, purchased for the National Trust by way of funds raised by Octavia Hill. Turn right here (take care not to miss it) and follow the path along the edge of the field and, at the far side of the field, follow the path ahead, now going downhill, ignoring a path off to the left.

If you have enough energy for a short detour, then the path left leads to a viewing seat placed by Octavia Hill in memory of her mother. From the seat you will gain probably the best views on the walk and arguably the best in all Kent.

After approximately twenty metres, ignore another path on your left and continue your route downhill by way of some steps. At the bottom, turn left passing through a gate and follow a tarmac lane past "Froghole Oasthouse" on your right. This is the famous oasthouse which can be seen from Crockham Hill at the beginning of the walk.

Continue until the lane bends left beside another oasthouse and leave it here to take a signposted footpath directly ahead, marked to Crockham Hill Church, and next to "Buttles Steps Cottage".

The cottage before Buttles Steps, "Sparks Haw", was owned around 1900 by E.V. Lucas, a publisher. Whilst living here, Lucas received many literary guests, including H.G. Wells who apparently was a frequent visitor.

Descend Buttles Steps which we climbed at the beginning of the walk and from this point on, simply retrace your steps from the beginning of the walk to return to our starting point at Crockham Hill and if you have timed it right, a celebration drink at "The Royal Oak", for successfully completing "The Churchill Challenge" - congratulations!

ACCOMMODATION

The Kings Head, Westerham. Tel: 01959 562990

Virtually on the walk, this elegant hotel was once a Georgian coaching inn. The seventeen bedrooms are all luxuriously furnished and each one is individually designed. The hotel has a good restaurant and if you want something different, you can try the Bistro Bar in the cellar, once the village jail!

Corner Cottage, Toys Hill. Tel: 01732 750362

On the walk, this is a beautiful place to stay, situated at the edge of the Greensand Ridge with wonderful views across the Kentish Weald. The accommodation also has its own entrance and is en suite - very comfortable.

Youth Hostel, Kemsing YHA, Kemsing. Tel: 01732 761341

Approximately eight miles from the walk, the hostel was once a vicarage in an attractive village at the foot of the North Downs. Quite a large hostel with fiftyeight beds, it can be busy in summer with school parties, so be warned and book ahead.

Camping and Caravanning, Thriftwood Park. Tel: 01732 822261

Approximately fourteen miles from the walk, this is a pleasant site set in several acres of woodland. The camp also has purpose-built barbecues allowing you to continue to enjoy that "outdoor experience". Very well run, but make sure you take your muddy boots off before entering the shop!

IN CELTIC FOOTSTEPS

Distance: 12³/₄ miles (20.65km)

Time: Allow approximately 6 hours

Map: Ordnance Survey Landranger Map 177

START
BIRLING
40M

WHITEHORSE
WOOD
190M

LOWER
LUDDESDOWN
50M

FINISH
BIRLING
40M

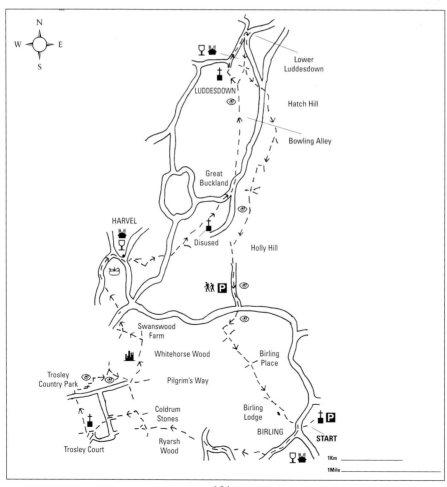

Walk Summary

"In Celtic Footsteps" as the name suggests, is to take a step into history. Following ancient paths and trackways, the route visits a number of sites of historical interest and in between, passes through some glorious countryside. There are wonderful views to be had, particularly from the North Downs escarpment, but these are not gained without effort and you must expect a couple of fairly stiff climbs. Other than that, it is fairly easy going with mud, as usual, being the only other obstacle. For those who are gluttons for punishment, the walk can be extended for several miles with a detour from Holly Hill, though taking this option would mean missing what is undoubtedly the best vista of the day.

Two pubs are passed en route and there is another at the start and finish, so for those who need a drink to keep going, you need not panic!

Start - GR. 680606 Map 177

The walk starts from Birling village which nestles close to the North Downs, north west of Maidstone. The village is fairly easy to get to and unless you are local, the best method of finding it is to head for junction 4 of the M20, the interchange with the A228. If travelling along the M20, this junction is signposted to West Malling. The turning for Birling is off the A228, just south of the M20 and is signposted to Grange Park College as well as Birling. Then, follow the road to its end, a "T" junction and turn right, obeying the sign for Birling. The road leads you to Birling village centre where at another "T" junction, I suggest you turn right again to arrive at the church where there is a public car park at the rear. The nearest railway station is at West Malling, though it may be quicker and easier to get a train to Maidstone and a bus or taxi from there. An alternative start can be made from Trosley Country Park car park, signposted from the A227. However, you will have to pay for the privilege and the car park is locked early evening, an annoying worry for such a beautiful walk, especially if you intend sampling the local beer. Another alternative start can be made from the car park at Holly Hill. However, this is quite hard to find and starts with the best view first - personally, I always like to keep this to last.

IN CELTIC FOOTSTEPS

To start the walk, you need to be the opposite side of the road and facing the village church. Before we set out though, I believe it is worth detailing a little about Birling itself.

Birling (GR. 680606 Map 177) is a linear village straddling a road running parallel with the North Downs. The village name is of Saxon origin after a man called "Baerla", probably a Chieftain. The road running east to west through the centre is also probably Saxon. This is one of several routes at this point running parallel with the North Downs and by studying the map, it is fairly easy to see how preferences have changed over the centuries. The earliest route still visible today is the one closest to the North Downs, known as the Pilgrims Way, though it goes back way before that period. After this, a succession of parallel routes with the North Downs can be seen, each a little further away as life became safer and speed of travel more important. The latest, of course, is the M20.

Dominating the village is the stout village church. Set on a sandstone mound, its huge tower is a well known local landmark. On Midsummer's Day the church is directly in the line from the Neolithic Coldrum stones (visited later) of the rising sun and it is likely that before the church, the sandstone mound was a place of some importance to Neolithic man. The church essentially dates from the 13th century with the tower having been added during the 15th century. Inside the church, is the entrance to the Nevill family vault. The Nevills first came to Birling in 1435 when the family gained the manor through marriage. They have lived here ever since and still own most of the land. The Nevills are one of those great English families which have, in their time, played a major part in English history, though few recognise the name today. The family is perhaps better known under their title, Earls of Warwick, and undoubtedly the most famous Earl was Richard "The Kingmaker".

Richard earned his other name, Kingmaker, after his virtual domination of The War of the Roses. At this time, as Earl of Warwick and of Salisbury which he inherited after his father's death, Richard Nevill was probably the richest and largest landowner in England and consequently, wielded great power. At the beginning of the war, he supported the Duke of York (of nursery rhyme fame) and after a complicated series of events, was instrumental in bringing him to the throne as Edward IV in 1461. With Warwick's help over the next three years, the Yorkshire Red Rose had virtual control over the whole country and the defeated Henry VI was captured and thrown in the Tower.

Edward IV was well aware that without Richard Nevill, Earl of Warwick, he would not have been King and this unnerved him. Instead of rewarding the Earl therefore, in his fear, he banished him to France where the Earl had once controlled the Calais Garrison. It was a great mistake on the King's part, as Warwick returned with an army and routed the King, returning Henry VI to the throne, thus giving the Earl the title of "Kingmaker".

Warwick's newly found title was short lived however, for Edward returned and at the resulting Battle of Tewkesbury, Warwick was killed in action. Henry VI was once again deposed and this time murdered at the Tower. Warwick's main accomplice, Edward's brother, Duke of Clarence, was also murdered, being drowned in a Butt of Malmsey, a sweet syrup-like wine, popular at the time.

As recently as the second World War, the Nevills lost another family member in action. he was Michael Nevill and his name now takes its place on the war memorial outside the church. As a mark of respect, the name of the village pub was changed from "The Bull" to "The Nevill Bull". The bull incidentally, forms the main part of the Nevill family crest and examples can be found in the church.

"The Nevill Bull" pub, Whitbread, is the only place in the village offering refreshments and is a good place for a celebrational drink at the end of the walk.

To start the walk, as mentioned, facing the church from the opposite side of the road, turn right to pass the old village forge, noting as you pass the upside down horseshoe on the door. This is rather rare, as old superstition dictates that if you held a horseshoe upside down the luck with which a horseshoe is normally associated, would fall out! Almost immediately after the forge, ignore a road on your left (probably the road by which you entered the village) and continue to pass "The Nevill Bull" pub. Keep to the road, heading west, and ignore all further turnings off, passing, as you progress, a pleasant mixture of ancient, old and modern houses, highlighting the continuous growth and changes within this thriving village. Later, the houses give way on your right to open fields, affording views across to the North Downs and on meeting the last house on your left, "Charlton House" (the most westerly house in the village), leave the road by turning right to pass through two cut down telegraph poles and enter a field. Walk diagonally left across the field in the direction of a yellow arrow, to go over a rise and then head for the far left hand corner and a stile, which should now be visible. Go over the stile and ignore a path on your left to cross another stile ahead immediately after and therefore, continue ahead along the right hand perimeter of a field. As the perimeter turns sharp right, leave it to continue ahead, bearing very gently diagonally right, heading for the far right hand corner of the field. Ahead now are some lovely views to the North Downs and to your left, unfortunately, some less attractive views of the M20 motorway.

At the field corner, go over a stile and follow a path beside a stream to, after a few paces, turn left, crossing the stream into a field. Continue ahead along the left hand perimeter of the field, heading for a collection of houses ahead and walking parallel with the North Downs. At the far side, follow a track ahead

i between some attractive cottages to soon arrive at a lane and the northern tip of Ryarsh village. You are fortunate in visiting the prettiest part of the village which is mainly famous for brick making. Bricks from Ryarsh house the lions at London Zoo!

Turn right along the lane, at first noting the cottage on your left still with its old wooden closet room which overhangs the lane, and follow it as it bends left, ignoring a signposted footpath on the right. Thereafter, keep to the lane as it leads uphill passing, at intervals, a couple of ponds on your right, the first hidden in a copse and the second, much prettier, surrounded by willows. In between the ponds, ignore a marked footpath signposted off to your left and follow the lane until you arrive at a "T" junction at another pretty collection of cottages. Note the yew hedge here on your right in the shape of a duck.

Turn right at the "T" junction and after approximately ten paces, left to join a marked footpath (yellow arrow), by going over a stile and after the stile, follow a well trodden path ahead through Ryarsh Wood. The path soon descends and later crosses a wooden plank footbridge after which you should continue ahead (do not turn right), to after a few paces, arrive at a stile on your right. Go over the stile and immediately after, turn left, in the direction of a yellow arrow, to walk through a field which, at the time of writing, has been left fallow with absolutely superb views right to the North Downs. For some admiring the view, the only dampener is the knowledge that during our walk today, we will be climbing the steep escarpment at least twice!

On reaching the far side of the field, go over a stile and follow a path ahead, once again walking through Ryarsh Wood. Sometime later, we leave Ryarsh Wood, by way of a stile into a field where once again, there are excellent views right to the North Downs. Continue straight ahead across the field and at the far side, go over a stile beside a gate to thereafter turn right along a track. After approximately fifteen metres turn right onto another track, marked by a yellow arrow and a blue arrow with "WW", the latter indicating that you are now following the Weald Way, and continue until the track meets a concrete drive. Turn right along the drive, now heading for the North Downs, and take time to enjoy the magnificent views on your right, where the fields like a carpet at the foot of the North Downs, sweep towards the Medway valley. At the time of writing, these fields are used predominantly for the crop, rape, creating a beautiful sea of yellow in late spring and early summer.

After approximately thirty metres, if you can take your eyes away from the view, look out for a stile on your left and a National Trust sign for Coldrum Longbarrow. Go over the stile to immediately be confronted by a grass mound with some large sarsen stones at its head. This is Coldrum Longbarrow.

Coldrum Longbarrow (GR. 654607 Map 177) is a Neolithic burial chamber,   *i*
probably of a King or Chieftain and his family. The modern day equivalent would be a family vault. Then as today, the more important or wealthy the person, the grander the memorial. Around five thousand years ago when the longbarrow was made ready for its recipients, ordinary people were simply buried beneath the earth or burned. The longbarrow though rare for the South East is one of several Neolithic remains in the immediate area. It is believed they are the work of the earliest Neolithic settlers in England, known as the Dysser people, a race which came from an area known today as Denmark. It looks as though they did not travel much further than the Medway, for there are few Neolithic remains elsewhere in Kent. Around one thousand years later, a much greater flow of Neolithic tribes entered Britain from the south and left their mark over an area we now call Wessex, the original England. It is in Wessex that we can still today find near perfect examples of longbarrows, particularly at Avebury and "Waylands Smithy" on the Ridgeway. Coldrum Longbarrow was constructed from twentyfour large sarsen stones and covered with earth, the stones in front of you formed the entrance. When excavated in 1910, it was found to contain the skeletons of twentytwo people as well as a number of animals. In later longbarrows the bodies were cremated and stored in pots giving rise to the expression "Beaker people". Longbarrows eventually gave way to the more familiar and easier to build, round or bell barrow.

It has always been a mystery as to why and how sites were chosen for Neolithic burials and religious monuments. Physically, there appears to be no continuity, they are found on hill sides, in valleys, on plains, but never on obvious landmarks and sometimes miles from any settlement. One theory put forward, originally dismissed as "crackpot" but growing in acceptance is that they were constructed along Ley lines. These are supposedly invisible lines of energy which cover the earth. The dowser's stick (water diviner), for example, is said to use this energy to find water. At Coldrum, a Ley line is said to run directly underneath from east to west. The line is said to also run directly underneath Trosley church and this fits in with local legend which recalls a tunnel with hidden treasure running from the church to the longbarrow. Legend or fact? A similar legend regarding a Ley line existed at Glastonbury and a tunnel was later discovered. As already mentioned, on Midsummers Day, the longbarrow is also directly in line with Birling church and the rising sun. Was the position of Coldrum chosen because of energies we no longer understand or was it simply a pleasant site? We shall probably never know, but it is interesting and fun puzzling over an answer.

After going over the stile, circum-navigate the longbarrow by climbing the steps on your left which take you around the back of the longbarrow itself allowing you to appreciate its size as well as the determination of those who built it with their limited tools. After descending some further steps, go over a stile at the bottom and turn left to once again follow the concrete drive. After a few paces, leave the drive as it bends right and continue ahead along a wide track. After approximately thirty metres, fork left, thereby leaving the Weald Way, to go up a bank into a field and follow a well used path across the centre. At the far side, pass through a gap in the hedge and continue to follow the path ahead, at first through a copse and then between fields to, after passing through a gate, arrive at a small car park. Carry straight on past the car park, between houses, to shortly arrive at a lane.

Cross the lane, go over a stile the other side and follow a path ahead across the centre of a field where not only can you enjoy views to your right of the North Downs but to your left you also have your first real view to the Greensand Ridge and beyond. As you continue, another lovely scene comes into view ahead, namely Trottiscliffe church. Being within earshot of the busy M20 it is almost as though this scene has been transported from another time.

At the far side of the field, exit between some wooden posts and descend to a lane, onto which you should turn right to pass a pair of lovely 18th century cottages. Note the stones in the wall of the upper storey. These are dated 1758 and indicate the cottages were built by or for Thomas and Sarah Whitaker. The cottages are still called "Whitakers". Immediately after, we arrive at Trottiscliffe church.

Trottiscliffe Church (GR. 646605 Map 177) sits between cottages on one side and the elegant Georgian "Trosley Court" the other, is one of those rare forgotten corners of England, unscathed by the 20th century. The Georgian house is "Trosley Court" and Trosley is oddly, how Trottiscliffe is pronounced. The church is worth visiting in its own right, but a look inside is doubly worthwhile for it acts also as a sort of makeshift museum displaying the finds of Coldrum Longbarrow. There is

Trottiscliffe Church

also an unusual story surrounding the pulpit. Daringly, it was taken from Westminster Abbey and only when it was in place here at Trottiscliffe, was permission requested for its removal from the Abbey. Probably to avoid scandal, permission was duly granted.

In the churchyard is buried the controversial artist, Graham Sutherland. Some of his more famous works are portraits of Sir Winston Churchill and Somerset Maugham as well as the tapestry, "Christ in Majesty" which hangs in Coventry Cathedral.

After the church, continue ahead passing through a gateway into the farmyard of "Trosley Court". The virtually unaltered Georgian farmhouse is worth more than just a momentary pause. Continue ahead through the farmyard (do not fork left), and just before the last barn ahead, turn right to follow a marked footpath (yellow arrow) along the right hand perimeter of a field, following a line of telegraph poles and heading for the North Downs. At the far side of the field, pass through a kissing gate and maintain your direction ahead, now along an enclosed path which later brings you out to a narrow tarmac lane. Cross the lane, go up some steps the other side and after a few paces, go over a crossing path and over a stile to enter "Trosley Country Park".

***Trosley Country Park** is run by Kent County Council and at the park's car park* *i* *(not on our route), there is a small visitors centre with basic information on the park's formation and wildlife. Unfortunately, although offering protection to the countryside within its boundaries, it also attracts hoards of people all seemingly nervous to explore anything outside the park boundary - you have been warned!*

Follow a path ahead for a few paces to, after passing through some typical chalk scrub, arrive at open grass hill side and here you should take the second path on your right. (To make this clear, the first path right leads gently downhill to follow the edge of the scrub at the base of the downs. The second path on your right, probably the more prominent, follows the edge of the downs but a little higher up). As a further guide, as you continue, you will find yourself virtually the same height as a line of telegraph wires on your right. If the country park is not too busy with visitors, this is a lovely part of the walk, particularly in summer when the chalkland flowers are in full bloom and the butterflies are out in colourful force. Continue to follow the path along the edge of the downs, ignoring any paths to the left and right, ascending or descending the scarp slope until sometime later, as you approach a fence ahead to your left (as a guide, this is almost aligned with a line of houses which lead away from the North Downs on your right), turn left going up the side of the scarp slope, heading for a kissing gate in the fence, approximately twenty metres away (take care not to miss it).

Pass through the kissing gate, go over a crossing path and climb some steps the other side to immediately after, turn left. After approximately ten paces, turn right to climb some more steps to soon reach a narrow crossing path. Do not make the mistake of going over the crossing path and needlessly climbing some steps the other side, but turn right along the crossing path to once again, walk along the edge of the downs, though this time through scrub. After a short distance, pass through a kissing gate to soon after, arrive at more open hill side, this time above some chalk workings. There are excellent views here. Directly below you is the village of Trosley, "Trosley Court" and church, in fact you can follow the early line of our walk from Birling. Also visible are the factories at Maidstone, the Medway and beyond in the distance, the line of the North Downs stretching towards the Kent coast. The Greensand Ridge is also visible and on a very clear day, you can just see the South Downs.

Continue to follow the path, which climbs gently from here along the edge of the downs, to soon pass through a kissing gate beside a five bar gate on your left. After the kissing gate, continue ahead up some steps to shortly arrive at a crossing track beside a post, marked as number "8" and "Red Walk". Turn right along the track, the North Downs Way, which virtually runs along the top of the downs though any view is now obscured by woodland. After a few paces, ignore a marked path on your left and continue to follow the track, ignoring any other turnings off, to soon arrive at a kissing gate beside a field gate. A marker on a post here, indicates that you are still following the North Downs Way (GR. 649614).

Pass through the kissing gate thereby leaving Trosley Country Park and after a few paces, turn right onto another track in the direction of the North Downs Way sign. The track almost immediately leads downhill, at some points between banks. Though today the track is known as the North Downs Way, it is also one of Kent's most ancient tracks, probably Saxon but possibly even older. On nearing the base of the downs, the track passes through an avenue of yews before coming out at the end of a narrow tarmac lane, perhaps Kent's most famous ancient thoroughfare, the Pilgrims Way. Turn left here, still in the direction of the North Downs Way sign, leaving the tarmac to follow the Pilgrims Way, via a well walked path. If the undergrowth is not too thick, then look out for a Pilgrims Way sign on your left, with the emblem of a scallop shell.

i   **The Pilgrims Way** *until recently was believed to have been a continuous track from Winchester to Canterbury. It is now apparent that this was almost certainly not the case and that the route was simply by way of very local paths and tracks. It has even been suggested that the pilgrimage from Winchester to Canterbury was no more than Victorian fantasy. I for one, if only for personal pleasure and the enjoyment of treading a path once used by pilgrims, prefer not to believe this.*

The Pilgrims Way is reputed to have come into being after the murder of Thomas a Becket on the alter at Canterbury Cathedral. Becket died in defence of his faith and the church, against his one-time friend, Henry II, who wished to be King of the church. Becket's murderers further attempted to demonstrate the King's power and contempt of the church by spreading his brain over the cathedral floor. Their ugly deed backfired and Thomas a Becket became Saint Thomas, his tomb in the cathedral becoming one of the most important shrines in Europe. As a result, in theory, the Pilgrims Way was born with pilgrims making their way from Winchester, our country's ancient capital, along one of the oldest routes in the land to Canterbury. Tradition has it that Henry II even started the pilgrimage, when as an act of repentance, he walked the route barefoot in 1174, though this is now also hotly disputed by modern historians.

Much of the modern belief stems from the fact that the Pilgrims Way is marked as a long distance route on the Ordnance Survey maps. The man responsible for this was Captain Edward James and it is now evident by his notes, that whilst surveying in Surrey, he became fascinated by the story of the Pilgrims Way and promptly marked his own interpretation of the route on the map. Thus, almost overnight, unintentionally, he created supposedly the best evidence that the Pilgrims Way existed.

There is however, evidence on the ground that pilgrims did travel from Winchester to Canterbury. Along the way, there are several roads called "Pilgrims" which pre-date Victorian fantasy and Ordnance Survey maps and several churches give hints to there once having been a pilgrimage. For example, churches dedicated to St. James, the patron saint of pilgrims, pre-dating the Victorian era are dotted along the route. One of the most famous churches is in Surrey. This is St. Martha's which uses the scallop shell as its emblem, a symbol from another famous and ancient centre of pilgrimage, Compostella in Spain. The scallop shell emblem is the same one on the sign beside the track where you are now standing.

Whatever the truth, what we do know is that this part of the Pilgrims Way really is an ancient track, frequently referred to as the "Old Road" and over the centuries, used by our Neolithic ancestors, Romans, Saxons and Danes, if not pilgrims.

Follow the Pilgrims Way for only a few paces to go over the first stile on your left, thereby leaving the ancient footpath, to once again rejoin the Weald Way (indicated by the yellow "WW" arrow). Once over the stile, go up some steps to almost immediately commence your second ascent of the North Downs. You may be cursing me by now, but remember this is supposed to be, as the title of the book suggests, an "adventurous walk"! After the steps, the path runs diagonally up the slope, the climb is not too difficult, the only downside being that you are walking through scrub which except in winter, means the views are fairly limited. At the top, continue ahead, going over a narrow crossing path, and join a track ahead which runs through a coppice in the direction of the yellow Weald Way arrow. Regaining your breath, you will probably be pleased to know that you are now at the highest point on the walk.

After approximately fifty metres, leave the track as it bends left and continue ahead along a narrow path, still following the yellow Weald Way arrows. Stay on the path for some distance until you meet a crossing path marked by a yellow arrow. Turn left, thereby leaving the Weald Way, and keep to the path, ignoring any minor turnings off. Later, the path graduates into more of a track before eventually arriving at a semi-tarmacced track onto which you should turn right, again in the direction of a yellow arrow. After a few paces, turn right again and go over a stile onto a rugby/playing field. The footpath goes straight across the playing field in the direction of a yellow arrow though if there is a game or training session taking place, do not risk the wrath of the teams, instead ensure you walk around the edge of the playing area! Whichever route you take on the day, you should arrive at the far corner of the rugby/playing field where, after crossing a stile, you will meet a road (GR. 652623).

Cross the road and turn right to almost immediately pass the beautiful thatched "Swanswood Farm"and after the farm, turn left onto a signposted public footpath which at first runs through a copse that in spring is carpeted by a mixture of bluebells and the less common wood anemone.

i   **The Wood Anemone** *has delicate white flowers which close and hang like a bell in dull weather and open to the sky when the sun shines. They are also known as windflowers as according to the ancient Greek writer, Pliny, the flowers only open when the wind blows. After walking this way on an extremely blustery day, I can conclude that he was wrong!*

The roots of the flowers are extremely poisonous, though during the Middle Ages the leaves were collected, then crushed and used on a poultice (a hot flannel used to apply ointment to the skin) to relieve muscular pains and chest ailments.

On entering a field, continue straight ahead to cut across the right hand corner of the field (the farmer here is normally very good and marks the way - if however, you are in doubt, then simply follow the right hand field perimeter). On reaching the far side, go over a stile and continue ahead across the centre of the next field, heading for a gate at the far left hand corner, just to the left of a house.

On reaching the field corner, pass through the gate and turn right to follow a lane for approximately a third of a mile, passing along the way, "Harvel House Farm", to arrive at the village of Harvel in front of the unusually named "Amazon and Tiger" pub, a freehouse which offers home cooked food and real ales. Turn right in front of the pub and follow another lane through the village, to soon pass the small Post Office which also doubles as a general stores, your last chance apart from a pub to restock with some provisions. Stay on the lane, passing some of Harvel's most attractive properties to soon arrive at the village pond and green. The pond is home to a rabble of ever-hungry ducks which locally are renowned for their poor road sense! Ignore Dean Lane on your left beside the pond but join the green the other side and walk diagonally across its centre, noting as you progress the two unusual oasthouses on your left, best described as upside-down ice cream cones! On reaching the far side of the green, turn left along a narrow lane and after approximately twenty metres, right to join a signposted public bridleway (ignore a marked footpath on your left as you join).

The bridleway leads down to a shallow lush valley, in summer a myriad of greens, and turns left to follow it for a short distance and then right (ignore a footpath on the left here) to cross the valley floor, between fields. It then continues gently uphill the other side, through scattered woodland, and you should keep to it, ignoring a short way on tracks on either side. Continue ahead to soon pass to the left of some farm buildings before arriving at a lane (**GR. 659633**). Cross the lane, go over a stile the other side and walk diagonally left across the centre of a field, now once again following our old friend, the Weald Way. At the far side, pass through a kissing gate, cross a tarmac drive and join and follow a fenced path ahead (do not turn left) which later leads out to the corner of a field at the edge of a deep valley. Do not descend into the valley but turn left instead to follow the left hand perimeter of the field, along the top of the valley side.

At the far side of the field, pass through a gap (at the time of writing) in a rather dilapidated fence to then follow a marked path (yellow "WW" arrow) diagonally across the centre of another field. At the time of writing, this field has been left fallow. At the field end, join and follow a prominent path through the particularly attractive Luxon Wood, a wood matured from a disused coppice. Sometime later, the path begins to descend to meet and follow the line of a field with views over scattered dwellings in the valley below. Together, they make up the hamlet of Great Buckland, though many years ago there was a thriving village here called Dode.

The Tragedy of Dode. The furthest building on the right was the village church. I say this because the church is no more than a restored ruin today. Dode village thrived until 1349 when its population was virtually wiped out by the Black Death. Just three years after the disease had taken hold the village was deserted and fifteen years later, after hoping for re-population, the Bishop of Rochester reluctantly closed the church. Dode then fell to ruin until, in the 20th century in 1901, one George Arnold restored the church to something like its original appearance, except for the roof which would have been thatched and not tiled. What happened here at Dode was an extreme rarity. Contrary to popular belief the Black Death wiped out very few villages, in fact the loss of nearly all villages in England was as a result of changes in farming methods and uncharitable landowners as opposed to any disease. The people at Dode were therefore, very unlucky indeed. Today, gazing across the tranquil valley floor, it is hard to believe that such a tragedy ever took place. Ironically, the valley is now often referred to as "Happy Valley".

The path initially skirts around the edge of the field before bending left to run between two more fields, at the far side of which you should cross a stile and continue ahead through another field to soon after, cross another stile beside a gate. Maintain your direction through the next field to eventually arrive and cross yet another stile beside a gate to arrive at a lane. There are lovely views here up a part of the valley known as the Bowling Alley. Turn right to follow the lane downhill, ignoring a signposted footpath on the left as you continue, to soon after pass the unusual "Great Buckland Farm", which has one of the most imposing garages I think I have seen anywhere in the country, let alone Kent!

After the farm, ignore a footpath on your right and continue along the lane to shortly join another lane onto which you should turn left, thereby maintaining your direction. Follow the lane for about twenty metres and then turn left onto a marked public footpath, still the Weald Way. Follow the path down a bank, over a stile and into a field, where you should continue diagonally right across the centre of the field, in the direction of a yellow arrow, although as this is part of a long distance walk the way is usually fairly clear.

Eventually, upon reaching the far side of the field, go over a stile and maintain your direction across the next field, cutting across the left hand corner, to reach and cross a stile at the left hand perimeter. Turn immediately right thereafter, to follow the right hand perimeter of a third field and soon after, go over a stile ahead into a fourth field where you are instantly rewarded with a marvellous view ahead over a meeting of valleys. Continue diagonally left across the field, cutting across the left hand corner, and on meeting the left hand field perimeter, continue ahead and follow it to reach the far left hand corner and cross yet another stile to carry straight on along the left hand perimeter of the next field.

After approximately fifty metres, go over a stile beside a gate on your left into another field. You are immediately rewarded with a tremendous view over the magical village of Luddesdown. To the left of a church is the ancient "Luddesdown Court" and together, they make one of the most picturesque scenes in Kent. Once in the field, turn right along a track and after a few paces, ignore a stile ahead to turn left instead and proceed along the right hand field perimeter, now going downhill and heading directly for "Luddesdown Court". At the bottom of the field, go over a stile and continue ahead across a smaller field to, at the far side, cross another stile to arrive at a brick driveway.

Turn right along the driveway admiring the cleverly designed house ahead with its glass topped roof and a few metres on, pass through a gate on your left into the churchyard. Welcome to Luddesdown.

i **Luddesdown (GR. 670662 Map 177),** *apart from a collection of cleverly designed buildings to the east of the church, remains virtually unaltered since its heyday in the 11th century. Even before the 11th century, the site had been continuously occupied since the Stone Age. Relics from both the Stone Age and the Celts have been found and there are Roman tiles in the lower parts of the walls of the church tower. Before the Norman conquest, "Luddesdown Court" (private) next to the church, was the home of Lewin, King Harold's brother. After the death of Harold at the Battle of Hastings, "Luddesdown Court" was given by William the Conqueror to his half brother, Odo, Bishop of Bayeux. Bishop Odo was also made Earl of Kent and continued to be the King's right hand man, acting as Regent whenever William returned to Normandy. It is believed that whilst living at "Luddesdown Court", Odo commissioned the famous Bayeux tapestry. The house is to some extent much as Odo would have remembered it (outside that is) and is amongst the longest continually inhabited houses in England.*

The church is dedicated to St. Peter and St. Paul and is normally locked, though a key can be obtained from a nearby house.

To continue, facing the church, turn right to follow a red brick path through the churchyard which leads to a small car park. Carry straight on, passing through a metal gate, to arrive at a lane. Turn left along the lane, ignoring a signposted footpath the other side and after a few paces, fork right to arrive at a "T" junction. turn right and follow another lane for approximately a quarter of a mile, to arrive at "The Golden Lion" pub, at the tiny modern day of Lower Luddesdown. Note the sign recommending Benjamin's good food. After maybe trying the food (it's not bad), carry straight on past the pub, ignoring a road on your left and at the end of the pub car park, turn right onto another lane, signposted to Great Buckland. Note as you turn, another signpost with a hedge cleverly cut around it. The lane leads uphill and after approximately one hundred metres, leave it to join a signposted footpath on the right. The footpath, at first, runs along the right hand perimeter of a field, with good views right over the "Old Rectory" and beyond. When the field perimeter bends left, continue straight on across the field centre and after a short distance, on once again meeting the perimeter, maintain your direction, now with the field perimeter on your right. Keep to the field perimeter, later ignoring a marked path right and just after this, a crossing path, to continue your route along the right hand field perimeter. If you are a "closet" train spotter then keep your eyes left and you may be lucky enough to catch a glimpse of the Eurostar.

After a short dip the path begins to climb the other side of the Buckland valley and as you climb there are superb views right up the valley itself to "Great Buckland Farm", passed earlier. At the corner of the field, you will arrive at a lane which you should cross to join a track the other side, marked as a byway. The track takes you up the other side of the valley proper and at this late stage in the walk you may find it somewhat testing! Be re-assured however, by the thought that this is the last significant climb on the walk. A little further up, ignore a track the other side of a gate on your right and keep to the track you are on, still climbing.

The track climbs steadily to the top of the valley side, known as Hatch Hill and on eventually levelling out, it follows the line of a field on your left. After a short distance, the field ends and you should ignore a marked footpath on your left, signposted to Upper Halling, to continue following the track in a straight line through Horseholders Wood. The track which now runs along the top of the hill, is often churned up by horses and the wheels of four wheel drive vehicles and in wet weather can be extremely muddy, though there is normally a path on one side or the other enabling you to avoid the worst of this.

Later, the track forks as it meets a field ahead. Take the right hand fork where soon after, the track bends right and then left to pass under two sets of electricity pylons. As the track bends left do not make the mistake of following another track ahead - if you have not passed beneath the two electricity pylons or find yourself going downhill, you have made an error and should retrace your steps. Shortly after the pylons, the track continues in a straight line through some particularly attractive woodland to eventually, after approximately a third of a mile, arrive at a crossing path. You should ignore this and carry straight on, along what is now once again part of the North Downs Way. The track continues through more attractive woodland which in late spring like most of the woodland encountered today, has a floor carpeted with bluebells. Sometime later, the track runs close to Buckland valley side and where the trees thin you can enjoy good views across the valley itself to the other side and the earlier parts of our walk.

Stay on the track, ignoring all turnings off (if in doubt, simply follow the North Downs Way signs), to eventually arrive at the hamlet of Holly Hill. The first sign of the hamlet is in the form of a garden fence on your left, shortly after which the track becomes a lane, at the same time passing the entrance to the west wing of "Holly Hill House". After this, you will arrive at two signposted public footpaths, one either side of the lane. Our way here is straight on along the lane. However, if you want a view of "Holly Hill House", take the public footpath on your left for a few paces to gain a better vantage point, though please remember this is private property.

You can also, by taking this path, add a few miles to the route by following it to "Crookhorn Bungalow" and then right along the Pilgrims Way until you rejoin the official route **(GR. 669620)**.

To continue on the official route, follow the lane ahead later passing the driveway to "Holly Hill House" where there is also a superb view to your left across the Medway valley. Shortly after this, you will pass the Kent County Council Holly Hill car park on your right (alternative start). Carry straight on along the lane still enjoying magnificent views left and behind. On a clear day it is even possible to pick out Rochester, Chatham and the Thames Estuary. Eventually, the lane arrives at a "T" junction. Cross the lane and go over a stile the other side and follow the path ahead, in the direction of a North Downs Way arrow. After a few paces, cross another stile to arrive at open hill side, known as White Horse Hill. Taking a few paces left here will allow you to enjoy an excellent panorama, undoubtedly the best view on the walk. Before you lies a checkerboard of fields, disturbed only by the industrial units within the Medway valley area. Some may complain about the latter, but remember industry has existed within the Medway valley virtually since Neolithic tribes arrived in the area. Directly ahead of you, just visible, is the village of Birling and its church - a welcome sign in terms of the end of our walk and the prospect of a visit to "The Nevill Bull".

To continue, follow the path and North Downs Way downhill, taking great care not to slip as you descend, as it is quite steep in places and can be slippery in wet weather. Near the foot of the downs the path bears right, shortly after which you should cross a stile to then follow the path along the foot of the downs, heading west. Sometime on, go over a second stile and follow a fenced path between fields, now walking south, away from the downs, heading directly for Birling church which, on a good day, is clearly visible.

At the far side of the field you will meet a crossing path, our old friend the Pilgrims Way and where the detour rejoins our official route. The North Downs Way turns right here to follow the Pilgrims Way. Our route however, is straight on, over the crossing path, thereby leaving both the North Downs Way and the Pilgrims Way. Cross a stile the other side and thereafter, continue ahead along the left hand perimeter of a field, at the far side of which cross a concrete drive to carry straight on, along a grass track. As a tall hedge on your left gives way there are excellent views on the same side to the ancient "Birling Place" with its huge stone garden wall and stone mullion windows. From its appearance, one feels that this building should not be in Kent at all but perhaps better off in Devon, Cornwall or even Scotland.

The track leads down to a field where you should go over a crossing track to continue ahead along the right hand perimeter of the next field. Even at this low level the views around you are still very good, to your left is the escarpment of the North Downs heading for the Kent coast and behind is the ever changing view of "Birling Place" and ahead, like a beacon guiding you home, the striking Birling church. Halfway across the field, ignore a marked path on your right to continue straight on and later, after skirting a garden and pond, go over a small bridge and then a stile, into another field. Once again, you should continue ahead along the right hand perimeter of the field with the church at Birling, even on the most miserable of days, now clearly visible. At the far side of the field, go over a stile to arrive at the top of some steps, now directly in front of the church and take the opportunity to have one last look back to the North Downs. It is also a good time to look back on the day's achievements and encounters. Encounters that have brought you close to people who influenced the early part of our history and people who first started to shape this land, nearly five thousand years go. Gazing at the North Downs you cannot help but wonder what the next five thousand years will bring.

Returning to the present day, go down the steps to make the most enjoyable entrance back into the village of Birling. Turn right along the road and pass the church to arrive back at the entrance to the old forge and our starting point.

ACCOMMODATION

Wateringbury Hotel, Wateringbury. Tel: 01622 812632

Approximately six miles from the walk, the hotel is ideally situated to explore the beautiful Teston valley, unfortunately not covered in this book. A friendly local concern with comfortable rooms, the hotel also has a sauna to ease the rigours of your adventure.

The Stable Block, Birling. Tel: 01732 873437

Virtually on the walk, accommodation is in a charming ragstone house converted from stables. The house has two comfortable guest rooms and is ideally situated allowing you to discover more of the surrounding countryside. The local pub is only a few minutes walk away.

Youth Hostel, Kemsing YHA, Kemsing. Tel: 01732 761341

Approximately ten miles from the walk, the hostel was once a vicarage in an attractive village at the foot of the North Downs. Quite a large hostel with fiftyeight beds, it can be busy in summer with school parties, so be warned and book ahead.

Camping and Caravanning, Thriftwood Park. Tel: 01732 822261

Approximately five miles from the walk, this is a pleasant site set in several acres of woodland. The camp also has purpose-built barbecues allowing you to continue to enjoy that "outdoor experience". Very well run, but make sure you take your muddy boots off before entering the shop!

BEATING THE BREW

Distance: 13½ miles (21.75km)

Time: Allow approximately 7 hours

Map: Ordnance Survey Landranger Map 188

START
LAMBERHURST
40M

COUSLEY WOOD
140M

FINISH
LAMBERHURST
40M

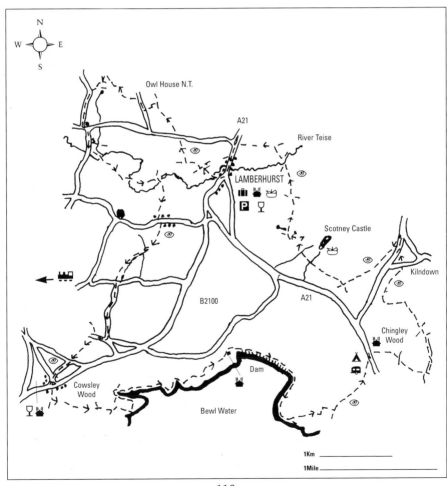

Walk Summary

A drinker's paradise, that's what the beautiful countryside around Lamberhusrt should be remembered for! Instead of wheat or corn, the fields yield grapes for wine, apples for cider and hops for beer. Do this walk in late summer and you will doubtless come across temporary campsites for the hop and fruit pickers. It is not uncommon to be offered a swig of locally produced cider as you walk through an orchard, though if this happens to you take my advice and treat it with respet, or you may not "beat the brew"!

Apples, grapes and hops aside, the walk also passes through some gloriously untouched woodland and open parkland with, at times, some surprisingly good views. A short stretch takes us into East Sussex and along the shores of Bewl Water, before the undoubted finale, "Scotney Castle". There is never a dull moment, passing several famous landmarks along the way and yet, at other times, one can feel very remote. There are no high climbs but mud and the length are to be taken into consideration when starting out. Apart from Lamberhurst at the start, there is only one pub en route, roughly half way round, so bear this in mind when planning your day. Good luck!

Start - GR. 676364 Map 188

The walk starts from in front of "The George and Dragon" pub at Lamberhurst. Lamberhusrt is easily reached, being on the main A21 London to Hastings road, south of Tunbridge Wells. From the north, the A21 connects with the M25 and M26 at junction 5, though be warned, you cannot join the A21 at this junction if coming from the east along the M26. If coming from the north east, it is best to use the B2126 and from the east the A262. If coming from the south or south west, the A267 from Eastbourne and the B2100 are your best bet.

Lamberhurst has a public car park which, at the time of writing, is free. It is well signposted and the entrance is beside "The Chequers" pub on the A21. The nearest railway station is at Wadhurst between Hastings and Tunbridge Wells. From there it is about a three mile walk to join the route at "The Old Vine" pub at Cousley Wood.

An alternative start can be made from the visitors centre at Bewl Water, but you may have to pay for the privilege.

BEATING THE BREW

The walk starts from in front of "The George and Dragon" pub, on the main A21 at the centre of Lamberhurst village. First though, I believe it is worth knowing a little about Lamberhurst.

Lamberhurst (GR. 676364 Map 188) is an attractive village set on the side of a hill surrounded by orchards, hop fields and woodland. Some of its beauty is lost due to the busy A21 which runs through the village centre, but a few steps from the main road and you will find peaceful weatherboarded cottages and fine ragstone houses, all oblivious of the rude 20th century invasion.

The name "Lamberhurst" is of Saxon origin and means "wooded hill where lambs graze". The description is still true today and the village has an abbotoir specialising in this market. Lamberhurst was also once the centre of the iron

117

industry and evidence of much of this industry can still be found in the surrounding countryside and on the Ordnance Survey map. The other two industries for which Lamberhurst was and still is famous, are fruit and hop picking. Plums and pears as well as apples can be found growing in the surrounding orchards and hops still hang between tall polls, just as they have done for centuries.

Not surprisingly, Lamberhurst used to have its own brewery and there is still a "Brewers" street, though the art of beer making has long since left the village. Instead, the village now has a vineyard, perhaps the most famous in the country. It produces a fine range of wines all of which can be purchased direct from the vineyard, which also offers winery tours. There is also a shop and restaurant, "The Country Pantry", which are open all year. If you wish to visit the vineyard it is off the B2100 at the southern tip of the village, on the way to Wadhurst. It you get a taste for the wine and enjoy your visit, then it is a good idea to join the "Winemakers Selection" wine club (for more information, telephone: 01892 890890).

It is a sign of the times that the village is now most famous for producing wines. It is a far cry from the days of the last century when hop growing was so important that the villagers voted for Lamberhurst to come wholly under the Council of Kent, where hops could demand higher prices. The vote took place in 1874, before which time the village had been half in Kent and half in East Sussex. The river Tesse, which still dissects the village, before 1874 acted as the county boundary.

Beer may no longer be brewed in the village but real ales are still served in all the village's hostelries. The two hostelries you will easily find are "The George and Dragon", a freehouse and "The Chequers", Shepherd Neame, which stand side by side on the A21, divided only by the river Tesse. Both were old coaching inns and date, incredibly, from the early 15th century, though "The George and Dragon" is a reconstruction having burned down in 1901. There is not a lot to choose between them, though I'd say that "The George and Dragon" has a slight edge in terms of atmosphere. This could be because of the various ghosts which are said to haunt the pub. Apparently, one of the ghosts was once so upset that it hurled some saucepans at the chef who took some persuading before he would re-enter the kitchen. Bear this in mind if your food is late being served! The real ales on offer are normally Flowers and Courage Directors as well as two guest ales. "The Chequers" serves the Kentish brews, namely Master Brew, Spitfire and Bishop's Finger. If visiting on a hot day, both pubs have pleasant riverside gardens.

Another pub close to the village centre a little way up the Wadhurst road, is "The Horse and Groom", Shepherd Neame. A friendly local pub which apart from the beer, serves some good value food including, quite often, trout fresh from nearby Bewl Water.

Before any more talk of food and drink makes us abandon our walk to indulge in quite different delights, with your back to "The George and Dragon", cross the A21 via the traffic light controlled pedestrian crossing and once the other side, turn left along the A21. After approximately fifty metres, fork right onto the B2100, signposted to Wadhurst, to almost immediately pass a large General Stores, a good place to stock up. Shortly after this, you will pass a bakers and then a newsagents and just after the newsagents, you should turn right onto a gravel drive between a half tiled cottage on one side and a weatherboarded cottage on the other. After a few metres, when the gravel drive ends, continue straight ahead along a narrow path between gardens, to shortly cross two bridges in quick succession, taking you over the river Teise, one of many such crossings today.

After the second bridge, bear diagonally right across the centre of a field heading for a stile the other side. As you cross there are good views to your right of Lamberhurst and the clock tower of the village school. The large building to the left of the village is the abbotoir. At the far side of the field, go over the stile and turn left along a track for a few paces, passing in front of a barn, immediately after which you should turn right to follow a fairly well defined path diagonally across a field, going gently uphill. At the far side of the field, pass through a gap in the edge into another field and turn right to continue uphill along the right hand perimeter of a field, with a hedgerow on your right. Ahead of you now, just above the brow of the hill you are climbing, is the tip of a modern oast. When the hedgerow ends, maintain your direction following a well defined path dividing two fields. As you near the top of the hill, ensure you take time to enjoy the views over the Teise valley behind, before proceeding to pass through a gate onto a lane **(GR. 669367)**.

Turn left along the lane and after a few paces, go up some stone steps on your right, beside the drive for "Barnsfield Oast", belonging to Hoathly Farms, a traditional Kent fruit grower. At the top of the steps go over a stile and follow a fenced path which shortly bends left, affording fine views over another valley on your right. Just after the bend go over a stile and continue in the same direction, now along the right hand perimeter of an orchard, later with the perimeter of a wood on your right. In spring, the wood is carpeted with bluebells and the orchard (a mixture of apple and pear) white with blossom, an incredible scene. At the far side of the orchard, pass through a gap in a hazel hedge ahead and maintain your direction thereafter, along the perimeter of the next orchard, still with the wood on your right. At the far side of the second orchard, pass to the right of a tennis court to shortly after, follow a fenced path along the side of the wood.

On meeting a stile on your right do not cross this but turn left instead to go uphill, still keeping to the perimeter of the orchard. To your right now, through the trees, is an ornamental wooded garden, part of the gardens to "Owl House". The orchard perimeter soon does an "S" bend before approaching a house. Keep right here and follow a fenced path, which can be somewhat overgrown in summer, passing to the right of the house to shortly walk through a yard of a fruit farm and packing plant, before arriving at a lane. Turn right along the lane to shortly pass through the gateway to "Owl House Gardens".

Owl House Gardens (GR. 664372 Map 188) *were created by Lady Dufferin in the 1950's. They surround a beautiful 16th century smugglers cottage, "Owl House", which has a chimney that looks as though it will collapse at any moment. The gardens are beautifully laid out with much sympathy to the local landscape and are open to the public (the "Owl House" is private), every day of the year, except Christmas Day, Boxing Day and New Year's Day.*

Shortly after, after passing a weatherboarded house on your right, turn left through a gate beside a sign, "Beware Heavenly Pekinese with Suicidal Tendancies"! The footpath and gate are also marked by a yellow arrow. Continue between a white fence on your left and a hedge on your right and after crossing a stile, continue ahead, once again walking along the perimeter of an orchard.

At the far side of the orchard (at the time of writing, the far side of the orchard is a low fence which could easily be taken away in the future - it is approximately one hundred metres from the point at which you joined the orchard), look out for a narrow path entering the wood on your right. This is indicated by a small yellow arrow on a tree, often hidden in summer (take care not to miss it). Take the path which runs downhill through the wood, where in spring the floor is covered by wild ramsons giving off their normal pungent smell, to later arrive at a hillside clearing at the edge of a valley with a derelict weatherboarded cottage the other side.

Turn right to go down the side of the valley. This is quite steep in places and care is needed to avoid a long slip downwards, especially if you have already been persuaded to try some local cider! Once safely at the bottom, cross the valley floor to a point in front of the derelict cottage the other side.

i   *Note the corrugated roof, which would once have been thatch but was probably replaced during the second World War to stop sparks from stray bombs setting it alight. This happened to many thatched cottages in Kent, usually by order of the Council. After the war, thatch was often too expensive to replace and tiles were used instead or, as in this case, the corrugated roof remained.*

Turn left, passing in front of the cottage, along the right hand perimeter of a field and follow the perimeter round as it bends right, shortly after which you should bear diagonally left ahead across the field heading for the far right hand corner and not the left hand corner which is an easy mistake to make. (If the field is recently ploughed, then it is only a short detour to walk, as an alternative, around the field perimeter).

At the time of writing, the valley is used for breeding grouse, pheasants and partridge for game hunting and you will more than likely find these birds scattering from your path as you walk. Amongst the birds will also be numerous squirrels who have quickly learned how to raid the bird feeders!

At the far side of the field, you will meet a track marked by a yellow arrow (this is on your right if you have had to walk around the perimeter), which you should follow, going over a stream to do so. After the stream, the track runs gently uphill through woodland and soon passes to the left of another derelict building, this one being brick. Almost immediately after the building, turn left (at the time of writing this is unmarked) to walk across a grass clearing, the other side of which you should go over a high narrow bridge, somewhat hidden among some trees, to cross a stream. This takes you into a wood where you should continue ahead, in the direction of a yellow arrow, along a narrow path to arrive at a track in front of a field with a kidney-shaped lake (hidden when the crop is high) ahead to your left.

Go over the track and straight across the field (if the field is freshly ploughed, it is only a short walk right along the track around the perimeter) and at the far side, follow a track ahead (right if you have followed the perimeter), ignoring a marked path on your left. The track proceeds uphill through more woodland where you should ignore any turnings off to soon arrive at a lane **(GR. 656374)**. Turn left along the lane, enjoying fine views ahead to your left as you walk, and follow it as it descends gradually, passing through a wood and a pond visible through the trees on your left. The pond is a left-over from the iron industry. The lane then bears sharp left where a track on your right at this point leads to the remains of Bayham Abbey.

Bayham Abbey was founded in 1200 by Robert de Truneham and Ela de Sackville.　　*i*
It housed an order of monks originally from Germany called "The Premonstratensian Canons". They were an extremely strict order, far stricter than the more common Augustians. Bayham Abbey was one of the first settlements in England for the German order and by the time Henry VIII dissolved the monasteries, they had thirtyfive settlements in the country.

The monks were commonly referred to as "white canons" due to their thick robes of undyed sheeps wool. Few people would ever have seen the monks as part of their doctrine was to isolate themselves from the outside world. According to local tales, ghostly images of the monks are supposedly seen regularly walking up the old nave of the abbey.

The track leading to the abbey from the lane is private. However, the abbey ruins and gardens are open to the public and if you wish to visit later, access is possible from the B2169. Even with visitors, it is still a silent place with plenty of atmosphere and it is easy to see why there are tales of hauntings.

Do not join the track which, as mentioned, is private, but keep to the lane as it bends left around the pond and shortly after, ignore another lane on your left signposted to Lamberhurst. In other words, keep to the lane you are on, which is signposted to Wadhurst, to soon pass "Hoathly Farm" and a converted barn and some magnificent converted oasthouses. A few metres after passing "The Oast House", turn left onto a tarmac track, signposted as a public footpath (low stone post), and continue to later pass over the beautiful river Teise once more. After the river, keep to the track ahead, ignoring another track off to the left, the latter

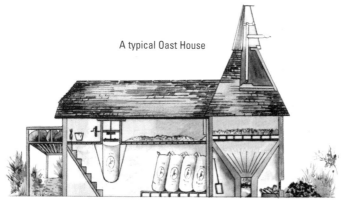

A typical Oast House

121

i leads to some caravans used as summer accommodation for hop pickers. After a short distance, the track bends left to follow what looks like a now virtually dried up river bed. It is in fact all that remains of a 16th century canal, created to provide water to work hammers at a nearby foundry, our next destinaton. Later, the track passes to the right of a barn (used for separating hops) and at this point, you should ignore a track leading off to the left. Shortly after, as the track bends right into a hop field, leave it to continue ahead along a narrow path, heading for some brick buildings.

On meeting a tarmac drive, carry straight on to walk between an old oasthouse and some outbuildings, to soon after arrive in front of what looks like a lovely old weatherboarded barn. Welcome to Furnace Mill.

i **Furnace Mill (GR. 662362 Map 188)** *today is a pretty collection of white weatherboarded buildings and oasthouses and together with a couple of graceful willows, makes a pleasant and typically Kentish scene. Furnace Mill however, has a place in history. In the early 18th century, as the name suggests, Furnace Mill was a foundry. At that time it was called Gloucester Forge, after one of Queen Anne's children. The foundry provided a range of iron based products but was famous for producing the railings which once encircled St. Paul's Cathedral. In total, there was half a mile of railings which weighed 200 tons. During the Victorian era, the railings were sold to Canada but only few reached their destination, the ship being wrecked close to the Canadian shore.The few railings which were recovered are now in a park in Toronto. Still at St. Paul's Cathedral and produced by Furnace Mill, are the screens in the aisles.*

Furnace Mill's demise came when the authorities found that it had secretly been producing and smuggling cannons to France for the French navy. The foundry already had contracts for the British navy which were immediately revoked and the owners heavily fined. As a consequence, the foundry went bust and iron has never been forged here since.

To continue, turn left to go over a stile into a field (take care not to miss it). The field, known as Pond Field, was once the hammer pond to the foundry. Continue straight across the field, in the direction of a yellow arrow, taking time to look back at the picturesque Furnace Mill. At the far side of the field, cross the river Teise again by way of a rather grand footbridge and thereafter, follow a path through a wood to, after a few paces, enter a field.

i *You may notice that the small strip of woodland beside the river is on a bit of a bank. Apparently, canon balls were once fired at the bank to test the strength of the canons produced at Furnace Mill.*

Once in the field, turn left to follow the left hand field perimeter and at the far side, at the field corner, pass through an old gateway ahead and then turn immediately right onto a concrete track to arrive in front of an old corrugated building on your right, all that remains of a hovel.

i **The Hovel.** *Hovels were and are a common name given to temporary accommodation for hop pickers. They were also known as Hopper's Huts.*

Hops were first introduced into England from Flanders in the 15th century, though it was not until one hundred years later that the production of hops for brewing really took hold. Hop growing peaked around the 1870's when over 70,000 acres (29,000 hectares) of land were dedicated to hops. Today, it is around 4,000 hectares, though with the growth in popularity of real ale, Britain's hop growing future looks brighter. For the uninitiated, it is the hop which puts the "bitter" into bitter.

Hop growing and cultivation was and still is labour intensive and during the 19th century, literally armies of people would converge on Kent looking for work. Gypsies, traditional hop pickers, would bring their caravans but hundreds of other workers came with no accommodation and no money to rent a room. At first, farmers would simply put the temporary workers in cattle sheds or even pig stys, but with the constant attack of disease (something which affected efficient collection of the harvest), a group of hop producers formed a society with an aim to improve the standard of accommodation for hop pickers. It was agreed that all hop pickers should have accommodation made of brick with rooms separated by wood or corrugated iron screens and that the minimum size of each living quarters should be 8 ft by 6 ft.

As there was a brick tax at the time, most hop producers were reluctant to build accommodation of brick, but when this was abolished in 1850, bricks were more frequently used, along with corrugated iron. The huts beside us are of this construction. Separate huts were normally built for washing and cooking. The hut over to our left appears to have been the cook house. When hop picking was at its height, there would have been many more huts and no doubt, tents as well, but these have long since disappeared.

Apart from the rough accommodation, hop picking was hard work. An average day would last around ten hours and during this time, the huts were out of bounds - everyone had to work, even children. The pickers would normally be woken up at around 5.00 a.m. by a manager running a stick along the corrugated iron walls. Breakfast from the cook house would normally be at 6.00 a.m. and work would start at 7.00 a.m. The earliest one could expect to finish was five in the evening. The only bonus was that free beer was sometimes allowed at the end of the week and there would normally be a grand party at the end of the season. The same went for fruit pickers and when farms were mixed (hops and fruit), there were no doubt some heavy heads the next day! There is a saying in Kent supposedly derived from pickers, "cider on beer makes you feel queer" - and believe me, it is quite accurate!

Looking around at the sad, dilapidated huts, it is hard to imagine that this was ever a hive of activity with hundreds of people living in squalid conditions. Todoay, gypsies still come to Kent to pick hops and fruit, though conditions have much improved and in some cases, people even pay for the experience of picking through the increasingly popular working holiday. The good thing is that tradition is still alive and during the season, especially around Lamberhurst and Plaxtol (see "The Soar Feat"), you will often meet up with seasonal workers, an increasing number of whom are from Europe, here for the social scene as much as the experience. What a change since the 19th century, when thousands of people, mostly from the East End of London, would descend upon Kent simply to earn enough money to see them through the winter.

To continue, keep to the concrete track, ignorning a couple of grass tracks on your left, to shortly cross the river Teise yet again. After the river, you should continue to follow the concrete track uphill, sometime later ignoring a stepped footpath on your left. On nearing the top of the hill, pass through a gate and continue ahead between buildings to shortly pass through another gate ahead (do not follow the concrete drive right) to arrive at a road, the B2169. Cross the road and turn left to follow it for approximately twenty metres and then turn right onto a signposted footpath beside the drive to "Misty Meadow Farm" (no connection with Morning Mist!). If you need to stock up on provisions, then the farm specialises in a variety of free range produce.

The path, at first, runs parallel with the drive to"Misty Meadow Farm" with a field on your right and soon goes over a rise, enjoying fine views ahead. Thereafter, the path descends gradually between fields, at the far side of which you should cross a stile to follow a fenced path, sheltered by a line of beech trees, with a newly created pond on your left. Go over a small bridge across a stream and follow the path as it continues through woodland, passing over another footbridge and a stream to enter East Sussex. Cross a stile into a field and once in the field, carry straight on, climbing the left hand perimeter of the field and at the far side, go a little way up a bank and then over a stile on your left to follow a fenced path along the edge of the bank, with a second man-made pond on your left. A little further on, go over a crossing track and cross a stile the other side to continue along a fenced path, passing a third pond on your left. Continue, passing yet another smaller pond and go over a stile, across a track and over another stile the other side, to continue ahead along the right hand perimeter of a field. At the far side of the field, pass through a gateway to carry straight on along the right hand perimeter of the next field and at the field end, on drawing level with another man-made pond, pass through a small gateway at the field corner and continue for a few paces to meet and cross a stile. Follow a fenced path after the stile, ignoring a marked footpath on your right, and keep to the path now walking through a small copse before arriving at a lane **(GR. 661348)**.

Turn left along the lane and after a few paces, fork right just opposite the entrance to the unusually named house, "The White Magpie". The lane is known locally as Hog Hole Lane, an obvious clue to the farming once practiced here. It is lovely in itself, being more suitable for walking as opposed to vehicles. After passing between fields, the lane continues through a beautiful deciduous wood where in summer ferns reach out from the mossy banks bordering the lane. Keep to the lane as it later climbs out of the wood to continue between tall hedgerows and later arrive at a crossroads. Turn right here, along another lane, in the direction of a sign for Bells Yew Green.

The field on your right is another used, in summer, to house fruit and hop pickers.

After approximately fifty metres, turn left onto a bridleway marked by a blue arrow on a telegraph pole on your right. The bridleway, one of East Sussex's older routes, is lined by ancient hedgerows and runs between fields. Later, it begins a gradual climb where, if you are tall or when the hedgerows are bare, you are afforded excellent views back across the Weald to the North Downs. The bridleway eventually meets a lane which you should cross to follow another lane ahead. As before, this is one of those lanes better designed for walking than the car and as you walk there are glorious views left across to Bewl Water, the largest lake in England south of the river Thames.

After enjoying the views across to Bewl Water, keeping to the lane brings you to a cluster of houses at a "T" junction. Turn left here, along another lane to soon after fork right and arrive at a road, the B2100, and the centre of the village of Cousley Wood. Much more important, the other side of the road, is the beautiful weatherboarded pub, "The Old Vine", Whitbread.

The Old Vine despite being on what many would term as a main road, is a fine pub. Anyway, being the only hostelry en route, a visit is virtually a must. Inside, a number (it is difficult to say how many exactly) of cosy bars cluster round a central serving area. The main bar has a fine original brick floor and a well preserved inglenook fireplace. The smallest and darkest bar, "The Tack Bar", nestles at the rear of the pub. Four well kept real ales are normally on offer and the substantial pub grub is very well priced.

To continue, after crossing the B2100, follow a track the other side signposted to "Little Butts Farm". This runs to the left of the pub. After passing a number of pretty cottages the track bends left where you should ignore another track leading off, ahead. Keep to the track as it begins to descend between fields, later affording more good views ahead over Bewl Water, at one point ignoring a marked footpath off to your left (yellow arrow). Shortly after this, after passing a pretty cottage on your left, go over a stile on your left, just as the track bends right, as a guide this is directly in front of "Bewl Water Oast", to follow a fenced footpath downhill.

After a short distance, go over a stile and maintain your route thereafter, still going downhill, along the left hand perimeter of a field. At the far side of the field, bear left along a path to shortly go over stile, after which you should ignore a path on your left to carry straight on. A few paces on, pass through a gap in a fence to arrive at "T" junction in the form of a prominent path, a path which skirts Bewl Water. Turn left along the path and after a short distance, turn left again. It is now simply a matter of keeping to the path which skirts Bewl Water but to ensure you are clear, I will continue to describe this part of the walk.

Sometime on, just before the path bends sharp right round Seven Pound Creek, there is a good view left to the oasthouses of "Little Butts Farm". Shortly after this, the path leads over a stream before twisting to follow the shoreline with attractive views across the lake. You should ignore a marked footpath off to the left just before this. After a long stretch of open shoreline the path continues through woodland, passing between the lake and a pond as it enters.

When I last walked this way, I saw a kingfisher sitting, motionless, on a branch over a pond in the wood on the left. It stayed like that for just a few seconds before flying off in a flash of orange and blue. Though it only lasted a few seconds, the moment is one I shall treasure for some time to come.

Later, you will arrive at a "T" junction in the form of a now dis-used tarmac lane. As you can see, the lane leads to the lake and before it was flooded, it used to lead across to "Bryands Farm" the other side. Turn left up the tarmac lane for approximately one hundred and fifty metres, and then turn right onto a marked footpath (yellow arrow), also signposted as the Sussex Border Path.

After going down some steps, the path continues to lead through woodland and continues a short time on, up some more steps to arrive at a parking area for

Bewl Bridge Yacht and Rowing Club. Turn right here, in the direction of the "Round Bewl Water Walk" sign, and after passing the building housing Bewl Bridge rowing club, turn left, still following the signs for the "Round Bewl Water Walk". After a few paces, turn right onto a path signposted to a public carpark and follow it through an area of woodland to later go over a tarmac drive and continue through woodland the other side. You should ignore all turnings off to the left or right to shortly arrive at a grass picnic area and a Visitors Centre ahead. You will probably at this point be greeted by hoards of people, particularly at weekends. You have been warned!

Follow the path ahead to pass round in front of the Visitors Centre which, for your information, has an exhibition, a small shop, cafeteria and public lavatories. It is also a good time to tell you a little more about Bewl Water.

i *Bewl Water is the largest lake in England, south of the river Thames and was formed by flooding the Bewl vally in the mid-1970's. When full, the dam holds back over 6,900 million gallons of water. The Visitors Centre is the hub of a number of activities centred on and around Bewl Water, including walking, riding, rowing, diving, sailing, cruises and perhaps most famous of all, fly fishing. Across the other side of the water you can just see a number of oblong tanks. These make up a fish farm which releases around 5,000 rainbow and brown trout into the lake each year, making Bewl Water one of the most important trout fishing waters in the country. Fishing can be from the shore or from boats which are available for hire. For novices, the reservoir authorities run some very good one-day cruises. If you are making good time, you may want to take a short cruise around the lake. A small ferry departs at regular intervals from the jetty below the Visitors Centre.*

Apart from all the aforementioned, Bewl Water organises several one-off events each year, including Dragon Boat Racing, open air theatre and very popular, a firework and laser symphony concert. For further details on any of the activities mentioned, telephone:- 01892 890661.

Once you are in front of the Visitors Centre, with your back to it, walk across the car park bearing gently towards the right hand perimeter and the lake and continue until you see some steps on your right. At the top of the steps, you can enjoy a marvellous view across the dam which holds back Bewl Water. Go down the steps, over a track and down some more steps, at the bottom of which you should turn left to walk along the top of the dam. The dam with its impressive size and strength, can give one a real feeling of insignificance. If you can take your eyes off the lake, to your left you can watch the water spraying into the tiny river Bewl, which in turn later joins the river Teise. On a clear day there are good views up the Bewl valley to the North Downs. Also, through the trees on your left you can just make out Scotney Castle, visited later en route.

Half way across the dam, we re-enter Kent and at the other side of the dam, follow the track as it bends right to pass through a gate. If you look across the water here, on a clear day, the church spire at Wadhurst is just visible and below it to the right is "Little Butts Farm", where we first joined the lake. The track now leads through Chingley Wood and continues to hug the shore with ever changing views across the water. You should keep to the track until you see a marked footpath (no. WC62, yellow arrow) on your left, signposted to Post Boy. This is approximately half a mile after the dam.

Leave Bewl Water at this point and join the marked footpath by going over a wooden stepped stile and continue thereafter, along a path now going gently uphill, through Chingley Wood. Ignore all turnings through this truly unspoilt deciduous wood and on nearing the other side of the wood, pass through a sweet chestnut coppice before arriving at a field. Continue ahead along the left hand field perimeter and keep to it as it later bends left with the wood. At the next field corner, turn right and continue following the perimeter where there are now lovely views over a section of Bewl Water, a wonderful place for a break and perhaps a snack or a bottle of beer! On eventually reaching the far left hand corner of the field, turn left through a gap in the hedge to join a track the other side. Ignore a marked footpath right at this point and follow the track ahead between fields.

Sometime later, go over a crossing track and then a stile and continue thereafter along an enclosed path with a line of hazel on your right. After crossing another stile follow the path as it runs between gardens to arrive at a track, with a cottage and twin oasthouses on your right. Follow the track ahead to shortly pass "Chingley Manor" on your left and continue along the track to its end at the main road, the A21, beside "Cedar Gables", a Camping and Caravanning site. Turn left along the A21 and after approximately thirty metres, cross the road just before a Little Chef restaurant and join a signposted public footpath the other side by going over a stile beside a pair of gates and continue ahead along a track through Cats Wood.

After a short distance, follow a path well marked by yellow arrows (make sure you pay attention to the arrows as it is easy to divert onto wood clearing tracks), through the wood ignoring all minor turnings off to eventually, after crossing a couple of wooden plank bridges either side of a stile, arrive at a field. Continue ahead for a few paces and turn left in the direction of a yellow arrow, through a gap in a hedge, to walk straight across another field. At the far side, go over a stream, then over a stile and at the same time, through a gate (you will see what I mean). Thereafter, continue ahead along the left hand perimeter of a field which, at the time of writing, houses hundreds of free range hens. If you are eating a sandwich at this point, you are in for a hard time! (DOG OWNERS - PLEASE KEEP YOUR DOG ON A LEAD). At the far side of the field, cross and go through another combined stile and gate and continue straight across a track between two commercial chicken sheds and pass through another stile and gate to the left of the chicken shed on your right. After the stile and gate, turn left to follow the perimeter of another chicken field, descending into a valley, heading for a stile and gate visible at the bottom.

At the bottom of the field, pass through the stile and gate, cross a track and go over a stile the other side, to thereafter follow a narrow path ahead. After a few paces, turn left onto a narrower path and after going over a footbridge and then a stile, come out at another track. Cross over the track to follow a narrow marked (yellow arrow) path the other side which proceeds in a straight line, close to the bottom of a valley, through dense undergrowth. Eventually, it bends left and crosses a stream via a footbridge, after which you should go over a stile to arrive at open space in front of another chicken field. Turn right, with the field on your left and continue to follow the field fence to its end (or where it bends left), where you should continue ahead, passing through an old gateway, into the beautiful Shearnfield Wood. Thereafter, follow a narrow path through the centre of the wood. Although easy to follow the path is not that well used and may as a bonus, afford a sighting of some local wildlife, particularly deer. At one point, the path dips in and out of a valley crossing a narrow stream via a wooden plank bridge at the bottom, a beautiful moment. After this, keep to the path as it continues in a fairly straight line and ignore all minor turnings off, including at one point a crossing path, being sure at all times to follow the yellow arrows. After approximately two thirds of a mile, you will eventually reach the far side of the wood where, just before you meet a field gate ahead (GR. 697344) you should turn right, still in the direction of the yellow arrows. This continues to take you through the wood, now a sweet chestnut coppice.

i *As you walk, the coppiced sweet chestnut trees look very young in comparison to the rest of the wood. This is misleading as many of the trees are several hundred years old. To tell the age of a coppiced tree, one has to measure its base. For every foot in width, the tree is roughly one hundred years old. For full details on coppicing, see "The Soar Feat".*

The path continues along the top of a valley side, the valley sloping gently away to your right. After approximately two hundred metres, you should turn left onto a narrow marked (yellow arrow) path and follow this gently uphill with a line of holly bushes on your right and heather at your feet. The path soon leads up to a stile which you should cross into a field. Thereafter, turn right to follow the perimeter. Ahead to your left now are the first buildings of Kilndown village (in particular, a fine oasthouse), our next destination. Do not get too excited about the "PH" marked on the map - sadly, the village hostelry has recently closed. At the far side of the field, continue ahead along a fenced track and then go over a stile into another field. Here you have a beautiful view through a gateway on your right over Shearnfold Wood and beyond to Bedgebury Pinetum. Bedgebury is the largest collection of pine trees in Europe.

After admiring the view, continue ahead along the right hand perimeter of the field and after passing a pretty tile hung cottage, cross a stile at the far side. Turn left thereafter, along a track to shortly meet and cross a lane, joining a signposted footpath the other side. This runs alongside some picturesque half weatherboarded cottages with good views to your right, before arriving at a cul de sac. Go straight across the cul de sac and follow the footpath the other side, between gardens, to arrive at a road. Turn right along the road and continue to a point almost opposite the village's Victorian church, where you should pass between a metal rail on your left, the other side of the road, to enter the unusual village park, though first you may wish to visit the church.

i **Kilndown Church (GR. 701353 Map 188)** *is quite grand for such a small village and its spire can be seen for miles around. The real shock however, is on entering, for instead of the modest decor of most English churches, the interior is a splash of colour. Rich carving is everywhere and virtually everything is painted - even the font is a mixture of red, gold and blue. The stained glass windows too are rich in colour, depicting characters from early Saxon christianity. The rich decor is* *quite unique and it may not surprise you therefore, to learn that much of the work was done by craftsmen from Munich in Germany, where colour is an important feature in churches.*

Stepping outside once more, you are almost surprised to find yourself still in England. It is as though for a brief moment, you have been transported to another world.

To continue, after entering the park, descend some steps to then follow a pleasant path along the left hand edge of the village pond. After approximately twenty metres, just before you reach some picnic benches and a table, turn left through a gap in a fence and then turn left again along a track.

The local hostelry "The Globe and Rainbow Inn" is right along the track for a few metres. It has recently closed but may open again and you may wish to try your luck - let me know if you strike gold!

Sometime later, after passing a row of cottages, the track narrows to become a wide path, where you should maintain your direction along the path, ignoring all turnings off, to later enter Kilndown Wood. At first, you will follow a magnificent line of beech trees after which the path meets a track which you should, in turn, follow ahead, now going downhill in the direction of the footpath sign for Scotney Castle. A few metres on, the track passes to the left of a cottage and shortly after, still going downhill, you are treated to some surprising views ahead over Bewl Water.

On nearing the bottom of the valley ignore a couple of tracks leading off to the right and carry straight on in the direction of the sign for Scotney Castle. A little later on, at a "T" junction, turn right along another track, still following the signs for Scotney Castle and sometime on, ignore a track forking off to the left to continue ahead along a less defined track. A few paces after, go over a stile beside a gate to enter the idyllic parkland of Scotney Castle.

The park would befit any Jane Austen novel. Trees planted to give the appearance of a natural landscape grace a well grazed valley, descending in elegant folds to the sparkling waters of Bewl Water. Cows and sheep move slowly amongst the trees, intent only on finding a richer blade of grass, blissfully unaware that they are an integral part of a peaceful English scene. The picture is worth more than a moment's pause.

To continue, carry straight on, along a track, through the parkland now descending into Bewl valley. At the valley bottom pass through a gate and cross the pretty river Bewl by way of a stone bridge. After the bridge, continue to follow the track the other side where ahead to your right is Scotney Castle "mark two", the original castle with its much photographed moated tower being visible, in autumn and winter only, through the trees on your right. In summer, if you want to see the original castle, you will have to pay for the privilege.

Sometime on, pass through a gate and over a second stone bridge across a marshy arm of the river Bewl, and continue along the track as it bends right to lead up the other side of the valley. Ignore a marked footpath to Lamberhurst on the left here. As you climb gently there are fine views to your right over the beautiful landscaped valley. Near the top, pass through a gate to arrive at a drive and to your right the entrance to the castle gardens.

i

Scotney Castle (GR. 687354 Map 188) is perhaps Kent's most photographed landmark and not to be outdone, features on the cover of this book. The house, beside the National Trust shop and entrance to the castle and gardens, was built in 1837 which would normally be of interest in itself, but here pales into insignificance when compared with the romantic ruin of the moated castle. Ironically, the ruin is somewhat deliberate as the old castle was partly deliberately taken down to make a perfect garden feature - the planners succeeded!

The name "Scotney" is believed to have come from the original owner of the manor, Lambert de Scoteni, in the early 12th century. It is debatable whether he actually ever had a house at Scotney, though some believe it may. have been on the smaller of the islands protected by the moat. The de Scoteni family disappeared during the "Barons War" in the 13th century, with one of the family, Walter de Scoteni, being hanged at Winchester for poisoning two of the powerful de Clare family. One of the de Clare's was Gilbert, who was instrumental in forcing King John to sign the Magna Carta. The de Clare's are strongly featured in "10 More Adventurous Walks in Surrey" (see "In Search of Lost Castles").

It was just over a hundred years later, in 1378, that one Roger de Ashburnham, who inherited the land, started building th first Scotney Castle. Ten years later a close friend and colleague of Roger, Sir Edward Dallingridge, started building Bodium Castle which has often been compared in style to Scotney. The castle originally had four fortified towers, but today only one remains, the one that is featured in so many photographs. It is approached by a stone bridge over the moat which surrounds the castle, created by diverting the river Bewl. The diverting of the river caused some confusion for the river also acted as the county boundary. When a maid tragically drowned in the moat, a heated argument ensued as to which county was to bear the cost of her burial.

In the 16th century, the Dorrell family inherited the castle. They were staunch Catholics and remained so, even after the Reformation. They build a clever priest hole in the old house attached to the original fortified tower with several false priest holes to confuse anyone searching the house. One famous story tells of a Father Blaunt, who hid for over ten days in the priest hole whilst JP's searched the house. He eventually escaped by climbing over the wall and swimming across the moat, whilst a member of the household created a diversion. Another story concerning the Dorrell family, took place in 1720. At the funeral of Arthur Dorrell, a man in a black cloak was heard to whisper, "that is me they are burying". Many years later, the grave was exhumed and the coffin was found to contain nothing but stones! Nobody has ever explained what happened to Arthur.

The last owners of Scotney Castle, the Hussey family, acquired the castle in 1778 from a Mr. Richards who had purchased it at an auction in 1774, held at "The Chequers Inn" at Lamberhurst. In 1836, Edward Hussey decided to build a new house and this was completed in 1843. Below the house he set about planning what is perhaps today Kent's most attractive garden. Except for a few minor alterations, the garden today is much as it was originally planned. In 1970, the castle and gardens passed into the hands of the National Trust who now maintain it for all to enjoy.

A visit to Scotney Castle is a must and a unique experience, for it is unusual for such a colourful landscape to have an equally colourful history.

To continue, turn left along the drive and follow it, going steadily uphill, for approximately two hundred metres where you will see a marked footpath (yellow arrow) on your right. Take this, going up some steps to do so and follow the footpath through woodland, at first passing a small lake on your left. After the lake, keep to the footpath, ignoring all minor turnings off, to soon arrive at the far side of the wood with a stile ahead. Go over the stile into a field, ignoring a marked "woodland walk" on your left and go straight across the field to shortly meet and follow the field's left hand perimeter ahead. As you progress there are good views right across the Bewl valley and visible at the far side, just rising above the trees, is the top of the church spire at Kilndown. Later, as the field perimeter bends left, you should bear diagonally left to follow a line of horse chestnut trees at the end of which you will arrive at the corner of the field, where a bench allows you to enjoy the fine views in comfort.

Pass through a "V" stile at the field corner and turn right to follow the right hand perimeter of a field to shortly meet another stile which you should cross into the next field. There is now an excellent and famous view ahead to the church at Lamberhurst and beside it, "Court Lodge".

At the time of writing, this famous scene is under threat of being home to a bypass. There is much opposition to the plan and hopefully, this madness will be quickly shelved.

Continue ahead along the right hand field perimeter, going downhill and ignore a marked footpath left. As you descend, over to your left now the houses of Lamberhurst, our final destination, come into view. At the far side of the field, pass through a gap beside a gate and cross over a concrete drive to a house on your right. Thereafter, continue ahead to follow a well walked path across the centre of a field, at the bottom of which you should cross a narrow bridge over our old friend the river Teise.

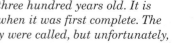

approaching
Lamberhurst Church

After the river Teise, continue ahead across the next field heading for the church at the far side. At the field end, follow a path ahead into the churchyard where you should fork left along the edge of the churchyard to soon arrive at the church entrance.

The Church of St. Mary the Virgin (GR. 682365 Map 188) *dominates the skyline. Built in the 14th century, it is well preserved and contains many original features, including some fine arches. Perhaps the most dominant feature however, is the fine solid oak carved pulpit which is over three hundred years old. It is magnificent today but must have been splendid when it was first complete. The pulpit originally had three floors or decks as they were called, but unfortunately, the lower deck is missing.*

To continue, carry straight on along a tarmac path, passing between a golf course on your left and the magnificent "Court Lodge" on your right and at the far side of the golf course, follow a tarmac drive ahead to soon arrive at the busy A21. Turn left along the road, following a tree lined pavement downhill and continue to follow the A21 back into Lamberhurst and "The George and Dragon" pub, our starting point. Congratulations, you have "beaten the brew", so why not celebrate by having one!

ACCOMMODATION

The George and Dragon, Lamberhurst. Tel: 01892 890277

On the walk, this is a fine 15th century coaching inn. There are six bedrooms, four of which are en suite. Close to the A21, nights can be noisy so ensure you ask for a room at the rear of the inn.

Hook Green Pottery, Hook Green. Tel: 01892 890504

Approximately a quarter of a mile from the walk, this is a lovely 18th century farmhouse with fine views over a valley of wooded farmland. A warm welcome is assured as well as some good home cooking. Perfect.

Youth Hostel, Black Boys YHA, Uckfield. Tel: 01825 892607

Approximately six miles from the walk, this is a lovely hostel popular with YHA members. Accommodation is in simple wooden huts in a small Sussex village. One major attraction is the local pub, one of the best in Sussex.

Camping and Caravanning, Cedar Gables, Flimwell. Tel: 01892 890566

On the walk, this is a small farm site close to Bewl Water and Scotney Castle. The facilities are a little basic but very clean and the owners are extremely friendly.

THE TOADS TERROR

Distance: 16 miles (25.75km)

Time: Allow approximately 7 hours

Map: Ordnance Survey Landranger Map 188

START
RUSTHALL
CHURCH
130M

STONE CROSS
100M

FINISH
RUSTHALL
CHURCH
130M

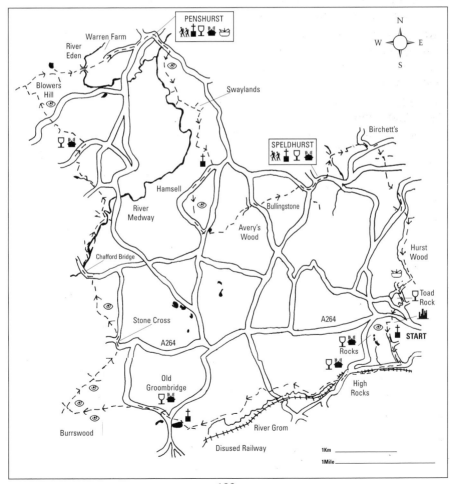

Walk Summary

Though this is by far the longest walk in the book, it is by no means the hardest. It is also probably my favourite in the collection passing, at times, what one can only describe as some quite unique scenery. There are also some spectacular views and in between, the route discovers the quieter more charming corners of Kent. No fewer than six pubs are passed en route, all with their own merits and as a finale, a short detour at the end brings you to a most unusual pub with an outstanding view. Despite the fact that there is in excess of one steep climb, you are more likely to be bothered by mud than the scale of an ascent. This walk, like several others in the book, is also excellent if walked in reverse, with the views being quite different. No matter which way you do this walk, take time to admire the scenery and you will have a memory to savour for months to come.

Start - GR. 566393 Map 188

The walk starts from Rusthall church on the A264, close to Toad Rock (marked on the Ordnance Survey Landranger map). Rusthall is just west of Royal Tunbridge Wells and the church (St. Paul's) is signposted from the A264, the Tunbridge Wells to East Grinstead road. A "no through" road leads from the A264 to the church where there is ample room for roadside parking. Numerous A and B roads converge on Royal Tunbridge Wells or the A264 close to Rusthall, making the start, from most directions, easily accessible.

The nearest railway station is Royal Tunbridge Wells from where you can take a taxi, though if you do not mind the distance, it is quite a pleasant walk to Rusthall church. The most obvious alternative start, if you have a car, is Penshurst. I recommend you avoid Speldhurst as a place from which to start as street parking can be difficult.

THE TOADS TERROR

The walk starts beside St. Paul's church, a somewhat austere Victorian affair softened only by the local sandstone from which it is constructed. The church could quickly be forgotten except that it marks the highest point on our walk. In theory therefore, it should be all downhill from here, though I have the feeling you do not believe me!

To start, facing St. Pauls church and war memorial, turn right to, after a few paces, leave the drive passing between some posts to thereafter, follow a path ahead through woodland (part of Rusthall Common), with the wall to an old school (now a beauty centre) on your left. Keep following the wall as it bends left, ignoring a path forking right (this leads to "The Beacon" pub, a recommended place of celebration for the end of the walk). Thereafter, continue straight on to shortly start descending. A little later on, ignore another path on the right (you may want to detour here to visit some sandstone cliffs through you must retrace your steps to rejoin our route), to pass between some metal railings and follow the path ahead to come out at a rather smart residential road. Go straight on along the pavement and ignore a turning left later, to continue until the road abruptly ends. Here, maintain your direction, now following a path which continues from the end of the road and after a few metres, fork right onto a much narrower path (take care not to miss it). Follow the path until is comes out at a road and turn right to follow the road, taking care of the traffic along the bottom of a valley, affectionately known locally as Happy Valley.

Keep to the road for approximately three hundred metres until you pass a stile on your right and immediately after this, turn left to follow a track under the now disused Tunbridge Wells to Three Bridges branch line **(GR. 564384)**. At the other side, cross over the river Grom (more a stream) and thereafter, turn right along a crossing path, the High Weald Walk Link Route. After a few paces, the path forks and the choice is yours as they rejoin later. However, the right hand fork is probably the better of the two as it follows the river Grom. Sometime later, ignore a path on the left leading to a road outcrop, to continue along the bottom of the valley, to shortly follow the path up and over a bank where there are even more rock formations. This landscape is quite dramatic and you may want to spend more than a few minutes exploring the rocks or testing your climbing skills. Also not to be missed is the view to your right across the valley to an old oasthouse.

Continuing along the path (the High Weald Walk Link Route), you will shortly meet and follow a fence enclosing an area of particularly impressive rocks. They are aptly named High Rocks and are famous in the climbing world. The path continues to follow the fence until eventually, after descending some steps, you come out at a road on a bend where you should turn left, to shortly arrive at "The High Rocks Inn". The inn is a large ivy-clad freehouse with a restaurant, a large garden and several function rooms. At weekends it can become very crowded - so be warned! Opposite the pub is the entrance to High Rocks and tickets to visit the rocks can be purchased from the bar at the inn.

High Rocks (GR. 559383 Map 188) are an amazing number of high sandstone   *i*
cliffs, some having the most peculiar shapes and were formed from water currents
when the sea covered the area millions of year ago. Years after the sea receded,
Stone Age man made his home here and later still, the Celts build a fort above the
rocks. In later centuries, the rocks became a tourist attraction and in the late 19th
century, an hotel ("The High Rocks Inn") was built opposite to accommodate the
large numbers of visitors. The rocks also attracted climbers from all over the
country, eager to test their skills on the unusual sandstone face. One of the most
famous of these was Julie Tullis, perhaps Britain's best known female climber and
the first woman to climb K2.

Julie first came to High Rocks in November 1956 on a casual visit to meet her
sister, who regularly practised her climbing skills at the rocks. She arrived cold
and tired just as the hotel was closing with her sister no-where to be seen. As she
wondered what to do, a tall bearded man emerged from the entrance to the rocks
themselves and enquired if she wanted a cup of cocoa to warm her up. After Julie
had accepted the offer, he said "I think you should hold my hand", an offer to

guide her to where he and his friends were camped. Julie, who was at first suspicious, took his hand and in her words "have been holding hands ever since". They were married in 1959.

Julie and her husband spent many years at the rocks, with other climbers, practising their skills in preparation for more serious climbs. At night, they would camp in their shelter much as man had done thousands of years before. Later, they started a climbing school at nearby Bowles and Harrison's Rocks. Although Julie went on to climb peaks thousands of feet high, she never forgot her days at High Rocks and often amused herself by conquering heights - High Rocks at 45 feet and K2 at 28,250 feet!!

At the age of 45, Julie became the first British woman to climb over 8,000 metres, but her burning ambition was to climb perhaps the world's more unforgiving mountain, K2. After two failed attempts she set out, in 1986, for a third try. Several groups of climbers of various nationalities were also making the climb at the same time, though none of them knew that they were about to be part of mountaineering's most tragic episode. Julie realised her dream on 4th August, 1986 when, with her climbing partner Kurt Diemburger, she reached the summit of K2. Sadly though, her joy was short lived, for the next day they were trapped in a storm close to the summit. During the night of 6th August, after spending the previous four nights above 8,000 metres, a testing feat, Julie finally succumbed to the elements and died in her sleep. Six other climbers were to die on the mountain in the next couple of days, though Julie's partner, Kurt, was one of only a handful to descend safely. In all, eleven climbers died on K2 in October of that year - a tragedy which thankfully, has not been repeated since.

On 27th September, 1986, Julie's husband, Terry, held a remembrance service for his wife at High Rocks, the place at which they had first met. Over five hundred people attended the ceremony, including many climbers from around the world, one being Kurt, who had been with Julie on the night of her death on K2. Many had brought trees and shrubs to be planted in her memory at High Rocks and Harrison's, nearby. Although today, there is no plaque or stone to remember Julie Tullis, the trees and shrubs planted by her friends and the climbing world grow strong in her name.

Sadly, serious climbers are no longer welcome at High Rocks and an admission fee is charged simply to view them. Harrison's Rocks however, only a few miles away, continues the tradition of testing the skills of budding climbers.

For those who would like to know more about Julie Tullis, her autobiography, "Clouds From Both Sides", is published in paperback by Grafton Books.

To continue, carry straight on past the inn and High Rocks and after approximately thirty metres, leave the road to join a signposted public footpath on your right, marked as the High Weald Link Route to Groombridge Place. The path leads downhill, later passing under the old railway line and shortly after crosses the river Grom via a wooden footbridge. Thereafter, follow the path through an area of natural vegetation (this means nettles in summer!), to soon bend left following the course of the river Grom, which from here on, marks the boundary between Sussex and Kent. This is a particularly lovely part of the walk, passing through beautiful deciduous woodland of silver birch, hazel and maple, with the river Grom meandering gently to your left. Ignore all minor turnings off to later go over a stile and thereafter, continue in the same direction through a field. After a short distance, the path bends right (look out for the yellow arrow) and continues across the field to go over a stile beside a large old oak tree at the far side. Continue in the same direction through the next field, at one point meeting up with the river Grom, after which you should head for a stile at the far side.

Go over the stile and turn left thereafter, along a fenced path. The path soon twists right to shortly after arrive at a track, onto which you should turn left in the direction of a blue arrow. Immediately after this, pass through a gate into a field and cross a bridge to continue ahead along the right hand perimeter of a field and at the far side, pass through a gate ahead onto a track. Follow the track ahead to soon arrive at a lane **(GR. 546382)**. Cross the lane go over a stile the other side to follow a signposted fenced footpath which skirts a local a sewage station (my apologies!!). On a hot day the presence of the sewage works will probably spur you quickly on by. On a better day however, take time to look about you. Sewage stations are fast becoming a botanist's delight, with all sorts of exotic plants taking root from seeds that have passed from the supermarket shelves and through the human food chain!

After the sewage works the footpath continues between thick hedgerows, normally bustling with bird life, before suddenly bending left to skirt a house and two converted oasthouses. Cross over the drive to the house and go over a stile the other side to thereafter, continue ahead along the right hand perimeter of a field. Lining the field perimeter are a number of willow trees which sadly are slowly dying off. The willow tree has a tremendous thirst and with the water table getting lower by the year, it will be not long before these trees are gone forever.

At the far side of the field, go over a stile and then a bridge across a man-made stream and at the other side, continue ahead with a canal now on your right. If you look carefully, the area the other side of the canal is actually a carefully landscaped garden, part of "Groombridge Place", our next destination. After approximately one hundred metres go over a stile beside a gate ahead and continue to maintain your direction, now walking along the right hand perimeter of a field, with "Groombridge Place" now clearly visible ahead. As you near the far side of the field you will virtually draw level with the magnificent building, a fine 17th century moated house, complete with drawbridge. At the far side of the field, pass through a kissing gate and go over another man-made stream to, after a few paces, arrive at the drive to "Groombridge Place".

Groombridge Place (GR. 533377 Map 188), as we see it today, was built around 1660 and has changed little over the centuries. Those who know "Igtham Moat" (see "The Greensand Grapple"), will immediately recognise the similarity between the two buildings. It is a magnificent house and the moat, still with water, adds a touch of magic.   *i*

There was a "Groombridge Place" on the same site long before the current house. In 1415, the then owner, Sir Richard Waller, set out from here with an army led by Henry V, on a campaign to France. The campaign culminated in victory at Agincourt, where they successfully captured a brother of the King of France, Charles, Duke of Orleans. The Duke was imprisoned in the Tower of London whilst his younger brother, John, Count of Angouleme, taken as a hostage three years earlier, was kept prisoner at "Groombridge Place" itself. The beautiful and natural gardens which surround "Groombridge Place" are credited to be the work of diarist and amateur landscape gardener, John Evelyn (see "10 Adventurous Walks in Surrey"), who was a frequent visitor here. In summer, the gardens are sometimes open to the public and if you can visit, I urge you not to pass the opportunity by.

To continue, carry straight on along the drive, ignoring a footpath off to the left, taking time to admire the magnificence of "Groombridge Place" on your right. As the moat ends, the drive forks and here you should continue straight on along a footpath with iron fencing on your right. After a short distance pass over a small rectangular lake, well stocked with fish and take time to look back and enjoy a very different view of "Groombridge Place", through an avenue of redwood trees. Continue ahead up some steps to then turn right, skirting a grand lake and after a short distance, go over a tarmac drive and pass through a small gate ahead, to thereafter bear diagonally left across a field, heading for the houses and church of Old Groombridge.

At the far side of the field, pass through a kissing gate and follow a fenced path past some fine weatherboarded cottages, with the church on your left, to soon arrive at a road, the B2110. In front of you is the village's much photographed lovely sloping green surrounded by picture postcard cottages and most importantly, overlooking it all and directly in front of you, the superb "Crown Inn", a freehouse which also offers B&B - a good place at which to say welcome to Groombridge!

i
†
■
   ***Groombridge (GR. 530377 Map 188)** must rate as one of the prettiest villages in Kent, even with the noisy B2110. The simple 17th century church, once the private church to "Groombridge Place", has a number of simple treasures. The central window in the south chancel remains the original and depicts Sir Richard Waller and the Royal prisoner at Agincourt. Above the door is a memorial to William Cotton-Oswell, buried in the church and who accompanied Livingstone on many of his adventures to Africa. Above the priest's door in the chancel is an unusual memorial to Philip Packer, who is depicted sitting cross-legged with his head resting on one shoulder. The engraving is said to show the position in which he was found, dead, in the grounds of "Groombridge Place" in 1686.*

The village's other main building, "The Crown Inn", was built at roughly the same time as the church and reminds me of a rhyme recently relayed to me by a fellow walker of Irish extraction, the nation from where the rhyme originates:-

> *"Wherever God erects a house of Prayer,*
> *The devil also builds a chapel (pub) there,*
> *And it will be found in examination,*
> *That the latter has by far the larger congregation!"*

Whether built by the devil or not, "The Crown Inn" originated as a coaching inn and has received overnight guests, without a break, since the day it was built. During the 18th century, it was notorious for harbouring a gang of smugglers who also hid their "booty" there. Perhaps the inn's most famous guest however, was Sir Arthur Conan-Doyle, who would reside at the inn when visiting "Groombridge

Place". The pub is featured in a couple of his books, in particular "Valley of Fear".

For the modern-day adventurer, the inn offers some well kept ales of which there is always Harveys as well as a good wine list, with all wines shipped direct from France. For more solid refreshments one can choose from simple bar meals or enjoy a meal in the restaurant. For those who find themselves so in love with the place that they don't want to leave, the inn has a few guest rooms cleverly constructed in the roof.

To continue our walk, cross the B2110 and follow a brick path the other side, passing in front of the pub and continue thereafter along the top of the green to, at the far side, turn right along a lane. This lane takes you past more perfectly preserved cottages and soon after, the magnificent "Court Lodge", after which you should follow the lane for approximately a quarter of a mile, until you see a signposted footpath on your left **(GR. 523379)** - take care not to miss it. Join the path by going over a stile and continue straight ahead across a field, in the direction of a yellow arrow. As you progress, there are some excellent views ahead to your left over the Grom valley to the rolling hills of East Sussex and closer, hugging the hillside, the historic house of "Burrswood" is also visible.

At the far side of the field, go over a stile, down a bank and across a lane to ascend some steps the other side. Go over a second stile and continue to follow a narrow path along the edge of a wood, with a field on your right. Sometime later, go over a stile into another field and carry straight on, across the centre of the field, bearing very gently left in the direction of a yellow arrow. On reaching the far corner of the field, go over a stile and turn left to follow a narrow path which winds through some enchanting woodland. After a few paces, go over a crossing track and continue to follow the path the other side, now going downhill. At the bottom of the wood, after going over a stream, cross a stile and carry straight on across the centre of a field. At the far side of the field, cross another stile and bear right passing a secluded pond on your right, to cross the centre of another

139

field, keeping a low bank on your right as you walk. Careful attention is now required. As you near the far side, look out for a point where the bank on your right levels out where you should in turn look out for a stile on your right. (If you find yourself meeting and following the field perimeter fencing then you will have gone too far and should retrace your steps to find the stile).

Go over the stile to join the Weald Way, represented by a yellow arrow with "WW". The path leads uphill through a line of trees, after which you should cross a stile into a field, ignoring a gate on your right. Continue ahead, uphill, along the right hand field perimeter and after approximately seventyfive metres cross a stile on your right (take care not to miss it), into an adjacent field. Once in the field, turn left in the direction of the Weald Way arrow and continue, still going uphill, now following the left hand perimeter of a field. There are good views behind here if you want to take a short breather and as you continue to climb, there are also excellent views to your right.

At the field corner go over a stile ahead and continue in the same direction, along the left hand perimeter of the next field, still in the direction of the yellow arrow. As you approach the far side of the field, head for a stile beside a gate, visible ahead to your right. As a guide, this is roughly a third of the way down from the far left hand corner of the field. Go over the stile and maintain your direction along the left hand perimeter of the next field, again in the direction of the yellow Weald Way arrow. This field is long and narrow and at times is almost like a very wide grass track. On eventually reaching the far side, cross a stile beside a gate at the field's left hand corner and thereafter, continue following a hedged path with a garden on your right. After a short distance the path arrives at an open grass area with the first houses of Stone Cross visible ahead.

Carry straight on passing to the left of an outbuilding and after this, descend a bank to follow the wall of a house on your right and then a fence, before meeting and crossing a stile to arrive at a road, the A264 (**GR. 523389**). Turn left along the road, taking care of the traffic as you walk (do not turn right), and shortly after turn right onto a narrow lane signposted to Fordcombe. Follow the lane for just a few paces, passing through a gateway on your left, to join a signposted footpath (marked by a low stone post). At this point we now leave the Weald Way which takes another route on the opposite side of the road.

The path winds through a wood to come out at the far side, at the edge of a field, with fine views ahead over the Medway valley and Kent Water. After admiring the views, turn left going downhill, along the left hand perimeter of the field. As you continue, notice the overgrown and sunken track on your left, the original route when horse and cart was the primary mode of transport. At the field's far left hand corner, continue ahead passing through a gap in the hedge (there could be a gate or stile here in the future) and thereafter, maintain your direction along the left hand perimeter of the next field.

On reaching the far left hand corner of the field, go over a stile and as before, continue ahead, again keeping to the left hand field perimeter, now with a bubbling brook on your left. At the field corner, cross a tributary to the brook and carry straight on across the centre of the next field and at the far side, go over yet another stile to again continue ahead, this time following the right hand perimeter of the next field. In spring and summer this field is normally ablaze with buttercups. At the far side, go over one more stile to meet a lane (**GR. 517400**). Turn left along the lane, going downhill, to soon pass a line of idyllic cottages which overlook the river Medway on your left. Keep to the lane and cross over the Medway river via Chafford bridge, which replaced an earlier ford (see "The Leopard's Loop", Fordcombe).

Immediately after the bridge, go over a stile on your right into a field and once in the field, follow the river bank to reach and pass through a gate at the far side. Note, as you approach the far side, the unusual weir and a well concealed brick pill box with its own private beach! After the gate, continue ahead across the next field, keeping to the river bank, where as you progress you will pass another pill box, this time on your left, behind which and perched on the side of a hill is the pretty hamlet of Walter's Green. At the far side of the field, go over a stile and continue to follow the river bank through another field to later meet a bridge on your right where we also meet part of another route in the book, "The Leopard's Loop". Do not cross the bridge but continue instead to follow the river bank round to pass beneath some electricity pylons and just after this, as the river bends back on itself, follow it around the first part of the bend to then bear left diagonally across the field, heading for a point just to the left of a small group of trees at the field corner. Go over a small bridge at the edge of the field, into another field and carry straight on, across the centre of the field, following a line of oak trees and at the far side, go over a stile to arrive at a lane (**GR. 518415**).

Cross the lane, go over a stile the other side and continue thereafter along the right hand perimeter of a field with a large tiled and weatherboarded house above to your left. Keep to the field perimeter to soon walk through a small gulley, where a short distance on you should turn right over a small bridge across a pretty stream which rises from a nearby spring. After the stream, continue ahead along a narrow path, going uphill. In wet weather this part of the walk can often be very boggy due to several springs which rise here and you will be glad of your trusty walking boots! After passing through a grove of holly bushes, the path bends left to run along the side of a slope and a little later on, bends sharp right, in the direction of a yellow arrow, (look at your feet!).

After a few paces uphill, bear left to soon pass through a gate (the gate, at the time of writing, appears temporary and will probably disappear in the future), to enter and cross the centre of a small field, heading for a gate at the far side, with a yellow arrow on the gate post. As you cross the field, look out for the lovely half tiled Wealdon farmhouse on your left, "Tubs Hole". On reaching the gate, you are rewarded with an intimate view behind over the Medway valley. Pass through the gate and turn right along a tarmac drive, bordered by rhododendrons, going uphill. The tarmac drive soon bends sharp left to level out for a short distance, before climbing again to eventually arrive at a road. Turn right along the road and follow it, later passing some pretty weatherboarded cottages, before arriving at the highly recommended "Bottle House Inn". This is an excellent freehouse with a superb a la carte restaurant, probably one of the best in the area.

From the pub, we follow "The Leopard's Loop" in reverse for a short distance. To do this, after passing the pub, turn left through its car park and continue along a semi-tarmacced track, passing the occasional property on your left. Continue until you see a stile on your left which as a guide, is just before a gateway ahead to "Horns Lodge". Go over the stile and bear diagonally right across the centre of a field, in the direction of a yellow arrow and after a short distance, at the far side, cross another stile to maintain your direction across the centre of the next field. At the far side, go over a stile and turn right to follow the perimeter of a field. Behind you now, is a white painted triangulation point which marks the top of Blowers Hill, a height of 103 metres.

Follow the field perimeter which initially follows the line of a garden to a house on your right and when the perimeter bends right, leave it to carry straight on across the centre of the field. At the far side follow a narrow path through undergrowth before descending some stone steps to cross a lane and join a signposted footpath the other side. The footpath winds along the edge of a wood before meeting a stile, which you should cross into a field. Ahead now are excellent views across rolling hills to the North Downs. Carry straight on, in the direction of a yellow arrow, descending Blowers Hill across the centre of the field and half way across, pass through a line of trees, after which you should continue in the same direction, to the bottom of the field and go over a small footbridge across a small stream. Thereafter, you should continue across the centre of the next field, heading for the far left hand corner.

At the field corner, go over two bridges in quick succession across another stream and after the second bridge, turn left to pass a pond on your right. After the pond, carry straight on, going uphill, to follow the left hand perimeter of Penshurst Vineyard, with Courtlands Wood on your left. After a short distance, turn left with the perimeter of the wood and after approximately fifty metres, follow a path ahead into the wood, in the direction of a yellow arrow. Here, after crossing yet another bridge, continue along a narrow path the other side, going gently uphill with a field on your left. Later, on meeting a track at a bend, carry straight on along the track and after a few paces, leave "The Leopard's Loop" by turning right onto a marked footpath (yellow arrow), going over a small wooden plank bridge to do so (take care not to miss it).

After winding through an area of gorse, go over a stile and continue ahead along the left hand perimeter of a field with fine views to your right. At the far side, cross a stile and carry straight on along the left hand perimeter of the next field and at the far side, go over another stile and thereafter, bear right to follow a narrow footpath along the edge of a strip of woodland with a field on your right. Sometime later, the path begins to descend and passes to the right of a fine old Wealden farmhouse, "Salmans Manor", before arriving at a driveway beside the rather grand gates of the manor. Go straight across the drive and follow a track the other side to, after a few paces, go over a stile ahead beside a gate (do not make the mistake of following the bridleway which bends round to the left). After the stile, carry straight on along the left hand perimeter of a field and at the far side, go over another stile and bear diagonally right across the centre of the next field, heading for the far right hand corner.

At the field corner, cross a stile and follow a path ahead, which runs between a fence on your right and a stream on your left. Sometime on, the path meets and crosses the river Eden. Unless you have been studying the map, this is a pleasant and quite unexpected surprise. After the river, cross a small field and go over a stile the other side to continue ahead along the left hand perimeter of the next field, climbing gently. At the far side of the field, go over a stile and carry straight on through a farmyard to join and follow a concrete drive ahead, passing to the right of the beautiful "Warren" farmhouse and cottage with views behind over the Eden valley.

After the farm, the concrete drive becomes a narrow tarmac lane and you should follow it, until it meets the B2188, beside a school, a distance from "Warren Farm" of approximately half a mile. Turn left along the B2188, to enter the famous village of Penshurst, passing as you walk the village garage which doubles as a Post Office and General Stores on your right. This was once the village blacksmith, the reason for the horseshoe shaped entrance. Follow the road through the village, later ignoring another road leading off to the left, passing a Tea Room and far more important, "The Leicester Arms", a freehouse and a good pub for a half-way stop and an opportunity to learn about Penshurst. For information on Penshurst, see "The Chiding Challenge".

After the pub, continue to follow the road and keep to it as it bends right in front of the gateway to "Penshurst Place", with the beautiful and original "Leicester Square" on your left.

The archway beneath one of the buildings in the square leads to the village church.

Keeping to the road, cross an arm of the river Medway and shortly after the river Medway itself. After the second bridge, follow the road uphill for approximately fifty metres until you see a signposted footpath on your right, marked "To Poundsbridge". As a guide, this is beside a cottage, "Holly Bank", and opposite a fine old ragstone cottage. Take the footpath which is in the form of a track and follow it between fields, enjoying fine views right across the river Medway to Penshurst. After this, the track bends left, climbing gently and then proceeds to follow the course of the river Medway. Stay on the track, later ignoring a marked footpath on your right, after which the track quickly narrows to become a mere path and shortly after arrives at a stile at the far side of a field. Ignore another marked footpath right at this point.

Go over the stile and carry straight on along the left hand perimeter of the next field where there are more superb views right over the Medway valley. If you know your pubs in this area, then across the valley at the other side you will recognise "The Spotted Dog" at the top of Smarts Hill. Approximately two thirds of the way across the field, go over a stile beside a

Swale Cottage

143

gate on your left and thereafter, continue ahead along an enclosed path. After a short distance, the path begins to descend, following a tall stone and brick wall on your left, to soon arrive at a drive beside some cottages. Turn right along the drive, passing to the left of a superbly preserved half timbered Medieval manor house, "Old Swaylands", and thereafter a converted barn, "Swale Cottage" (recommended accommodation). The name "Swaylands" is after a yeoman, John Swayland, who lived here during the 16th century (in terms of class, a yeoman was one step down from a gentleman and was usually a small landowner). A few paces on, go over a stile on your left, just before a third house, and turn right thereafter to follow the perimeter of a field.

At the far side, pass through a gate and go over a grass path to meet and cross a stile the other side to enter a field. Bear diagonally right across the centre of the field and cross two stiles in quick succession to enter another field and thereafter, continue straight across the centre to, at the far side, go over another stile into a third field. Bear diagonally left, cutting across the left hand corner of the field, to soon meet and cross yet another stile at the field perimeter. After this, turn right to follow the edge of a hop field and at the corner, continue to follow the field perimeter round to soon cross a bridge on your right over a tributary to the river Medway. (Take care not to miss it as the bridge is often hidden). The bridge takes you into another field where the official route is directly across the field heading for a bridge visible the other side, where you should turn left back across the centre of the field. It is much easier however, to simply turn left on arriving at the field and follow the perimeter round, at first following the tributary and thereafter, a ditch and fence. To your left now the tiny church at Poundsbridge, our next destination, is visible. Keep to the field perimeter as it bends left at a point where it draws level with the bridge on your right and continue to follow the field perimeter, heading for a pair of gates at the field's left hand corner and the church at Poundsbridge.

At the field corner, pass through the smaller of the two gates and bear diagonally right across the centre of the next field, following a line of oaks and heading for a point to the left of the churchyard ahead. At the far side, pass through a gate and follow a track to, after a few paces, arrive at a lane beside the churchyard entrance **(GR. 537418)**.

The tiny church is normally locked. However, it is its position and the view from the churchyard which are its best and main assets.

Turn right along the lane where there are continuing fine views over the Medway valley and shortly after passing through a pretty hamlet and past "Hamsell Farm", join a signposted footpath on your left which leads diagonally right uphill, across the centre of a field. The path climbs to meet a stile at the field's right hand perimeter, where you may want to pause and catch your breath to take in the glorious views behind along the Eden and Medway valleys and the North Downs. To continue, go over the stile and maintain your direction across the centre of the next field and at the field perimeter, pass through a gateway to again maintain your direction across the centre of another field. At the far side, pass through a pair of gates to arrive at a lane.

After admiring the view one last time, say farewell to the Medway and turn left along the lane, still climbing, later passing "Little Hickmans Farm", before arriving at a "T" junction. Go straight across the road here (do not turn left or right) and over a stile the other side to follow a wide path beside a pond, with a yellow arrow marked with "WW" indicating that you have now rejoined our old friend, the Weald Way. After the pond, go over a stile on your left and bear diagonally right thereafter across the centre of a field, in the direction of the Weald Way arrow. At the far side, go over another stile and continue in the same direction across the next field. At the far left hand corner of the field, cross a stile and continue to follow a fairly prominent path through Avery's Wood, another truly beautiful part of the walk, especially in spring when bluebells line your path.

Sometime later, the path bends right and starts to descend into a valley. Take care from here on, as the descent can, at times, be very slippery. The path later bends left and levels out to continue its route along the side of the valley where, as before, bluebells are in abundance in spring. Later, the path begins to descend once more, though this time far more gently and then, after a series of natural steps formed from the roots of a beech tree, the path crosses a stream via a footbridge at the valley bottom. This is a magical spot, its beauty being difficult to express in a book. Instead, I will leave it to you to find your own words. After the bridge, continue to follow the path ahead which soon begins to climb the other side of the valley. Sometime on, on meeting a garden fence ahead, fork left in the direction of the Weald Way arrow, to follow the garden fence and arrive at a lane between two lovely 15th century thatched cottages, sitting in blissful ignorance of the modern world. Welcome to the hamlet of Bullingstone.

Turn right along the lane, continuing uphill, and after approximately forty metres, turn left onto a marked footpath (yellow arrow) marked also as the Weald Way and the High Weald Walk. The path which is fenced, leads gently uphill before levelling out to run between fields. Sometime later, go over a stile, after which you should maintain your direction, walking between two fields and making for the first houses of Speldhurst, visible the other side. At the far side of the field, go over a stile to thereafter follow an enclosed path which runs between gardens, at one point going over a crossing path before arriving at a lane ahead. Cross the lane and turn right to follow the pavement the other side and continue to soon arrive at a junction of roads in front of the entrance to the village church. The church is well worth a visit and is quite magnificent inside.

Speldhurst (GR. 554414 Map 188) sits at the top of a hill close to the Sussex border. Despite some modern houses, the village has retained its identity and is blessed with a majestic church and a fine hostelry. Ironically, in the past, both have been destroyed by fire.

The church was destroyed by fire in 1791, after being struck by lightening. All that remains of the original structure today is the base of the 15th century tower. The current church dates from 1871 and no expense was spared, as can be seen from the extensive wood carvings inside. Also worth noting are the beautiful stained glass windows by William Morris and Burne-Jones.

The village hostelry, "The George and Dragon Inn", faces the village church, from the opposite side of the road. It is claimed to be the oldest inn in the country,

although there is some doubt to this and certainly, "The Crown Inn" at Chiddingfold in Surrey is probably older. The original inn, like the church, was destroyed by fire and the current building is a clever Victorian reconstruction using many of the original materials. The fireplace, for example, is the original one and the grooves in its stonework are said to be from knights of

The George & Dragon

old sharpening their swords. In fact, "The George and Dragon Inn" appears to have been quite a meeting place for both crusaders and knights preparing for the battle of Agincourt. Whether you believe this or not, the original building does date back to the 12th century and the inn does have some secret passageways (now sealed), leading out to nearby woods. Today, the inn manages to retain the atmosphere of old and serves some very well kept beer. Upstairs in a beautiful old room is the restaurant, definitely one worth visiting.

To continue, at the road junction at the entrance to the village church, ignore a road right and continue to the follow the road you are on to arrive at "The George and Dragon Inn". Continue past pub and follow the road downhill (alternatively, you can walk through the churchyard) and after the church, ignore a road off to the left (Barden road). Before continuing, look out for a small red post box set in the wall of a building (the old Post Office) at the junction with Barden road. The post box has been cut in half to accommodate a larger window. To continue, follow the road downhill in the direction of the sign for Tunbridge Wells, passing between sandstone cliffs and shortly after passing "Wallers", a cul de sac, cross the road and join a signposted footpath on your left (take care not to miss it). The path which is fenced, leads along the side of a bank and later crosses a stile before continuing ahead along the left hand perimeter of a field. After approximately twenty metres, at a low stone footpath post (take care not to miss it), bear diagonally right to descend across the centre of the field, heading for another stone post visible at the bottom of the field. On reaching the bottom, cross a stream via a narrow footbridge and thereafter, follow a fenced, often very muddy path the other side. The path soon climbs the other side of the valley, at points assisted by steps, to eventually arrive at a track in front of a house.

Turn left along the track and after approximately twenty paces, turn right up some steps to join a signposted footpath which continues to climb, running between gardens. Go over a stile and continue thereafter along the left hand perimeter of a field and after approximately two hundred metres, look out for

and cross another stile on your left to thereafter, follow an enclose
skirts a garden, before descending some steps to reach a lane. Turn
the lane, going uphill, and follow it enjoying good views left, to soon
"T" junction in the form of another lane **(GR. 563420)**. Turn left at the
junction and follow the lane past some pretty cottages for approximate
seventyfive metres, until you see a signposted (low stone sign) footpath o   r
right, opposite the entrance to "Birchetts Court", a large house which once had
its own theatre, now converted into individual dwellings.

Join the footpath by passing through a kissing gate and a few paces on go over a
stile to continue ahead along the left hand perimeter of a field. At the far side of
the field, cross a stile on your right and thereafter, turn left in the direction of a
Weald Way arrow, to continue along the left hand perimeter of another field. At
the far side, turn left through an old kissing gate, thereby leaving the Weald Way
and follow an enclosed path for approximately thirty paces, after which you
should turn right to follow another fenced path with a large garden on your
right. Later, after going through an old iron kissing gate, cross a lane and join a
signposted footpath the other side. The footpath which is fenced, quickly
descends into a valley and near the bottom, runs alongside a wood on your left,
part of the gardens to Sir David Salomon's house.

David Salomon's House (GR. 568416 Map 188) is a fine Victorian villa built i
by David Salomon in 1852. Sir David Lionel Salomon, the younger, inherited the
house on his father's death and quickly started transforming it into one of the
most modern houses of its time. He was an important member of the scientific
community in England at the time and added a flamboyant water tower and a
science theatre to the house, the latter still perfectly preserved. In 1882, the entire
house was lit by electricity, the first house in the world to have this luxury.

Sir David was also a lover of the motor car and played a major part in
progressing the technology of the day. He owned sixtytwo different cars himself
and founded the organisation which was later to become the R.A.C. He also
started the original Motor Show.

Funnily enough, Sir David is not remembered for his remarkable scientific
achievements but rather the theatre that he founded at the house. Today, it is the
home of the Broomhill Opera Company which gives regular performances of both
classic and modern works. The preservation of the house and theatre is in the safe
hands of the David Salomon Society.

I always think it is incredible what one can discover during a stroll in the
countryside and the next time you need the assistance of a motoring organisation,
think back to this part of the Kent countryside and thank the man whose foresight
has brought such efficient assistance in your time of need.

At the bottom of the valley, the path levels out to follow a stream on your right,
passing through an avenue of laurels before eventually arriving at a road. Turn
right along the road, passing the entrance to "Redsheen Kennels and Cattery"
and thereafter, follow the road for just under a quarter of a mile where you
should turn left onto a signposted public footpath. This leads downhill between
banks later passing over a tumbling stream with a petite waterfall on your right.
Shortly after the stream, fork right to follow a fenced track between fields (a

reserve), later crossing a stile beside a gate and continue straight on
thereafter, through the beautiful Hurst Wood, ignoring a path on your right.
Later, on meeting and a crossing path with some old iron fencing on your left
(note how the beech tree has grown around it), carry straight on, over the
crossing path and thereafter, keep to the main path through the wood, ignoring
all minor turnings off.

Pass through a kissing gate beside a wider gate and continue ahead, again
keeping to the main path, now following a stream on your right, to eventually
come out at the other side of the wood in front of Hurst Wood Pumping Station.
Do not pass the pumping station but as you meet it turn right along a tarmac
path which leads up to a road. Continue ahead along the road and between
houses to soon arrive at a crossroads beside a General Stores on your right. Turn
left at the crossroads along Harmony Street, to soon pass the last pub actually on
our walk, the "Toad Rock Retreat", a Whitbread pub. The pub sign depicts Toad
Rock with a rather imaginative impression.

*The pub dates from 1700 when Rusthall was becoming a popular suburb of
fashionable Tunbridge Wells. A ghost is once said to have left sixpences (2 1/2
pence for those who cannot remember the old money) about the pub, but stopped
his fun when decimalisation took over! Although this is the last pub en route,
there is another pub only five minutes walk from the end of our route which I
highly recommend. If you intend finding this as well, then I suggest you tone
down any early celebrations at the "Toad Rock Retreat"!*

After the pub, keep to the road following it uphill through a green with an
amazing collection of grand sandstone rocks. The most famous, Toad Rock is on
your right, protected by iron railings. It really does bear a remarkable
resemblance to a toad. If you have the time and more importantly, the energy the
whole formation of rocks is worth exploring.

After Toad Rock, follow the lane as it bends right and almost immediately after,
as it bends left, leave it to follow a narrow path ahead. This path soon meets a
tarmac path onto which you should turn left to arrive at a road. Cross the road
and follow a tarmac path the other side through woodland to, after a short
distance, arrive at the main road, the A264. Cross the road and follow a tarmac
path ahead to arrive at St. Pauls church from where we started.

If you wish to celebrate the finish and the return to the highest point on the
walk by raising a glass in one last hostelry, then by following the path as though
starting the walk again, but forking right as the stone wall bends left and
following a path along the top of a sandstone cliff (good views), after a few
minutes (no more - I promise!) you will arrive at "The Beacon", an excellent
freehouse. Alternatively, if your legs will not carry you a step further, the pub is
signposted from the A264 (turn left out of the road from the church). The pub
was once the home of a former Lieutenant of the City of London and inside, it
still feels lived in. The bars have some incredible fireplaces but most famous of
all, is the view from the pub's terrace. I hope I've convinced you - cheers!

ACCOMMODATION

The Spa Hotel, Royal Tunbridge Wells. Tel: 01892 520331
Within walking distance from the start of the walk, this is a classic Regency hotel oozing with luxury. The rooms are superb and have fine views over open common. To ease those aches and pains at the end of your walk, the hotel has a useful indoor heated pool.

Swale Cottage, Poundsbridge. Tel: 01892 870738
On the walk, accommodation is in a beautifully converted Kentish barn. Awarded "The Best New Guest House in the South of England" in 1992, Swale Cottage offers three beautifully furnished en suite rooms. If you like a little luxury with peace and quiet then this is for you.

Youth Hostel, Blackboys YHA, Uckfield. Tel: 01825 892607
Approximately twelve miles from the walk, this is a lovely hostel popular with YHA members. Accommodation is in simple wood huts in a small Sussex village. One major attraction is the local pub, one of the best in Sussex.

Camping and Caravanning, Renhurst Farm, Mark Cross. Tel: 01892 852897
Approximately six miles from the walk, this is a small farm site situated in wooded countryside. Very friendly owners - a good choice.

FOR THOSE LOOKING FOR ADVENTURE

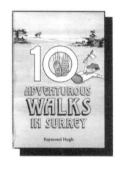 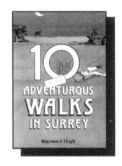 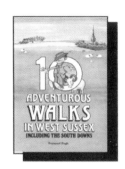

 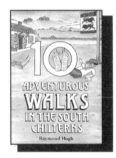 

SOME PUBS TO TRY

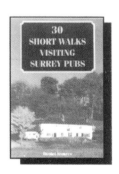  

WALK WITH US

Morning Mist Organise a number of one day, outings, short breaks and holidays at home and abroad. For a brochure please send a postcard with your name and address to Morning mist Travel PO Box 108, Reigate, Surrey RH2 9YP

KEEP UP TO DATE

If you would like a full list and to be kept updated on all the outdoor publications available from Morning Mist, please send a postcard with your name and address to Marketing, Morning Mist Publications, PO Box 108, Reigate Surrey RH2 9YP.